Pro Oracle Identity and Access Management Suite

Kenneth Ramey

⟨IOUG⟩
Independent oracle users group

Apress®

Pro Oracle Identity and Access Management Suite

Kenneth Ramey
Colorado Springs, Colorado
USA

ISBN-13 (pbk): 978-1-4842-1522-7   ISBN-13 (electronic): 978-1-4842-1521-0
DOI 10.1007/978-1-4842-1521-0

Library of Congress Control Number: 2016961691

Managing Director: Welmoed Spahr
Lead Editor: Jonathan Gennick
Development Editor: Douglas Pundick
Technical Reviewer: Arup Nanda
Editorial Board: Steve Anglin, Pramila Balan, Laura Berendson, Aaron Black, Louise Corrigan, Jonathan Gennick, Robert Hutchinson, Celestin Suresh John, Nikhil Karkal, James Markham, Susan McDermott, Matthew Moodie, Natalie Pao, Gwenan Spearing
Coordinating Editor: Jill Balzano
Copy Editor: Teresa F. Horton
Compositor: SPi Global
Indexer: SPi Global
Artist: SPi Global

Distributed to the book trade worldwide by Springer Science+Business Media New York, 233 Spring Street, 6th Floor, New York, NY 10013. Phone 1-800-SPRINGER, fax (201) 348-4505, e-mail orders-ny@springer-sbm.com, or visit www.springer.com. Apress Media, LLC is a California LLC and the sole member (owner) is Springer Science + Business Media Finance Inc (SSBM Finance Inc). SSBM Finance Inc is a Delaware corporation.

For information on translations, please e-mail rights@apress.com, or visit www.apress.com.

Apress and friends of ED books may be purchased in bulk for academic, corporate, or promotional use. eBook versions and licenses are also available for most titles. For more information, reference our Special Bulk Sales–eBook Licensing web page at www.apress.com/bulk-sales.

Any source code or other supplementary material referenced by the author in this text is available to readers at www.apress.com. For detailed information about how to locate your book's source code, go to www.apress.com/source-code/.

Printed on acid-free paper

*I would like to dedicate this book to my parents Don and Alice,
my bother Nick, and my wife Kathleen. They provided me the foundation, drive, and
encouragement to get me to this point in my life. All of them pushed me on and
kept me honest during the process of writing this book.*

About IOUG Press

*IOUG Press is a joint effort by the **Independent Oracle Users Group (the IOUG)** and **Apress** to deliver some of the highest-quality content possible on Oracle Database and related topics. The IOUG is the world's leading, independent organization for professional users of Oracle products. Apress is a leading, independent technical publisher known for developing high-quality, no-fluff content for serious technology professionals. The IOUG and Apress have joined forces in IOUG Press to provide the best content and publishing opportunities to working professionals who use Oracle products.*

Our shared goals include:

- Developing content with excellence
- Helping working professionals to succeed
- Providing authoring and reviewing opportunities
- Networking and raising the profiles of authors and readers

To learn more about Apress, visit our website at **www.apress.com**. Follow the link for IOUG Press to see the great content that is now available on a wide range of topics that matter to those in Oracle's technology sphere.

Visit **www.ioug.org** to learn more about the Independent Oracle Users Group and its mission. Consider joining if you haven't already. Review the many benefits at www.ioug.org/join. Become a member. Get involved with peers. Boost your career.

www.ioug.org/join

Apress®

Contents at a Glance

Contents

About the Author

Kenneth Ramey started his career with Oracle products in 1997 while serving in the U.S. Air Force. After an Honorable Discharge, he began focusing primarily on Oracle Application Server and Oracle Identity Management. He is currently working for Centroid as a consultant specializing in Fusion Middleware Products. During his career, Ken has presented regularly on the topics of Fusion Middleware Products, including WebCenter Content and Identity Management, at various events such as Oracle Applications User Group and Independent Oracle User Group Collaborate and the Rocky Mountain Oracle Users Group. As a consultant, he has worked on many projects from small businesses to large multinational companies. He currently lives in Colorado Springs, Colorado, in view of Pike's Peak with his wife Kathleen.

About the Technical Reviewer

Arup Nanda has been an Oracle database administrator (DBA) since 1993, dealing with everything from modeling to security, and has a lot of gray hairs to prove it. He has coauthored five books, written more than 500 published articles, presented more than 300 sessions, delivered training sessions in 22 countries, and actively blogs at arup.blogspot.com. He is an Oracle ACE Director, a member of Oak Table Network, an editor for SELECT Journal (the IOUG publication), and a member of the Board for Exadata SIG. Oracle awarded him the DBA of the Year in 2003 and Architect of the Year in 2012. He lives in Danbury, Connecticut, with his wife Anu and son Anish.

Acknowledgments

Throughout my career, I have had the chance to work with some of the best in the industry. These people helped put me on a path that led me to where I am now. There are people like my friend Jim Osborn, whose knowledge and experience helped me get through a number of projects, and his willingness to teach topics instilled the same willingness in me. The various project managers at Centroid (Ann, Carrie, Frank, Rob) with whom I have worked transformed my lackluster documentation skills into the ability to coherently convey complex project aspects. There are the owners of Centroid, who treat their employees like family. Scott Morrell and Paresh Patel, in particular, have mentored me and provided a work environment that encourages innovation and opportunity for professional growth. Jim Brull and Eric Reed have been there to show that the company is willing to let me mold my skills in ways that are mutually beneficial. I cannot forget to mention Ajay Arora, who has helped build my confidence as a leader and provided valued advice and technical knowledge many times.

Outside of work, there are the many friends and family who have been around throughout my life and provided encouragement and a sounding board when I needed it. Special thanks go to Mike Gale and Neland North, who have known me throughout my career and helped guide me from being a new Airman to now, almost 20 years later. They are still trying to help me figure out this thing called life. I will see you guys on the river and on the bike trail. If I did not mention your name here, the omission was not intentional. There are just far too many people to thank and acknowledge in a single book. Thank you all.

Introduction

Many organizations plan for security throughout the product life cycle for each product installed within the environment. Most products provide some sort of user storage mechanism. These individual user stores can be used, and might be a viable solution for smaller environments with few implemented products. However, this can often lead to multiple identity stores, replication of data across business units, and management headaches in larger organizations. In addition, the use of individual user management functions can lead to users maintaining multiple usernames and passwords for all of the products they use. In the end, these users are going to use less secure passwords, or worse, write a list of usernames and passwords and place it under their keyboard.

The solution is to implement a single source for identity data that all applications can leverage for authentication and authorization. The Lightweight Directory Access Protocol (LDAP) was designed to provide a standard way to look up information in an identity store. With LDAP, applications now have a standard way to authenticate and authorize users from external stores, provided it is compliant with the LDAP standard. Business units can now implement software that is LDAP compliant and access the central user store and no longer require users to maintain multiple accounts. Oracle Internet Directory (OID) is Oracle's implementation of a generic LDAP directory. Other Oracle products such as E-Business Suite, WebCenter Content, and OBIEE are designed to work with OID. Being a generic LDAP-compliant directory, OID can be leveraged by other third-party applications as well.

Oracle went a step further and introduced Oracle Access Manager (OAM) to provide single sign-on functionality. Now, instead of each application requiring a separate login request, they can be set up to utilize an existing browser token to authenticate, thus relieving the user from multiple credential entries. OAM supports the Security Assertion Markup Language (SAML), so it can be configured to provide authentication services to third-party cloud-based applications. This also means that Oracle cloud-based solutions such as Human Capital Management can be integrated with an organization's OAM single sign-on environment.

No implementation is complete without some sort of identity life cycle management. In the past, each application was responsible for its own identity store. This led to users having multiple accounts that had to be created and maintained for each application they accessed. When users on-boarded, it could take days to weeks to get access to everything they needed. Conversely, when a user left the organization, there was the possibility that his or her accounts might not be decommissioned in a timely manner, if at all. This posed a large security risk. Oracle Identity Management (OIM) was introduced to bring a new level of governance to enterprise-level identity life cycle management. OIM provides a central interface for the management of user identity data. It can connect to a standard LDAP directory, or by using Oracle Virtual Directory, it can manage data from multiple stores. The automation capabilities provided by OIM can reduce the amount of work required to on-board users and ensure access is removed when a user leaves the organization.

The Oracle Identity and Access Management Suite combines the key elements discussed here to provide an end-to-end solution for user management. Although it should be simple to implement this, there are a variety of steps required to get everything working properly and efficiently. This book is intended to provide a guide to getting the Identity and Access Management Suite up and running in your environment. It demonstrates installation and configuration, along with some architectural discussions to help determine what is required in your environment.

CHAPTER 1

■ ■ ■

Oracle Identity and Access Management Suite Overview

Oracle Fusion Middleware products are deployed within WebLogic Server architectures. WebLogic Server provides a scalable environment, allowing the enterprise to deploy and manage Oracle products and Java applications with the ability to access database and messaging services. WebLogic Server operates as the application server tier. The capabilities delivered by WebLogic include clustering, high availability, manageability, monitoring, security, and database integration.

The Oracle Identity and Access Management Suite consists of multiple components, each serving a very specific purpose. These components consist of directory services, access management or single sign-on (SSO), identity management, and self-service portals, as well as provisioning, governance, and reporting services.

This chapter provides an introduction to the Oracle Fusion Middleware WebLogic Server environment and the major components involved in configuring the Oracle Identity and Access Management Suite. You will also be presented with a description of the Oracle Identity Management components relevant to the rest of the book.

WebLogic Server

Oracle's WebLogic Server (WLS) is a fully J2EE-compliant application server that will support the Oracle Identity and Access Management Suite components. This environment provides the components necessary for the deployment of custom applications as well as Oracle Fusion Middleware Products like Enterprise Content Management and Oracle Identity and Access Management. As WebLogic Server is an application server, users are able to access these applications via a web browser using the deployed application ports or through an HTTP server serving as a reverse proxy.

To provide enterprise-level service, WebLogic Server supports a number of environmental features.

- *Programming models*: WLS supports a Java EE deployment environment, web services support, Java Messaging, Extensible Markup Language (XML) capabilities, Java Database Connectivity (JDBC) connection resources, and other components.

- *High availability*: This is supported using WebLogic Clusters to distribute work across multiple servers and the ability to detect overload and manage overload conditions. The persistent store and store-and-forward services allow the ability to temporarily store JMS messages and deliver them across services distributed across the cluster.

© Kenneth Ramey 2016
K. Ramey, *Pro Oracle Identity and Access Management Suite*, DOI 10.1007/978-1-4842-1521-0_1

- *Security*: WLS provides a built-in Lightweight Directory Access Protocol (LDAP) 2.0 identity store that can be used to manage access to services deployed on the server. Beyond this, WLS can be configured to authenticate against a number of different external data stores such as Oracle Internet Directory, Active Directory, and so on. Furthermore the WLS framework allows the integration of identity asserters such as Oracle Access Manager (OAM).

- *Diagnostic framework*: Affords the ability to collect and analyze runtime data about the processes running on the server. This can be used to diagnose issues and tune for better performance.

For the purposes of the Oracle Identity and Access Management environment, this book discusses how to use the following components.

- The administration server provides a graphical user interface (GUI) for managing all components of the deployment. Each WLS domain has one administration server that can be run on any of the WebLogic hosts. The administration server manages the configuration data for the domain, clusters, managed servers, data sources, security settings, and application deployments.

- A domain is a logical unit of management for server resources within the WLS. All aspects of the environment are contained within a domain, including the managed servers, database sources, messaging services, application deployments, machines, and clusters.

- Machines represent a physical host that houses managed servers. A single administration server can manage multiple machines. The administration server communicates with each machine's node manager for start and stop operations of each managed server. A single physical host can have multiple machines configured listening on different ports if necessary.

- WebLogic Clusters consist of one or more WLS instances that work together, providing high availability and the ability to scale the environments laterally.

- A managed server is a logical WLS construct where applications can be deployed.

- Data sources are JDBC connections configured within the WLS to be used by applications deployed within the various managed servers. Targeting a data source at specific managed servers makes it available to only those specified.

- Security realms define authentication providers and asserters that protect the application resources. Security groups, users, and policies can all be defined within the WebLogic security realms.

Oracle Directory Services

Oracle Directory Services makes up the core of Oracle Identity and Access Management. Consisting of multiple options, Directory Services provides identity and policy storage, directory synchronization, and virtualization functionality that can be leveraged by various applications in use by the enterprise. These options include the following:

- *Oracle Internet Directory (OID)*: Database-based fully LDAP-V3 compatible identity directory.

- *Oracle Unified Directory (OUD)*: Java-based LDAP-V3 compliant identity directory.

- *Oracle Virtual Directory (OVD)*: Directory integration that enables management of multiple sources without the need for data replication.

Oracle Internet Directory

OID is a fully LDAP-V3 compliant directory using the Oracle Database for storage. This allows OID to leverage database features such as Real Application Clusters and Multimaster Replication in conjunction with OID clusters and the Fusion Middleware architecture to provide a highly available and scalable environment. The Oracle Directory Services Manager provides a standard front end for the maintenance of users, security groups, object classes, attributes, and policies within the OID. Figure 1-1 presents a basic high-availability environment of OID or OVD using a Real Application Clusters Database environment.

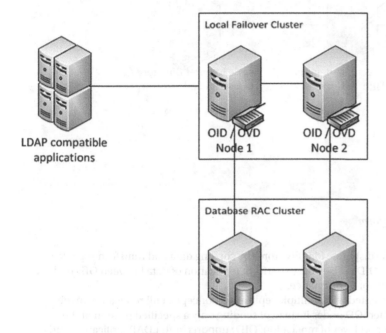

Figure 1-1. *Basic local high availability configuration*

OID allows the storage of disparate identity data through the ability to store multiple contexts. This allows data that might be stored in multiple sources to be managed in a single instance. For example, if the enterprise has implemented multiple Active Directory Lightweight Directory Service instances to manage users in various LDAP enabled applications, OID can be leveraged to provide a single LDAP source for all applications.

Using an Oracle database for the data repository, OID is able to leverage features such as Transparent Data Encryption and Database Vault to provide security at every level of operation. The ability to leverage these database features separates security duties by allowing the database to handle the data store and backup security.

OID provides the ability to synchronize other directories in use within the enterprise. The Directory Integration Platform, shown in Figure 1-2, allows administrators to create and maintain synchronization profiles for Active Directory, Sun eDirectory, OpenLDAP, and others. This enables the enterprise to consolidate user repositories and provide application security with a standardized general-purpose LDAP directory.

3

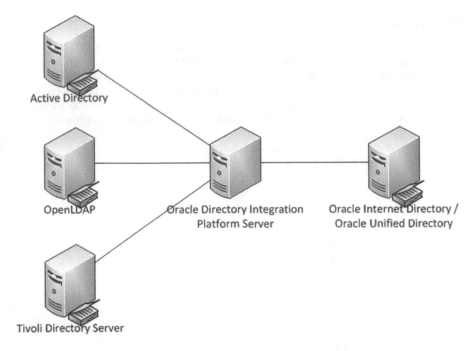

Figure 1-2. *Directory Integration Platform*

In addition to integrating multiple disparate identity stores by copying data and transforming it to match the needs within the OID store, OID is also able to perform replication of data between OID nodes to provide high availability and scalability for performance.

With OID, the organization is presented with multiple replication concepts. Full replication involves propagating the entire directory to other IOD nodes instead of sending only a specified portion of the structure to other nodes. For the transport layer of replication, OID supports both LDAP replication and Database Advanced Replication. The former relies on the LDAP protocol to convey data from one OID instance to another, whereas Oracle Database Advanced Replication requires the database to replicate the data between database instances. The last concept to be presented is the replication direction. OID supports single master, multimaster, and fan-out replication. As the names suggest, single master can be thought of as replication from a master node to all other nodes in one direction. Multimaster allows changes from any node to be replicated to the others. Fan-out is a sort of combination of the two previous directions, where a master node replicates out to other nodes and those child nodes can then replicate either full or partial data to other nodes.

Although OID has a long-standing history and is currently compatible with other Oracle Identity Management components such as OIM and OAM, along with Fusion Middleware products and applications, Oracle has indicated that the future direction of Directory Services is OUD.

Oracle Unified Directory

OUD represents Oracle's release of the industry's first Java-based, LDAP-V3 and Directory Services Markup Language (DSML) v2 compliant directory service that combines storage, proxy, synchronization, and virtualization in a single platform. OUD provides a high level of performance and elastic scalability and high availability using commodity-level hardware and flexible deployment architectures. While providing this level of service, OUD is able to maintain high levels of security and monitoring.

OUD's architecture allows for global indexing, increasing its elastic scalability. This feature allows administrators to add servers; OUD will handle routing of new requests to the new servers and storage as needed. This eliminates the need for building new environments and migrating large amounts of data. Another benefit of this indexing is that sizing needs can be addressed on an as-needed basis. No longer do administrators need to determine the current size requirements and estimate growth over the next few years. Entries can also be distributed across multiple directory storage instances. Figure 1-3 shows an environment that has been distributed across mulitple nodes as well as clustered to provide failover protection.

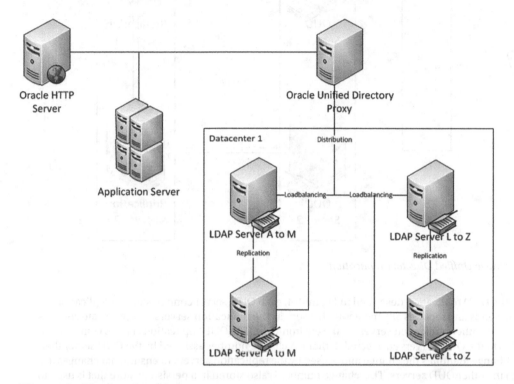

Figure 1-3. *Distributed architecture*

To support high availability while also promoting high performance, OUD separates the tasks of directory services and replication services. As discussed previously, OUD allows the distribution of servers across multiple data centers. To support this, OUD introduces replication servers shown in Figure 1-4. These are servers dedicated to replicating data across the entire environment, leaving client request handling to the directory servers.

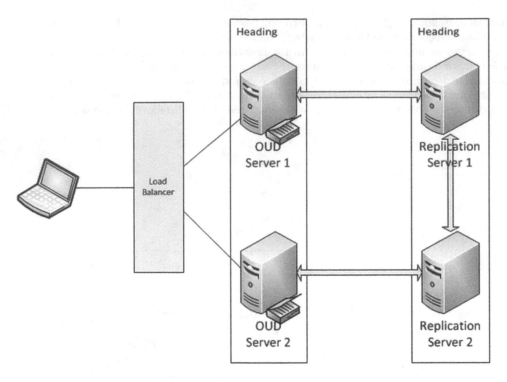

Figure 1-4. *Oracle Unified Directory replication*

During the OUD replication described in Figure 1-4, each OUD server connects to one replication server. It then sends and receives all changes to that server. The replication servers communicate changes received to all the other replication servers in the environment. The OUD replication servers communicate these changes to the OUD servers connected to them. A change number assigned by the OUD server that initiates the change identifies the change and is used by the replication servers to ensure that changes are populated to the other OUD servers. This change number is also stored in a persistent store that is used to populate changes to OUD servers that might have been disconnected from the replication servers. If changes occur on both OUD servers at the same time and cause conflicts, each OUD server will replay the changes until all conflicts are resolved.

The replication server manages connections to the OUD servers and listens for changes from other replication servers. These changes are populated to the directory servers connected to it. These replication servers are created automatically when an OUD server is configured for replication. As such, these can run on the same Java virtual machine (JVM) or host. To save resources, an OUD server can be configured to perform both directory and replication server functions. However, for larger environments, Oracle recommends these functions be separated to different servers.

Much like OID, the Directory Integration Platform can be used to copy identity data from third-party LDAP repositories to provide a central data store for application authentication. It should be noted that this is the same functionality presented earlier for OID. As such, it is producing a copy of identity data that must be maintained. Some organizations might not wish to manage multiple copies of LDAP data. This is addressed with OVD.

Oracle Virtual Directory

OVD provides a method of presenting multiple identity stores as a single source without the need for synchronization and replicating data. Presenting a single source enables enterprise applications to access identity data from multiple sources such as the database, EBS, Active Directory, and OID.

Aggregation of multiple data sources allows the enterprise to leverage existing identity data across multiple sources without the need for replicating data or setting up complicated synchronization tasks. Because OVD presents multiple data sources without copying the underlying data, significant savings can be realized as storage costs are reduced.

A key capability of OVD is its ability to transform identity data into application-specific views. Thus it can present non-LDAP data such as database or web services in the proper format required for the various applications in place in the enterprise. For example, OVD can be leveraged to present Siebel Customer Master data as an LDAP source for authentication of other applications. The translation capability not only allows multiple applications to view the data as needed, but it also allows the organizations to retain control over how they manage and share identity data within their own repositories.

Not only can OVD present multiple data stores as a single source, it can support the concept of split profiles. For example, an enterprise might store all identity data in Active Directory. However, applications such as EBS might require additional metadata for authorization stored in OID or the human resources database. The OVD adapters will allow applications to view this data as a single entry. Figure 1-5 shows a representation of multiple directory sources being consolidated with OVD. As this environment is virtual, it is all done without replication.

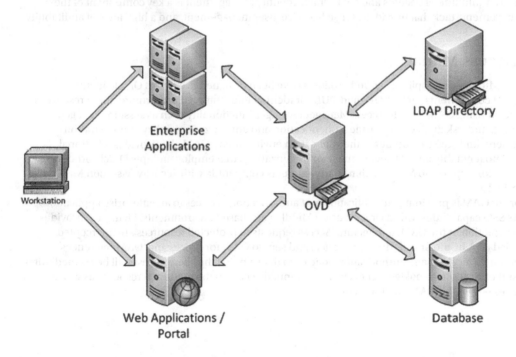

Figure 1-5. Data flow between application and identity sources through OVD

Built to be scalable and highly available, OVD can support the enterprise, no matter how large. Scaling for performance can be as simple as adding additional nodes to the cluster. This can be done in a central location or geographically. High availability is supported not only within the OVD environment, but it also supports load balancing and high availability of its data sources. Although this configuration allows a more streamlined environment with no data duplication, it can suffer from issues such as lost data if a user is removed from one source or orphaned accounts and groups.

Oracle Identity and Access Management

Most organizations require Identity Services such as an LDAP repository. Sometimes this is accomplished with a simple network directory such as Microsoft Active Directory. When considering application security, a more general-purpose directory is necessary. OID, OVD, and OUD, presented previously, can be used to provide this service. As more and more applications are introduced to the business, users can become inundated with authentication dialogs as they switch from one application to another.

OAM, a component of the Identity and Access Management Suite, can be leveraged to provide SSO capabilities. This function can greatly reduce the number of times a user must authenticate during the day, thereby increasing productivity. This reduction can also be built on by incorporating external and third-party applications through federation.

With SSO through OAM providing fewer authentication requests, it is important that application users keep secure passwords and accounts. Account management becomes a necessity as single accounts could have access to a multitude of systems and data. Oracle Identity Management is a key component of the Identity Management stack that provides user self-service, user management, and a high level of auditability.

Oracle Access Manager

Oracle Fusion Middleware applications and products have been designed to support Oracle Identity Manager (OIM) components such as OID and OUD for identity information. Furthermore, these resources can be protected using OAM. Oracle Access Manager leverages functionality such as session management, identity context, and risk analysis to provide authentication and authorization, policy administration and enforcement, and SSO capabilities to the application environment. OAM also provides additional functionality, most notably an SSO environment for organizations that employ multiple Oracle products and Identity Federation support to integrate third-party products compatible with Security Assertion Markup Language (SAML).

The core of OAM is providing authentication and authorization services to an enterprise application. It also allows SSO capabilities within Oracle Fusion Middleware-based environments. Figure 1-6 provides a high-level depiction of the OAM architecture. Access requests to protected resources are intercepted by a filter called a WebGate or a mod_osso instance, and sent to OAM for processing. OAM references configurable authentication and authorization policies to determine if the client access will be granted. After successful authentication, a cookie is set to ensure continued access to the requested resource as well as other resources within the OAM environment.

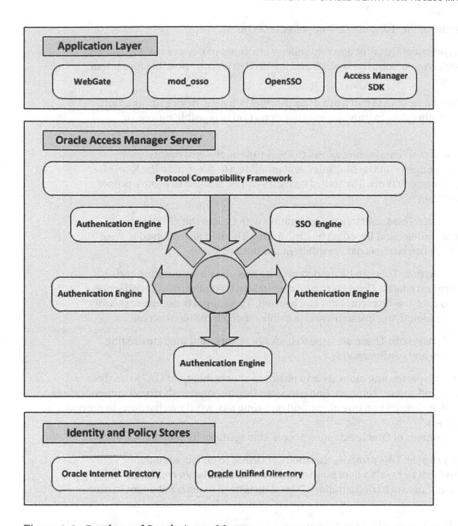

Figure 1-6. *Breakout of Oracle Access Manager components*

Oracle Adaptive Access Management

OAM does not only provide authentication and authorization services; it also enables the organization to increase security awareness and fraud detection across multiple levels of the organization's application architecture such as the web, data, and application tiers. Oracle Adaptive Access Manager (OAAM) strengthens the security of OAM's authentication mechanisms by adding the ability to learn behaviors and detect possible fraudulent activities. The real-time and batch risk analysis component of OAAM serves to verify user identities and the validity of activities using patterns, rule engine, actions, and transaction analysis.

The following are some of the risk analysis components of OAAM:

- *Device fingerprinting*: This functionality collects attributes of devices used to connect during a user's transaction. These attributes are used to identify possible fraudulent access requests.

- *Behavioral profiling*: OAAM can learn users' normal behavior, device information, locations, and other data to provide proactive detection of possible misuse or security breaks.

- *Risk engine analytics*: This feature allows the real-time analysis of events, user profiles, device fingerprints, geolocation, and other data to determine the level of risk during user interactions. The trail of analytics can be audited to ensure proper actions were taken.

- *Predictive analysis*: This facilitates the integration with Oracle Data Mining to provide anomaly detection based on historical data. This can also be used to base change decisions on analysis data as different models are tested.

- *Investigative forensics*: This can be used to provide sets of data for auditing and fraud investigation efforts. The data can be customized using Business Intelligence Publisher or out-of-the-box templates can be used. These reports can assist security investigators in identifying instances and possible related fraudulent access.

- *Universal risk snapshots*: These are used to back up, restore, and migrate existing security policies and configurations.

User-facing components preventing malware and phishing attacks augment OAAM analysis functionality to provide an end-to-end solution. End users can be presented with virtual authentication devices, knowledge-based authentication questions, and one-time password mechanisms to prevent unauthorized account access.

The user-facing components of Oracle Adaptive Access Management include the following:

- *Device fingerprinting*: This provides the ability of OAAM to collect metadata regarding users' devices. This data may include cookies, hardware configurations, geolocation, and network configurations. This data is used to detect changes in user behavior.

- *Knowledge-based authentication*: This provides a secondary form of authentication by requiring the user to answer security questions.

- *Answer logic*: This component enables OAAM to detect fundamentally correct answers to knowledge-based authentication questions even if they have minor typographical errors.

- *One-time password*: This functionality makes it possible for users to receive a one-time use password via short message service (SMS) or e-mail to be used for authentication to systems.

- *Self-service password management*: Users are empowered to create and reset their credentials using self-service.

Identity Federation

As companies move toward cloud-based services or employ external web applications, and other cross-domain services, the need to be able to authenticate to these services using the same credentials grows. Identity Federation enables the organization to simplify management of user access by eliminating the multiple sets of credentials traditionally required for a disparate environment where applications might exist in multiple domains. OAM supports federation with SAML, OpenID, form-fill, and OAuth.

The two functional components of Oracle Access Manager Identity Federation are the Service Provider and the Identity Provider. The Identity Provider component is responsible for establishing the users' identity, filtering attributes, asserting the identity information, and maintaining sessions. The Service Provider takes care of mapping the attributes, linking the identities, and passing identity information to the applications.

During login, as an Identity Provider, OAM first authenticates the user. If the user session has timed out, the Identity Provider will determine if the user needs to reauthenticate. Finally, the Identity Provider component determines if the partner application requires a challenge compatible with the level or scheme specified during the request. To support this, OAM allows the configuration of flexible authentication mechanisms. Identity Federation uses a federation authentication method and OAM Authentication Scheme mappings to control how the user should be challenged for authentication.

During logout, the Access Manager Identity Federation service provider supports two different flows depending on where the logout was initiated: from OAM or from the federated partner application.

During an OAM-initiated logout:

1. The user requests the logout via OAM.

2. OAM ends the Access Manager session.

3. OAM instructs the various WebGate instances to remove the user's session cookies.

4. The OAM federation services performs a logout operation causing logout of partner applications by either redirecting the user with an HTTP redirect or by sending a logout request via Simple Object Access Protocol (SOAP) message.

5. The OAM federation service terminates the federated session.

If the logout is initiated via the partner application:

1. The partner application redirects the user to the OAM federation service.

2. The federation service marks the session for logout.

3. The user is redirected to OAM for logout.

4. OAM instructs the various WebGate instances to remove the user's session cookies.

5. The OAM federation service performs a logout operation causing logout of partner applications by either redirecting the user with an HTTP redirect or by sending a logout request via SOAP message.

6. The OAM federation service terminates the federated session.

The Service Provider component of Identity Federation within OAM works in conjunction with the Identity Provider to deliver fraud and risk awareness in federated environments. When the Identity Provider authenticates the user, the Service Provider can be triggered to create a session with the appropriate authentication level as mapped with the federation authentication method. These attribute methods are supported as request attributes from the Identity Provider or mapping to an incoming assertion attribute name in the OAM session.

Oracle Access Management Identity Federation supports multiple federation technologies, including SAML, OpenID, OAuth, Social Identity, and form-fill.

- *SAML-based federation*: SAML is an industry standard open framework that allows the sharing of security information. It provides a standard method of transferring information across applications spanning multiple domains. It can also be used to link accounts belonging to a single user in multiple sites. The SAML protocol provides standard security tokens that can be used within multiple security frameworks. SAML also provides a standard method of representing a security token that can be passed among business processes or transactions. This is facilitated using XML documents.

- *OpenID-based federation*: OpenID allows any web site to leverage an authentication standard without the need to develop its own system. It employs the use of a single token that can be used by multiple systems. OAM supports the exchange of an OpenID identifier to exchange identity data. This can be done using a token containing the NameID and other optional attributes or by using the NameID format, a hashed user attribute along with a generated value stored within the data store.

- *OAuth-based federation*: This technology supports delegated authorization. It is an industry standard designed to transparently share private data on one site to another site. OAM supports OAuth within its Identity Federation component, Mobile and Social Security, and the API Gateways (APGs). Through these components, OAM provides token issuance, token validation, and token revocation services that are compliant with OAuth 2.0.

Mobile and Social Access

As today's organizations become more and more reliant on cloud and other web-based applications, their customers and internal users require access from multiple devices and locations including mobile devices. In addition to accessing enterprise resources from mobile devices, many organizations are deploying mobile versions of applications routinely used by their user base. Oracle has addressed this growing need with the Mobile and Social Access component of OAM.

Oracle's Mobile and Social Access leverages the core capabilities of OAM to secure applications. These include the credential collector, authentication and authorization services, and SSO. Designed with security as a platform in mind, Mobile and Social Access integrates with the Adaptive Access Management portion of the OAM stack to provide auditing, device fingerprinting, and risk analysis and authentication compatibility.

Mobile and Social Access allows the enterprise to provide the following capabilities:

- OAuth 2.0-compliant authorization delegation.

- Browser-based and native mobile applications access to identity stores.

- Interaction with cloud-based identity services such as Google and Facebook.

- A REST interface for LDAP operations that can used for user profile services.

API and Web Service Security

OAM delivers the ability to secure web services to support the industry's growing use of service-oriented architecture. Today more and more organizations are exposing web services that can be integrated into other applications in use elsewhere. For instance, a company might wish to include a stock market application in its own company intranet portal. These web services must be secured to ensure only authorized access to the functionality, lest they be misused. OAM offers standards-compliant functionality to protect web services and application programming interfaces (APIs) using the Web Services Manager (WSM), Secure Token Service, and APG components.

WSM protects Fusion Middleware Product and Application services using protocols such as WS-Security, SAML, and OAuth. WSM allows the enterprise to adjust to the ever-changing security landscape by defining policies, enforcing security, and monitoring events. These capabilities are further augmented by OAAM to help the organization identify possible security breaches and analyze risk to develop new security policies in real time. OAM WSM handles all aspects of web service security including authentication, authorization, confidentiality, and integrity using public key infrastructure to encrypt and decrypt data being passed.

The APG is used to secure access to services and APIs deployed in the cloud or within the enterprise. To do this, the APG is able to evaluate traffic for possible threats, selectively restrict requests that possibly contain threats, and actively scan content for malformed requests and viruses. The gateway also allows an enterprise to integrate LDAP identity and policy stores such as OUD or Active Directory to enforce authentication and authorization rules.

The Secure Token Service manages the relationship between a service provider and the service consumer by providing the token life cycle services; acquisition, validation, and cancellation. This service supports a trust between the web service and the API gateway, an SSO environment, or identity propagation enabled by the Secure Token Service between the client, token-issuing authority, and the token consumer.

Cloud Access Portal

The OAM access portal is designed to simplify access to partner applications and applications integrated with OAM. The access portal provides a cross-platform interface that allows users to access OAM protected resources from any device. The portal affords administrators the ability to automatically provision applications to users' accounts and gives them the ability to provide a catalog for users to select the applications to include on their personalized interfaces. In addition, the access portal will allow users to update their credentials online without the need to contact an administrator or help desk.

All of the OAM supported authentication types can be employed on the portal, thus maximizing the organization's investment and increasing user productivity. It is also able to provide access to federated partner applications and use form-fill authentication injection, which allows users to store credentials that will be used in software-as-a-service (SaaS) or web application login forms. The access portal provides the framework for organizations to deploy an SSO environment within the enterprise, increasing the productivity of their user base by giving them a central location to access their applications.

Oracle Identity Manager

As organizations grow and their user base has access to more and more resources online, the need for stricter controls and intuitive management tools grows. User productivity cannot come at the cost of enterprise security and governance. Businesses must be continually aware of who has access to what and how they received that access to stay on top of possible misuse or fraud. OIM makes up the identity governance component of the Identity and Access Management Suite of products.

The user identity life cycle must be tightly controlled to ensure users have the correct access on their first day and have that access revoked as needed when they change roles or leave the company. In addition, some users might require access that could be out of the ordinary for their job titles. Many of these roles can be granted based on a defined set of rules or selected by the user and approved by managers and administrators. However, tools are required and strict controls must be implemented to ensure correct access.

OIM is a provisioning tool that leverages the identity stores and access systems discussed previously. Whereas the rest of the Oracle Identity and Access Management Suite is dedicated to storing or virtualizing identity information and providing authentication and authorization services within the enterprise application environment, OIM streamlines the provisioning, life cycle, auditing and reconciliation services of the overall identity environment. This component completes the single identity management platform addressing all of the enterprise security needs.

To accomplish the task of improving user productivity and efficiency, OIM provides a full feature set, including self-service portals, provisioning and account management workflows, customization, and personalization.

Self-Service

The self-service features of OIM promote user efficiency by affording individual users the ability to manage many of their account details. These include the ability to reset and recover lost passwords, request new permissions, and register their accounts. No longer will employees need to open a help desk ticket when they have lost a password. Instead users can request a password reset by answering predetermined challenge questions. Users requiring new or additional permissions to systems can request them using the self-service portal referencing a catalog of possible authorization options. OIM also provides functionality that allows new users to register in the system and be granted the necessary predetermined default permission according to administrator-defined rule sets.

Workflows

In most organizations, users are granted permissions based on department or job title. The rules surrounding these grants can be defined in OIM and applied to new users as they are created. Furthermore, as employees request new permissions, complex workflows defined by the business can handle the approval matrices required before the actual grants are provided. These features ensure a maximum level of auditability to determine who has access to what and who granted the permission and when. All of this is very useful information when investigating possible misuse or performing security audits.

Delegated Administration

As organizations grow, the need to delegate administration becomes apparent. A single IT organization might not have the resources to handle all permission requests for a company. OIM provides the ability to spread administration tasks to the individual business units responsible for the content. Through the use of advanced security configurations, this also ensures that delegated administration is granted only to those areas needed. For instance, the finance administrators should only have access to the finance group of permissions and not be able to grant access to the legal department content.

Auditing

With all of the flexibility OIM provides, it is important to note how valuable frequent security audits become. OIM includes a host of features that make these audits manageable while providing readily usable information and services. The use of built-in reports and portals can give administrators and auditors a quick glance or detailed information about the state of security. Furthermore, orphaned or rogue accounts can be identified so that the required actions to reconcile the accounts can be taken.

Putting It All Together

Thus far, you have been presented with each of the major components of Oracle Identity and Access Management. These include the Fusion Middleware architecture, Directory Services, Access Management, and Identity Management. Although none of these products alone will provide everything an organization might need, these can be thought of as the building blocks of a full enterprise-level identity management solution, each providing its own set of functionality. As such, organizations whose short-term goal might be just providing authentication to Oracle applications can easily expand the functionality as requirements grow. In Figure 1-7, the overall architecture is presented as a single unit. It should be noted that this does not imply that all components must reside on a single server.

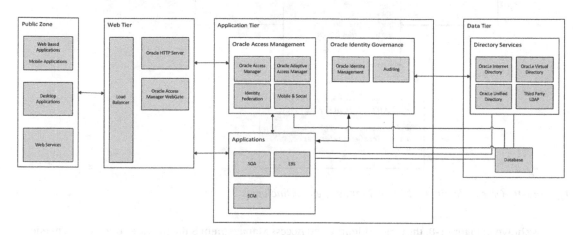

Figure 1-7. *Oracle Identity and Access Management overview*

Figure 1-7 shows how Oracle Identity and Access Management implements components throughout the application tiers to provide end-to-end security for the enterprise. Starting at the web tier, the Access Manager WebGate intercepts resource requests and determines whether or not authentication is required based on the authentication policies defined in Access Manager. If required, the Access Management server authenticates the user based on the background LDAP data tier. In addition, the Identity Management services track identity activities such as new user provisioning, authorization requests, and other governance tasks.

Summary

Oracle Identity and Access Management fills the need for highly secure, auditable, and reliable identity management within the enterprise. The components work together, forming a platform approach to identity management and thus reducing the complexity found in many situations that might have been built using multiple vendors and products as time and requirements increased. Figure 1-8 displays how data is shared between components of the Oracle Identity and Access Management Suite. With the knowledge that many organizations build security systems on an as-needed basis, Oracle ensured that the Identity and Access components are modularized. This allows companies to install the basic directory services needed and add access, SSO, and governance capabilities at a later date.

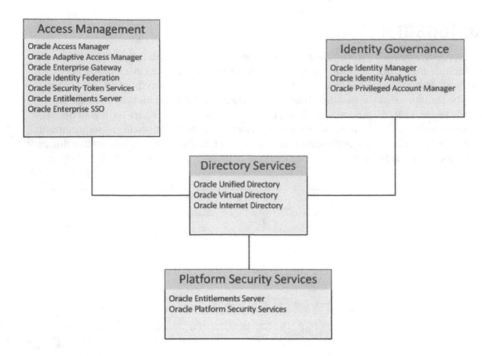

Figure 1-8. *Oracle Identity and Access Management technologies*

As shown in Figure 1-8, the Oracle Identity and Access Management Suite provides the services needed to handle all of an organization's needs pertaining to security. Access Management provides functionality such as Access Manager, Identity Federation, and Secure Token Services, increasing user productivity and application accessibility by allowing applications to share session information and provide SSO capabilities, thus reducing the number of times a user must enter his or her credentials. Identity Governance affords the organization the ability to automate many previously manual user-provisioning tasks and decreases time-to-work during employee on-boarding. Within the governance framework, Identity Manager reduces support calls by allowing users to perform their own password management and processing access requests based on a defined set of rules. Risk is also reduced with the ability to run periodic security audits and reconciliation tasks. Platform Security Services allows the organization to provide developers with standard methodologies to connect to and reference security information. All of this functionality uses Directory Services to store and access identity data. Oracle Directory Services consists of a Java-based identity store, OUD and the database-based OID. Both of these can be used to store application identity data and can be synchronized with existing enterprise LDAP identity stores. OVD allows organizations to consolidate existing identity stores without the need to copy data and provide a single point of identity data access to multiple applications.

CHAPTER 2

■ ■ ■

Preinstallation Considerations and Prerequisites

Capacity Planning

Implementing Oracle Identity and Access Management Suite or a part of the package to provide application security within an enterprise cannot be properly executed without proper analysis of the current environment and some planning for the future. This will ensure that not only the immediate requirements are met, but also that performance will not recede in the future as more users and applications are added to the environment. This chapter provides guidance for those in the planning phases of an Identity Management implementation

Fusion Middleware

Oracle Identity and Access Management, like other Fusion Middleware products and applications, relies on the WebLogic Server (WLS) architecture. As the backbone of the Fusion Middleware architecture, it is important to ensure that the WLS environment is properly configured. This starts with proper planning and analysis. There are a number of aspects to planning the WebLogic environment while deciding how to set up the environment such as memory, hardware, disaster recovery, and so on. These are discussed in what follows.

Performance requirements are an important point of consideration. One must consider what level of service the application users will expect for the applications deployed on the instance. Are the applications in question heavily dependent on identity or other data, are they memory intensive, or does the application have a specific response time requirement? Thought must also be given to the expected load the environment is going to experience.

Assessing Capacity Requirements

WLS must be installed and configured on a server that meets the minimum requirements. However, meeting the minimum requirements does not always guarantee that the applications deployed in the environment will perform at their optimum level and provide the level of service required by users of the system. While planning for a WebLogic implementation, one should work with the application planners or the developers to determine the number of expected users, number of concurrent connections, expected response times, and so on. Furthermore, it is quite helpful to gather information about the application itself, including transaction timing, transactions per second, and the application complexity. Also consider the application

© Kenneth Ramey 2016
K. Ramey, *Pro Oracle Identity and Access Management Suite*, DOI 10.1007/978-1-4842-1521-0_2

architecture, such as database connections and external service access. These will all be useful inputs in determining the necessary hardware requirements as well as software tuning for WLS. All of this might require installing a test environment and load testing it with these numbers in mind. This practice can also provide a solid benchmark to be used in future tuning endeavors.

Hardware

Capacity planning starts with calculating hardware requirements and ensuring the environment meets or exceeds these. A good place to start is the documentation included with the software that is planned for the environment. WLS requires a minimum of one 1-GHz CPU, but the requirements for the components to be installed will dictate the overall system requirements. For example, a distributed architecture where Oracle Access Manager (OAM) and Oracle Identity Manager (OIM) are installed on one host and the Lightweight Directory Access Protocol (LDAP) server is installed on another requires two physical hosts. The OAM/OIM host will require six or more cores, whereas the LDAP host requires only two.

Memory

WLS requires 8 GB available memory (4 GB physical and 4 GB swap). These represent the minimum requirements and will change depending on the number of managed servers and the software deployed in each. It is important to consider that the server itself has memory requirements as well. One can determine a starting point by allotting 3 GB for the Linux operating system (OS), 3 GB for the WebLogic Admin Server, and 3 GB for each managed server (this number will change based on what is deployed). This will provide an initial estimate of the required available memory for the WLS hardware. Further detailed discussion on memory is provided later in this chapter

Storage

Although WLS does not require a large amount of up-front storage, it is important to size the disk space to allow for growth. Again, one must consider the disk space requirements for all software that will be deployed within the WebLogic managed servers. The WLS installation requires approximately 580 MB and an additional 570 MB for coherence. The total space required is approximately 1.2 GB. As mentioned, consider the applications to be deployed. For example Oracle Internet Directory (OID) and the Directory Integration Platform and Directory Services Manager will require approximately an additional 800 MB.

Networking

Network load and network configurations on the host will have an impact on the perceived performance of the WLS instance. Oracle recommends WLS be installed on a gigabit network and the use of hardware load balancers.

Clustering

Increasing CPU and memory on the physical or virtual host will result in improvements within the WLS environment. These changes will also have an effect on the performance of the applications deployed within the managed servers. However, they do nothing to reduce the overall load on the individual server. Adding servers or clustering can result in greater performance improvements.

Clustering WebLogic environments consists of adding one or more additional hosts that run WLS and deploying applications within managed servers or multiple instances on a single multiprocessor server. However the performance would still be limited to the other resources on the physical server. An added benefit of clustering WebLogic environments across multiple servers includes increasing availability by providing failover support in the event of loss of a physical server. Adding a new separate host to a WLS cluster and load balancing the system will split the load among the multiple hosts. WebLogic will handle session information and cluster member monitoring to ensure data continuity. A properly configured WebLogic cluster will appear as a single instance to client applications.

The load balancing benefit of clustering evenly distributes application load across multiple hosts. This requires that the managed servers be deployed on every node within the cluster. It should be noted that each WebLogic instance within the cluster manages its own connections to database and underlying services. This capability further increases the performance of the overall environment, as each node handles its own set of application requests. Furthermore, additional cluster members can be added to the environment without affecting users, allowing for dynamic scalability.

The high availability improvement made by clustering allows for failover redundancy in case a node is lost because the WebLogic infrastructure handles session information and application state clusters can provide automatic failover capabilities. In addition, entire managed servers can be migrated to another node if needed.

In summary, ensuring a successful WebLogic environment requires considering the basic load that will be placed on the system in general. The single server must have at least the minimum required CPU and memory for WLS, but must also possess the requirements for the applications to be deployed. Further performance and failover capabilities can be seen with WebLogic clustering functionality. These features spread the load across multiple hosts, each handling a share of the work and taking up slack in the case of loss of one or more nodes. All of the components of the Oracle Identity and Access Management Suite require a WebLogic environment. General guidelines and considerations for the overall environment are discussed later in this chapter to assist with setting up a high-performance, highly available system.

Enterprise Deployment Topologies

Oracle Identity and Access Management represents Oracle's best of class offering of a comprehensive identity management suite based on state-of-the-art Oracle technologies. It increases user productivity while also providing a highly secure and easily adaptable environment. To support a wide variety of enterprise requirements covering performance, high availability, and scalability, Oracle Identity and Access Management leverages the Fusion Middleware architecture. With Fusion Middleware, the organization is provided with a number of options from single nodes that would be suitable for development environments to multiple-node clusters located in separate datacenters geographically located to support load and maximum disaster recovery. This section discusses the various Oracle suggested topologies along with some reasons why each should be used and how they can benefit the enterprise.

Single Node

Single node architecture describes an environment where all services run on a single WebLogic node. Although there might be more than one physical or virtual host involved, each host is running different components and no failover is provided. For instance OID would have only one instance running on Host_1. OAM might be running on Host_2. However, in this case all authentication requests would be routed through OAM on Host_2. OAM checks OID on Host_1. If either Host_1 or Host_2 goes down, all operations would halt. This topology does not provide any redundancy. At the same time, it provides no load balancing either. If the applications experience heavy loads, the single servers are required to handle the increased traffic. It is for these two reasons that single node topologies are usually only suitable for development environments.

Figure 2-1 describes the single node topology. Each level of the application environment consists of a single host/single WLS with two managed servers. As can be seen in Figure 2-1, no redundancy or load balancing is in place. This configuration is the simplest implementation and can likely be configured within a single day. Although this might be acceptable for a small organization, or one that does not anticipate high loads, a larger organization would normally require a higher fault tolerance and level of performance than provided by this architecture.

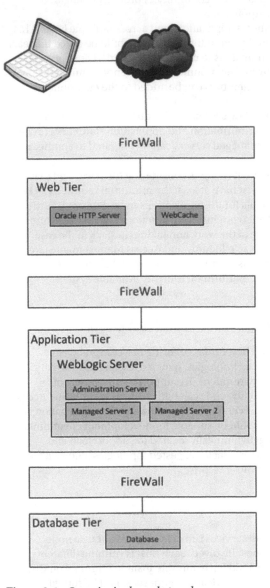

Figure 2-1. *Generic single node topology*

The image in Figure 2-1 describes a single node configuration with Identity and Access Management. Each level of the application environment consists of a single server. Requests are routed to the Oracle HTTP server with Access Manager WebGate. The WebGate determines if authentication is required for the requested resource. If the user has not yet authenticated, the request is routed to the single Access Manager server and authentication is handed off to the LDAP server. Within the enterprise, Identity Manager can be used to maintain the user repository.

In general, single node topologies work fine for environments with a tolerance for downtime or high availability requirements. For instance, development groups can use these to work on applications that require identity management. Development environments have the option to be taken offline without affecting the general user populations. By making frequent backups and having a good recovery plan in place, smaller organizations might be able to save some cost by running a single node environment if their user population is small or they do not require 24/7 availability.

Local High Availability

Oracle Fusion Middleware leverages WLS's cluster capabilities to allow organizations to implement clusters for redundancy and better performance. It was discussed earlier that a clustered environment provides scalability in that more nodes can be dynamically added to the environment to adjust to increased loads or to plan for future tasks. If an organization anticipates a higher load or growth, new nodes can be added and load balancing can ensure that the load is spread evenly across all members of the cluster.

A local high availability cluster is an environment located within a single datacenter or geographic location. This provides redundancy and load balancing capabilities and is the basic clustered environment. However, a power loss or disaster at the single datacenter will result in complete loss of service until the environment can be restarted or recovered. It should be noted that the environment could consist of two or more WLS. A typical load-balanced environment using multiple web tiers and a two-node application tier is shown in Figure 2-2.

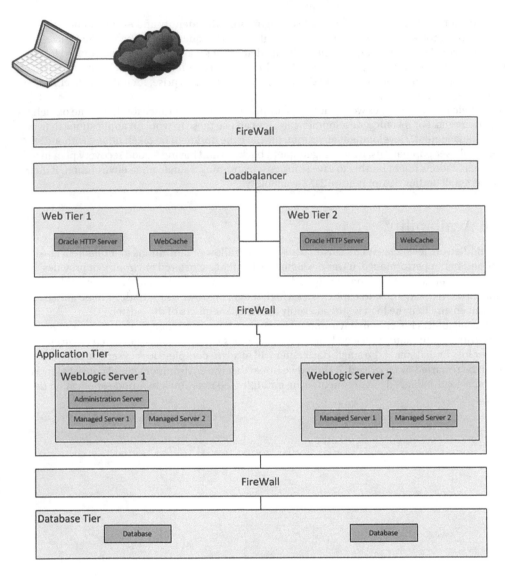

Figure 2-2. *Generic single-site cluster diagram*

Clustering objects within the Fusion Middleware environment also allows for higher availability. Nodes of the cluster can be added or removed with little to no impact for the users. For instance, if administrators notice that one cluster member is experiencing problems such as I/O or memory issues, that member can be brought offline to address the issue as long as there are other members available to take up the load. With the redundancy provided by clustering, server processes that fail can be automatically failed over to another member of the cluster.

Automatic server migration can be useful in instances where an application that is running on only one node fails. In this case, Fusion Middleware allows the server to be configured for automatic or manual migration. If WebLogic detects a failure of the service, the singleton service will be automatically migrated to another node. This is particularly valuable for services such as the JMS or JTA transaction recovery system, which can only run on one server.

Local high availability clusters provide for improved performance and redundancy against unplanned outages, and they can also benefit the organization by allowing for the application of system patches in a rolling fashion. Using clusters, organizations can apply minor patches without shutting down the entire environment. Nodes can be patched one at a time by shutting down a single node or directing the load balancer to remove it from the available servers and applying the patch. After the patch on that node is completed, it can be started back up and rejoin the cluster, and the next node can be completed without adversely affecting the user population.

These single-site multiple node clusters are perfect for organizations that need to address performance and provide a high level of availability. The environments handle loads by using a load balancer to split requests across multiple servers. The Fusion Middleware architecture provides web tier to application tier load balancing and application tier to database tier load balancing. This ensures that the server that is most able to process requests handles them. However, this is dependent on the type of server process.

Stateful Java applications such as WebCenter or ADF utilize the WebLogic proxy plug-in mod_wl_ohs to monitor server status, and the location of the session state replica information. In the event that a node is lost from the cluster, the WebLogic proxy plug-in will route requests to the available node and recover the session's state from the replica. Stateless applications rely on the load balancer to route requests to the available members of the cluster. In the case of stateful applications such as C-based components, no session state information replica exists. The load balancer preserves session stickiness and in the event of loss of a server, will route to the next available node. However, because no session information is available, the user will be required to begin a new session.

Local high availability clusters provide a high level of performance and reliability by spreading load across multiple server members. They also afford the enterprise the ability to apply patches and minor upgrades without adversely affecting their user populations. Through the Fusion Middleware architecture, high availability and load balancing are provided from the web tier through the data tiers.

Disaster Recovery and Maximum Availability

Although local high availability clusters are suitable for many organizations and provide a high level of performance and failover capability, some organizations require spreading load and providing failover across multiple geographical locations. This provides the greatest availability and fastest recovery in the event of loss of an entire datacenter. This topology can also be leveraged to provide better performance to geographically diverse user populations. This represents the most costly option to organizations, as it requires more hardware and multiple datacenter sites. It also increases the complexity and management. However, for the benefits provided to an organization that requires 99.999 percent uptime and has very high capacity and performance requirements, this is the ultimate solution.

Maximum availability is a requirement for organizations that do business around the world. These organizations cannot afford for their systems to go down or for security to be a bottleneck to service access. The information technology teams within these companies might choose to replicate data to multiple datacenters. An active–passive environment allows faster recovery. In case the primary site is lost, all traffic could be directed to the backup site during a failover process. When the primary datacenter is brought back online, all traffic is redirected to it, and replication begins again to ensure the backup site is consistent. Another option is to maintain an active–active cluster across datacenters. In this case, all traffic is load-balanced across all nodes in all datacenters. If a datacenter is lost, the load balancers automatically direct traffic to the remaining servers.

Clusters allow the added benefit of spreading computing power and tasks across multiple nodes. Many large corporations have huge amounts of identity data and users around the world. With the use of proxy servers and distributing data across multiple geographical locations, organizations can reduce network traffic and query times. For instance, locating a datacenter in New York and populating it with identity data for the North American region, while in Tokyo another datacenter handles identity data for the Asian region localizes data, reducing network latency for requests in Asian countries. Because the data source is smaller in each region, query times are also reduced. For organizations that might not have a geographically dispersed user population, but do have a large amount of data, this same functionality can be used to handle subsets of data on multiple servers, thus reducing the query time, while replicating the servers across multiple locations improve recovery time and reliability. An example of this environment is shown in Figure 2-3.

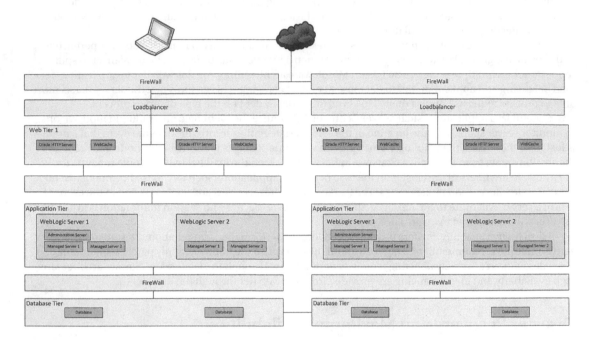

Figure 2-3. *Generic multiple datacenter maximum availability architecture*

Figure 2-3 depicts an environment where every level of the application architecture is clustered and distributed across multiple geographic locations. This replicates the local high availability cluster configuration to one or more geographically separate datacenters. Doing so increases fault tolerance and performance. It should be noted that Figure 2-3 does not go into detail about distributing data loads. These are discussed later in this chapter as they pertain to the Oracle Identity and Access Management topologies.

Topology Implementations

Up to this point this chapter has concentrated on generic terms of the Fusion Middleware environment and what can be done to increase performance and availability. The individual components of Identity and Access Management leverage these topologies to provide these benefits to the organizations. The following is a discussion of these as they pertain to the components of Identity and Access Management.

These recommendations are based on the Oracle Enterprise Deployment Guides (EDGs). EDGs represent suggested architectures that were developed by Oracle engineers to provide optimal performance and reliability. Although these do not give specific hardware or tuning requirements, they do give a general idea of how the environments should be installed and configured. These overall guidelines should be followed when determining the overall needs of the organization. Using these will also allow for a more standard environment, making it easier for new resources to be added, easier troubleshooting, and easier for new administrators to locate necessary components.

Oracle Directory Services

Oracle Unified Directory (OUD) supports multiple levels of load balancing and distribution. The most basic form is simple load balancing. This implementation allows for a proxy to determine which node should handle requests based on server status and load. This evenly divides the workload between one or more servers, thus providing failover and increased performance as shown in Figure 2-4.

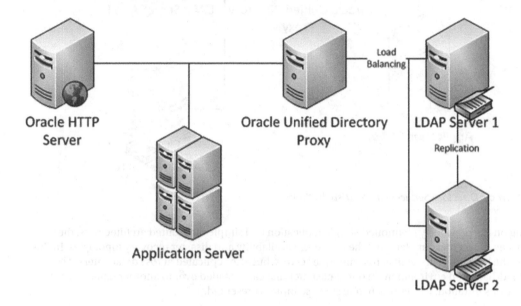

Figure 2-4. *Oracle Directory Services simple replication for load balancing*

Figure 2-4 describes a simple load balancing scenario. All data on LDAP Server 1 is replicated to LDAP Server 2. The Unified Directory Proxy handles load balancing between the two LDAP servers, thus reducing overall load on a single server instance. Load balancing, in this case, can be configured with a proxy. Using the Oracle Unified Directory Proxy, the environment can be configured to split the workload by data distribution. With a simple distribution, data is partitioned so that only part of the overall data is stored on each server. The proxy is aware of the contents of each partition and routes data to the nodes as appropriate.

Figure 2-5 describes an environment where identity information is split so that half of the alphabet resides on LDAP Server 1 and the other half resides on LDAP Server 2. This distribution unloads the server workloads by splitting the work according to what data is required. The distribution algorithms supported include numeric, lexico, and dn pattern.

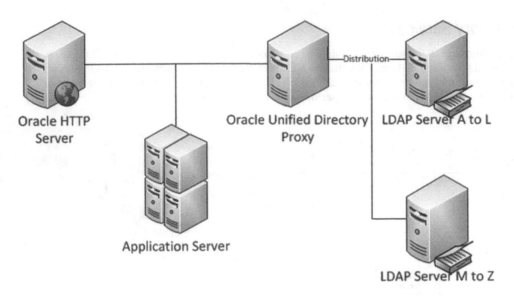

Figure 2-5. *Oracle Directory Services simple distribution*

Building on the previously mentioned simple replication and simple distributed architectures, the failover between datacenters implements the maximum availability and disaster recovery topologies. In this architecture, the load is not just split across multiple servers, but also replicated across datacenters. This provides a load-balanced environment in one datacenter that can be failed over to another datacenter in case of outage or saturation. In Figure 2-6, one such example is presented.

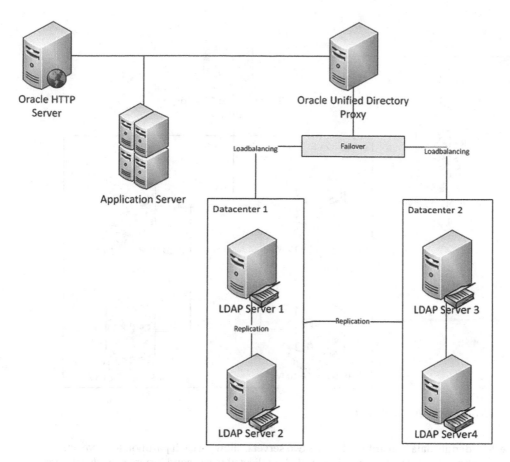

Figure 2-6. *Load balanced site with replica nodes*

Figure 2-6 depicts an environment where the LDAP servers are replicated within Datacenter 1 and that environment is replicated to Datacenter 2. The load balancing within each datacenter is configured based on the needs of the organization. The failover event can be configured to route requests to Datacenter 2 in case of loss of Datacenter 1. However, another option is to configure the failover for saturation events. In case Datacenter 1 becomes overwhelmed, requests can be sent to Datacenter 2 until the saturation goes back to normal levels.

The previous example provides load balancing between servers within each datacenter based on replicated data on each server. The next option involves load balancing distributed data between servers in a single datacenter. This option would be ideal for organizations that lack secondary datacenters, but have very large identity data needs and expect heavy loads. As seen in Figure 2-7, identity data is split across two LDAP servers alphabetically while multiple failover nodes provide stability and load balancing.

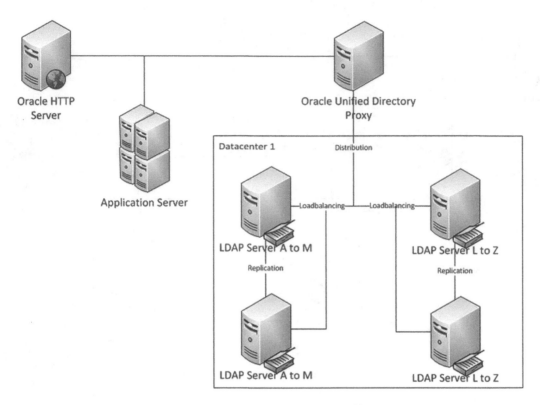

Figure 2-7. *Load balanced distributed data*

In Figure 2-7, identity data is distributed across two servers, allowing each partition to serve only requests based on the query string. Each partition is then replicated to a second instance to allow for load balancing. This architecture provides extremely fast performance as requests are directed to servers based on what it contains and the load placed on it compared to the others.

Although a load balanced distributed architecture provides a high level of performance and some redundancy in case of server issues, it provides little failover if a there is a problem at the datacenter. The ultimate in availability and performance combines all of these concepts to create a multiple datacenter load balanced distributed data environment. Figure 2-8 demonstrates the distributed architecture across multiple failover sites.

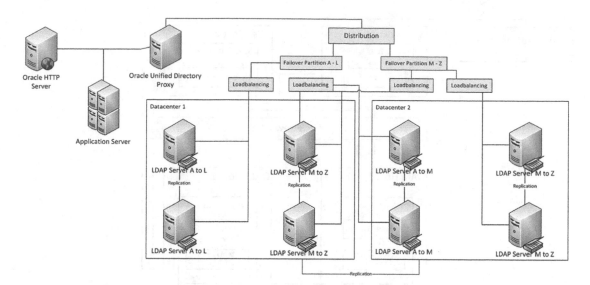

Figure 2-8. *Load balanced distributed data with failover between datacenters*

With the load balanced distributed data with failover between datacenters described in Figure 2-8, LDAP Server A to L is replicated within Datacenter 1. This data is then replicated to the two instances of LDAP Server A to L in Datacenter 2. This produces a load-balanced partition of identity data that can fail over to another datacenter in the event of an outage. As before, this reduces the load on individual servers by allowing each to handle a subset of the overall data. It then increases the reliability and performance by splitting the load for an individual data partition across multiple servers. Furthermore, the failover for each partition can be configured to redirect requests based on status or saturation.

Oracle Access Manager

OAM utilizes the WLS clustering capabilities to provide high availability and performance scalability. These features depend on proper setup from the web tier to the database tier. It should be noted that for higher availability and performance, a load balancer should handle all HTTP requests with session stickiness for HTTP traffic prior to the OHS web servers. OAM load balancing and simple failover is presented in Figure 2-9.

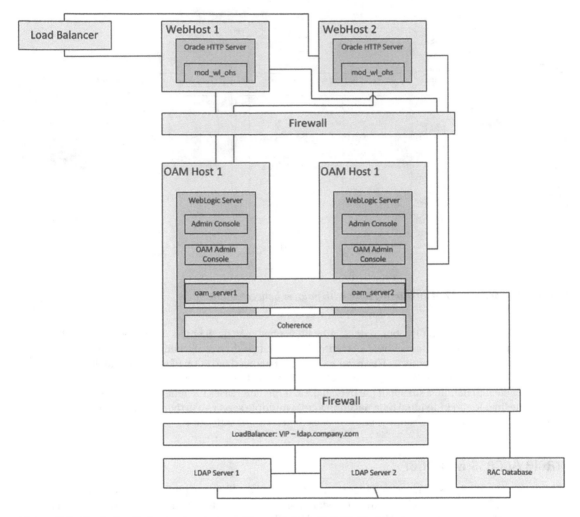

Figure 2-9. *Basic Oracle Access management local high availability architecture*

In the Oracle Access Management local high availability architecture shown in Figure 2-9, requests are first handled by the load balanced web tier consisting of two or more Oracle HTTP servers with the mod_wl_ohs module. The mod_wl_ohs module is configured using a file called mod_wl_ohs.conf, which identifies the location of WebLogic managed servers. If OAM protects the requested resource, the WebGate component configured on the OHS instance collects the necessary credentials and forwards them to OAM. It should be noted that HTTP session stickiness should be set at the load balancer to ensure that subsequent user requests are routed to the proper server.

OAM is deployed on a set of WLSs and clustered using the standard domain, machine, and cluster capabilities. As per a normal cluster, the Admin Server is installed on both WebLogic nodes. However, it only runs on one server at a time. OAM Server 1 and OAM Server 2 are deployed on machines configured on OAM Host 1 and OAM Host 2. Because both machines are part of the same WebLogic domain, they can be controlled by the single Admin Server instance running on OAM Host 1.

From the OAM Server instances, authentication queries are sent to the back-end LDAP server through a load balancer. As discussed in the previous section, the LDAP server can be OVD, OID, or OUD. For the best performance and availability, the LDAP server tier should be configured for load balancing as presented in the previous section.

Although a single instance of Oracle Access Management can support a large number of users while still providing decent performance, a multiple instance configuration can provide redundancy to provide fault tolerance and recovery as well as load balancing to provide better performance.

Oracle Identity Manager

Much like OAM, OIM relies on the WebLogic architecture for performance clusters and high availability. However, due to its reliance on Oracle service-oriented architecture (SOA), there is one more level of complexity. In addition OIM clusters configured to use a RAC database will require users to resubmit their requests if a failure at the database occurs. To provide high availability and load balancing for performance, OIM must be configured for clustering at every level from the web tier to the database and LDAP tiers. Figure 2-10 shows the Oracle Identity Management high availability architecture.

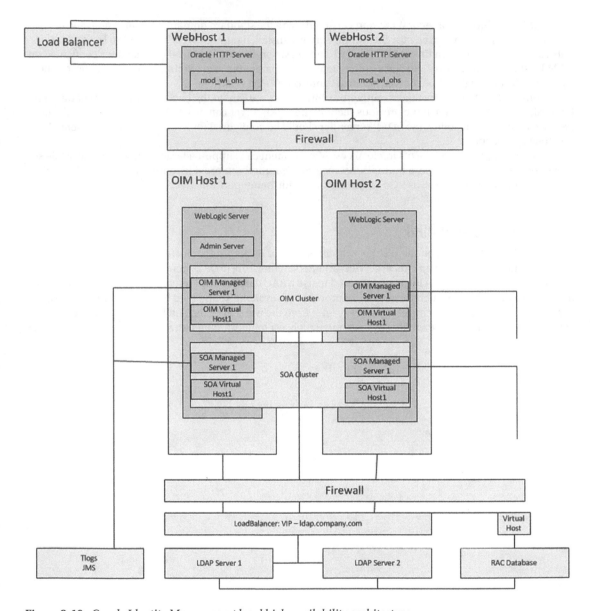

Figure 2-10. *Oracle Identity Management local high availability architecture*

A few details of Figure 2-10 should be noted.

- An OIM managed server has been deployed on both OIM Host 1 and OIM Host 2.

- An SOA managed server has been deployed on both OIM Host 1 and OIM Host 2.

- The Admin Server can be installed on both hosts. However, it can run on one node at a time.

- The RAC database is configured with a Java Database Connectivity (JDBC) multidata source on both nodes to protect against database node failure.

- The virtual host names configured for OIM and SOA allow for failover in case of loss of a node.

Using these architectures for each of the components of Oracle Identity and Access Management combined, the organization can create a scalable and highly available environment. Although each presents only a two-node cluster, they can be expanded to include more nodes and even extended to include multiple datacenters. Expansion to additional datacenters and providing data replication and partitioning, however, is outside of the scope of this book. They were discussed to allow the reader to consider these options prior to implementing the environment, as special consideration will be needed.

Each of the Oracle Identity and Access Management components was presented in a separate section, as each is a building block that can be implemented separately as the organization requirements grow. Although they can be installed on completely separate hardware or on single servers, installing them in separate WLSs will simplify software life cycles.

Implementation in phases as required allows the organization to install the minimum software to meet its needs. For instance, if the organization's short-term necessity is an identity repository to centralize management or application authentication, Oracle Directory Services can be utilized without the added overhead of Identity Manager or Access Manager. OAM can be added later to provide single sign-on (SSO), and later OIM can be implemented to complete the stack and provide access to the identity governance and full identity life cycle management.

Keeping the various components of Identity and Access Management in separate WebLogic environments simplifies the management of the software life cycle. There will be many times that the organization might need to upgrade one piece of the stack, such as Oracle Directory Services, while leaving OIM and OAM at their current versions. WLS might require a patch for OIM, although this patch could have adverse affects on OAM. In these cases, keeping each component in a separate WLS home will ensure that patches and upgrades can be performed and tested without risking the other functionality.

When determining how to implement these components, one must consider the complexity versus manageability of the chosen methodology. For some organizations, it might seem that installing each component within a separate WebLogic environment would be the best overall choice, other organizations might decide that combining OAM and OIM in the same domain while separating Oracle Directory Server is the best.

Prerequisites

As with any software, the Oracle Identity and Access Management Suite has its own set of requirements that must be met before a successful implementation can be performed. As with all of their products, Oracle provides a list of certified environments including OSs, Java runtime environments, application servers, and CPU architectures. Meeting these certifications will ensure that the environment performs at a baseline level and proper support if needed from Oracle.

Operating Systems

The Fusion Middleware suite of products and applications can be deployed on a number of certified OSs. Each organization has different reasons for running its chosen OS. Therefore, the scope of this book does not include OS recommendations. It is important during the planning phases to ensure that Oracle certifies the OS to be used. These certifications will also include any required patches and packages to make installation successful.

Fusion Middleware Hardware Requirements

Meeting the system requirements for Identity and Access Management begins with ensuring the hardware requirements for the Fusion Middleware environment are met. This includes CPU, memory, storage and network configurations. The information presented here represents the minimum requirements as provided by Oracle, but in most cases exceeding these minimums will provide room for growth and the ability to handle sudden changes in application load.

In its installation planning guides, Oracle provides a list of typical CPU configurations. For Identity and Access Management 11.1.2.x, it is recommended that the environments meet the following guidelines. The recommended architecture for each component is shown in Table 2-1.

Table 2-1. *Recommended CPU Configurations*

Managed Server	Processor
Oracle Access Manager	6 or more X Pentium 1.5 GHz or better
Oracle Directory Services	2 or more X Pentium 1.5 GHz or better
Oracle Identity Manager	6 or more X Pentium 1.5 GHz or better

In general, the Oracle Identity and Access Management products require a minimum memory availability greater than 4 GB. As such, 64-bit OSs must be used and installed on 64-bit CPU architectures. It should also be noted that 64-bit CPUs are capable of performing more calculations per second than 32-bit CPUs. Although in many cases, Oracle provides 32-bit versions of their products, the growth of 64-bit processing power and support affords many improvements in performance and scalability.

WebLogic Server

The numbers in this section are for the basic WLS. In general, the server requires 8 GB physical memory and 16 GB available memory. Additional memory will be required as managed servers and Identity and Access Management components are deployed. The specifics of memory requirements are shown in Table 2-2.

Table 2-2. *Fusion Middleware Minimum Memory Requirements by Operating System*

Operating System	Minimum Physical Memory	Minimum Available Memory
UNIX	8 GB	16 GB
Linux	8 GB	16 GB
Windows	8 GB	16 GB

In this case, available memory is equal to the physical memory plus swap memory. However, allowing more of the available memory to consist of physical memory will improve performance by reducing the I/O to swap memory stored on disk. This baseline is calculated assuming 4 GB is required for the OS plus 4 GB for WebLogic and the Administration Server:

```
      4 GB of memory for the OS
+     4 GB of memory for WLS and the Admin Server
      _____
      Total physical memory required
```

Storage requirements for the Fusion Middleware environment can vary significantly. At a minimum, 10 GB of storage is recommended by Oracle. It should be considered that logging and additional deployed software can increase this number. After installation and the environment has been stabilized, it might be prudent to reduce the log level configuration for any deployed applications and managed servers.

Oracle Directory Services

It is recommended that OUD be installed on a separate host from the Oracle Identity and Access Management instances. This is suggested to place the LDAP identity repository in the same internal network tier as the database. In the architecture diagrams shown previously, you will note that the LDAP and database environments are placed in a tier separate from the application middle tiers. For this reason, the memory requirements for Oracle Directory Services will be presented separately from the Oracle Identity and Access Management components.

OUD is a Java-based LDAP directory server. As such, like other Fusion Middleware products, it installs within a supported application server. The requirements in this section are for the software install and must be combined with the minimum requirements for Fusion Middleware. This is shown later.

Oracle recommends 2 GB physical memory for OUD to run at optimal levels in a production environment. This is in addition to the 8 GB required for Fusion Middleware. The Java Virtual Machine (JVM) for OUD can be configured to ensure sufficient memory is used without overloading the server and will be discussed during the installation section of this book. Calculating the overall memory requirements can be done simply as follows:

	4 GB of memory for the OS
+	4 GB of memory for WebLogic and the Administration Server
+	2 GB of memory for the OUD JVM

| | 10 GB physical memory required for OUD |

It is important to note that OUD uses a small database for the LDAP entries. This database requires a minimum of 1 GB of disk storage. Depending on the log configuration or replication, this can increase up to 30 to 40 GB. It is important to ensure that the log configuration and rotation are configured properly to prevent storage issues. Oracle also recommends that performance can be improved by sizing memory such that the entirety of the database files can be loaded into memory.

Oracle Identity and Access Manager

Although it is a good idea to keep the LDAP repository separated from the Identity and Access Management nodes, in most cases, Oracle Identity and Access Manager can be installed on the same physical hosts. Whether or not to install these into separate Fusion Middleware environments is up to the installers. However, the memory requirements will remain the same.

The minimum required memory for OAM is 4 GB physical and 8 GB available, and the host(s) serving OIM must also consider SOA. Thus the OIM host requires a minimum of 8 GB physical and 16 GB available just for the managed servers. This is in addition to the minimum required for the Fusion Middleware infrastructure, or 8 GB. Adding these together can give you the following calculation:

	4 GB for the OS
+	4 GB for WebLogic and the Administration Server
+	4 GB for OIM Managed Server
+	4 GB for SOA Managed Server
+	4 GB for the OIM Administration Server

| | 20 GB memory required for OIM |

If OAM is installed on the same host within the same WebLogic instance as OIM, an additional 8 GB will be required. Of the 8 GB, 4 GB is allocated to the OAM Administration Server and another 4 GB to the Access Manager Managed Server. Due to the required 4 GB for an additional WebLogic instance, it might be desired to install the OAM Managed Server within the same domain as the OIM instance.

Clustering Considerations

Within Fusion Middleware, clusters are defined as multiple WLSs working together to increase reliability and performance. As discussed previously, adding more instances to a clustered domain can be done on a single machine, provided enough resources are available, or multiple machines.

When determining clustering plans, it is important to strive to adhere to best practices. Implementing a clustered environment inherently increases complexity. Instead of single instances handling all services, additional instances are added, thus increasing the need for complex session handling, load balancing, distributed processing, and replication.

Host Configurations

Although Oracle recommends only one WebLogic instance per two CPUs, careful planning and capacity planning will ensure that the environment is able to handle the expected load. The linear scalability of the Fusion Middleware environment and Oracle's identity products allows for future growth as the organization's needs grow. It should be noted that the physical servers do not need to be configured with the same hardware. However, each server must meet the minimum requirements needed to support the deployed applications. It is also possible to deploy the clustered manage servers on different physical hosts.

For example Host_1 might contain the Admin Server, Identity Manager, and Access Manager, whereas Host_2 contains only Identity Manager, and Access Manager is deployed on Host_3. Depicted in Figure 2-11 is a basic breakout of identity management components on physical hosts.

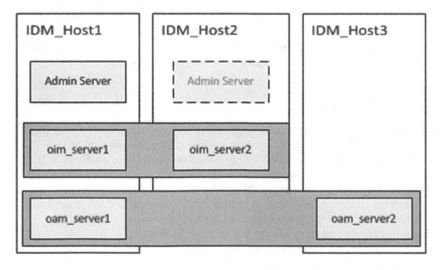

Figure 2-11. *Distribution of Identity Manager clusters on multiple hosts*

Network Planning

Network requirements increase for clustered environments as the number of servers grows. Depending on the organization's network topology (DMZ | Application Tier or DMZ | Application Tier | Data Tier, etc.), the number of firewalls and load balancers will change. At each level, firewalls will need to be configured to allow appropriate communication. In many cases, organizations have two main network zones: public zone/DMZ and an intranet or internal zone. For simplicity, this two-zone configuration is presented in this book.

The public zone or DMZ normally contains web servers that provide a front-end proxy to applications located in the intranet zone. This serves to separate the internal application zone from the public and protect resources by restricting internal communication to only approved protocols and ports. Within the DMZ, load balancers do the job of splitting the load between one or more web servers and firewalls serve to restrict communication. This provides tighter security, failover, and performance benefits.

Within the intranet zone, application servers and database servers provide services to the users. These are accessed via the proxy and web servers enlisted in the DMZ. Because the firewalls restrict access, the servers within this zone are usually configured to communicate only on designated ports. In some cases such as database servers, a load balancer might be required to handle failover and load balancing tasks. In other cases, the use of web servers configured with the WLS module can handle load balancing. Load balancers can also be used as a Secure Sockets Layer (SSL) endpoint, thus unloading the encryption handling from the underlying servers.

Whatever load balancing technology is used, the organization should ensure that it is capable of providing the following functionality:

- Monitoring HTTP and HTTPS traffic.

- Maintaining multiple virtual server names and ports.

- Detection of server status.

- Rerouting of requests in case of server outages.

- SSL management, acceleration, termination, and so on.

- Ability to add WL-Proxy-SSL : true to the HTTP Request Handler.

Summary

This chapter presented a number of concepts from hardware requirements to deployment topologies and preinstallation considerations. Instead of providing recommendations for options such as CPU architecture, OSs, and network hardware, this was presented in general guidelines. Each environment will have different requirements. However, the information provided should give an organization the ability to plan its deployment strategy.

In the chapters that follow, an installation with two node clusters is demonstrated. In some cases, multiple Fusion Middleware homes and instances could be installed on a single server. These are identified, along with the reasoning behind them.

CHAPTER 3

■ ■ ■

User and Policy Stores

Identity and access management systems are built around a core storage system capable of maintaining user information, roles, policies, and credentials. These storage systems can also be used to store information regarding network resources, peripherals, and applications. Most often directory stores use Lightweight Directory Access Protocol (LDAP)-based systems. Other storage methods include database stores and file stores. LDAP, however, provides a more widely accepted standard and compatibility with a wider group of applications.

LDAP defines a standard method of accessing information regarding identity data, network resources, peripherals, and even encryption certificates and services. The identity information can contain user credentials, contact information, and other pertinent data used to identify individuals. This data can be used by applications such as e-mail for e-mail addresses. Perhaps the most useful function is the ability to provide authentication and role definition. Applications can use directories and standard LDAP commands to ensure that users have access to systems and only the data they are authorized to use.

User and Policy Store Overview

Data stored within LDAP directories is often structured in an organized fashion providing easier access when browsing and querying information. Furthermore, the objects conform to defined formats including required and mandatory attributes. These attributes not only help identify a person or object, but also afford applications the ability to query for groups of users fitting certain criteria.

Although the LDAP does not define what data is stored or how it is structured, it does define how the data is accessed. LDAP-based directories have the advantage of being accessible to applications running on any platform. These applications can query the directory store using TCP/IP, LDAP protocols, and HTTP. As such, additional security can be afforded through the use of Secure Sockets Layer (SSL) and Transport Layer Security (TLS). This allows for faster development of applications by providing standard methods of implementing security. Multiple query tools exist for administration and browsing directories.

Other identity storage methods such as file-based security and database user stores do not provide a standard method of data access. This leads to inefficient application development, as the application must be developed with the identity store in mind and the developers must know how to access the necessary information. Furthermore, this can cause incompatibilities as organizations migrate from legacy systems to new products or development efforts.

As discussed previously, user information such as credentials and contact data can be stored within an LDAP directory. The data is normally stored in a tree-like structure that makes organization easier. In most cases, the base of the tree defines the organization or security realm. The base distinguished name (DN) can be set to something like dc=mycompany,dc=com, with DC standing for domain component. This provides a valid organization identification while being high level enough to break down the lower levels by region or business unit or other breakout defined by the enterprise. A directory tree could look something like Figure 3-1.

© Kenneth Ramey 2016
K. Ramey, *Pro Oracle Identity and Access Management Suite*, DOI 10.1007/978-1-4842-1521-0_3

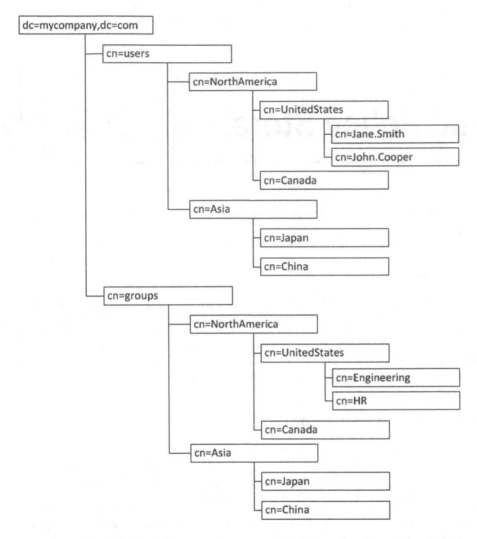

Figure 3-1. *Example LDAP directory structure users and groups by region (instead of using CN or common name, administrators could use organizational unit)*

```
dc=mycompany,dc=com
      ou=users
            ou=NorthAmerica
                    ou=US
                    ou=Canada
                    ou =Mexico
            ou=Asia
                    ou =Japan
                    ou =China
                    ou =Taiwan
```

It should be noted that these are examples. Individual organizations might wish to organize by region, country, business unit, or resource, as shown in Figure 3-2.

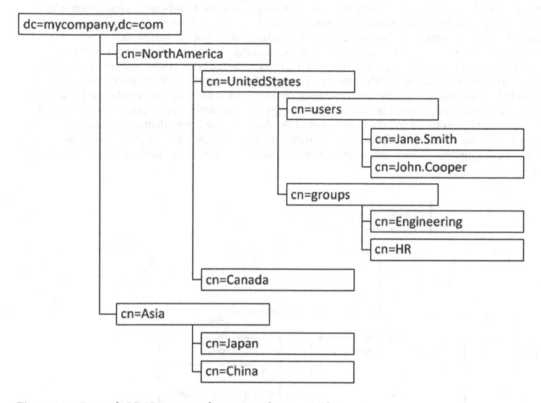

Figure 3-2. *Example LDAP structure for users and groups within region*

Because LDAP does not dictate how the data is structured or the granularity, companies are, for the most part, free to create the directory structure in a way that makes sense given their current and future situations. Design decisions might be made according to distributed administration or future plans of data partitioning or a host of other reasons.

User and resource entries are stored within these branches. For the most part, this is how user identities are stored. For instance, user John Daily might work for mycompany in the United States. In the first example, the entry could be uniquely identified by cn=john.daily,ou=US,ou=NorthAmerica,ou=users,dc=mycompany,dc=com. This is what is known as a DN. It is common to use a name-based approach to assigning a DN such as john.daily. However, other organizations might wish to create user accounts using an assigned identifier to simplify name changes or preventing duplicate user accounts if a second John Daily were to join the company.

Organizing user entries would have little use if the individual entries did not possess standard information that could be used to identify the users. Beyond storing contact information, user directories can also be used to maintain activity data such as last logon time, or last logon terminal. This data can be used to track history and in more advanced systems it can be used to identify possible fraud by alerting administrators or the user of deviations from normal activity. Along with this, information regarding failed logins can be utilized to lock accounts after too many attempts. To ensure that every entry of a certain type contains the same usable data, directories can be configured with object classes.

Object classes are used to define the standard attributes that must be configured for each entry. This can help enforce mandatory fields and optional data so that when querying a user, the client can be sure it will retrieve the same expected results no matter what user is returned. Object classes can be created for various types of entries including users, network resources, peripherals, and even meeting rooms. The definition of object classes is built by administrators and can be as simple as one or two mandatory fields, or it can include subobject classes and a combination of mandatory and optional attributes.

For example, object classes could define a person as requiring a Surname or sn, Common Name or cn, Given Name, and Date of Birth. An additional object class organizationPerson might be defined with the attributes manager, department, telephone number, and office location. More object classes can be created with different attribute profiles such as one called user, which might require attributes that are used for authentication such as password or failedLoginAttempts. Entries within the directory can be created with one or more object classes and entire branches of the directory tree can be defined such that all entries within the branch are created with the same combination of object classes, thus ensuring that all users within the North America OU are created with the Person, OrganizationPerson, and User attributes shown in Figure 3-3.

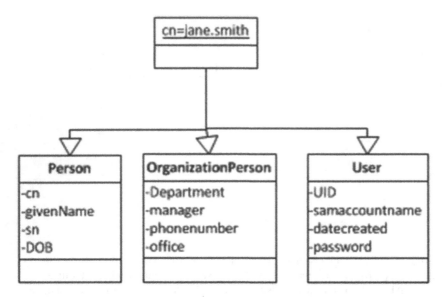

Figure 3-3. *Example of object classes and a user object*

Application permissions and authorization to network resources can be defined within a directory store. Much like user identities, roles and permissions are often organized into a directory structure. Although it is possible to grant users permissions within applications or other systems individually, the use of groups within an LDAP directory can provide the ability to grant many users the same permission. It also offloads the storage of users to permission mapping and processing to the LDAP directory.

Groups within the directory can be made up of user entries or other groups. Stored in the directory, applications can utilize standard LDAP application programming interface (API) commands to validate users' group membership before granting access to the requested resources. These application roles are normally mapped directly to permissions within an application.

The occurrence of multiple directories within the enterprise increases administration efforts and costs. When an organization maintains a network user directory and perhaps two or three application directories along with proprietary identity directories for other systems, each needs to be managed to stay on top of the constantly changing landscape. This requires more human resource time for each of the directories. In addition to the ongoing management, there is the time required for setup and configuration as well as the computing power and network resources necessary to keep them all running at their optimum level.

With the administration tasks required to manage multiple directories, it is very common for the various identity stores to become inconsistent. During the identity life cycle, setup, maintenance, and removal, ensuring user accounts are created across multiple stores can become very cumbersome. This leads to the possibility of accounts being created or removed from one directory but not others. As a result, it slows down new users when they attempt to access resources for which they have not yet received an account. On the other side of the scale, it opens the possibility that users who should have been deactivated still have access to confidential information.

As discussed earlier, multiple directories open up a number of security issues that can occur due to the difficulty in keeping all the instances synchronized. On top of this, it leads to data inconsistency. As directories are managed and user entries are modified across multiple locations, the entry attributes can become outdated. As a result applications might not have access to the most current information regarding the users or permissions.

Oracle Internet Directory

Oracle Internet Directory (OID) represents Oracle's database-based LDAP v3 compatible directory server. It is capable of storing identity data but also synchronizing with other existing data stores. Based on the Oracle database, OID is able to leverage advanced features to provide high levels of security even at the storage and backup level. Scalability of OID allows for large numbers of users, and transactions even in multisite environments. High availability is a key concern among organizations. OID provides mechanisms that assist IT departments to give their customers very high reliability. Overall OID affords an organization all of the identity and policy storage options it might need.

As a directory server, OID is built around LDAP v3 compatibility. This ensures that not only Oracle applications reference OID, but other third-party applications and services with LDAP compatibility are able to leverage an organization's investment. Unlike network access directories such as Active Directory or application-specific directories, OID is a general-purpose directory. General-purpose directories adhere to a common standard that can support disparate applications. Although Active Directory, a network, is an implementation of the LDAP standard, it is specialized for the network operating system (OS) and contains attributes required for network authentication and authorization. It is a more specialized tool and might be more difficult to adapt to a generic purpose. For this reason, OID provides a platform for companies to consolidate directories to use OID.

Security and Data Privacy

If an organization is considering Oracle Identity Management, security is high on their priorities. A high level of security should be maintained starting at the client/provider layer all the way down to the data storage and even backup levels. From the client application and authentication levels, OID supports SSL. SSL ensures that data is encrypted before it is sent over the network. From there, it provides the mechanism to determine that the recipient is authorized, decrypts the data, and ensures the integrity of the message.

Transmitting data in a secured manner as previously discussed ensures that the message cannot be intercepted and interpreted by a third party. Once it is received by the requestor or written to disk, data privacy concerns dictate the utmost care over securing the data even at these levels. Using the Oracle database as its data store, OID is able to leverage advanced database functionality to achieve this.

Oracle transparent data encryption (TDE) affords OID a method of encrypting data written to disk within the database. As OID data is written to the database, tablespaces configured with TDE ensure that the data is encrypted as it is written to the data files. The data is then decrypted as it is returned in result sets to the client. If the storage device or backup is lost or stolen, the encryption ensures the identity data remains private and secure. This layer of encryption occurs within the database. Users of authorized applications and with the correct authorization can view the data normally, with no added requirements. However, an unauthorized person or process attempting to bypass the applications and read data directly from the database files would only see encrypted data. All of this is transparent to the applications, meaning OID does not require any additional configuration changes to leverage the functionality within the database. Figure 3-4 is a depiction of a TDE environment.

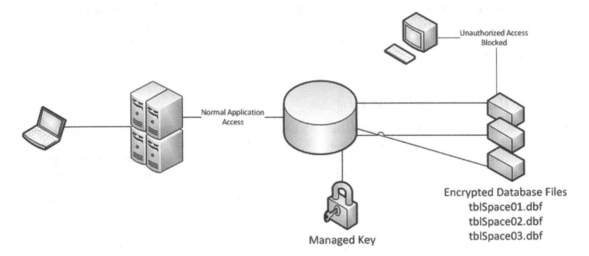

Figure 3-4. *Transparent data encryption*

Identity data not only requires security from intruders, but also occasionally must be protected from internal threats that could even include users of privileged database accounts. Unfortunately, most internal database accounts such as sys or system are known to a number of people, such as the database administrators (DBAs). This can lead to unauthorized access to key pieces of data, even if the access was unintentional. Oracle Database Vault allows administrators to effectively lock database accounts out of application data while still allowing those accounts to perform database management actions. Thus this increases security at the database layer by preventing privileged accounts from accessing private identity data used by OID.

Even outside of using TDE or Data Vault within the database, OID supports encryption of sensitive data elements out of the box. Sensitive attributes include `orclpasswordattribute` and the `orclrevpwd`. Values such as these are encrypted during storage operations and decrypted as needed. These are encrypted using AES256 if the Data Privacy mode is enabled within OID, which is the default mode.

Usability and Administration

Earlier in this book, it was discussed that security should not be a bottleneck in application performance or user productivity. Increased security should not require complicated interfaces or additional resources to maintain. OID simplifies administration tasks and environment management through the use of Oracle's Fusion Middleware Control interface and Oracle Directory Service Manager (ODSM). Using these graphical user interfaces (GUIs) along with a wide variety of command-line options, OID can be easily managed and monitored. This makes troubleshooting and ongoing maintenance simpler, as well as making day-to-day operations such as directory management more straightforward.

The ODSM interface is Oracle's standard web-based GUI that can be used to manage OID, Oracle Virtual Directory (OVD), and Oracle Unified Directory (OUD). The interface can be used as a basic LDAP browser for nonadministrator users, managing attributes, entries, and directory objects by administration users, and even managing configuration entries.

As a basic LDAP browser, ODSM allows nonadministration users the ability to view and search for other users. Any authenticated user, that is a user who exists and enters valid credentials, can browse the directory. Organizations do not need to develop custom applications or invest in expensive third-party products to allow their users to utilize OID to search for contact information on other users within the directory. It should be noted that when a nonprivileged user logs into the ODSM interface, he or she would only be able to view the Data Browser tab and not make any changes to the directory. This user's view will also be limited to only data he or she is authorized to access.

Administrative users can use ODSM as an administration tool. When the superuser account cn=orcladmin or a member of the DirectoryAdminGroup logs in, that user is presented with more data options than a normal authenticated user. Administrative users can browse the same data, but have the option of creating and modifying user and group entries, managing policies such as password policies, or even creating new object classes and new object types. These users are also able to manage system configuration entries.

Maintaining OID requires more than just managing the directory and keeping up with LDAP entries. There is a continual need to monitor the system for performance, monitor system status, and manage background processes such as the Directory Integration Platform (DIP). The Fusion Middleware Control interface is a web-based tool that allows system administrators to do just that.

If OID was installed within a WebLogic domain, WLS provides access to the control screens. Among the many functions Fusion Middleware Control provides, it allows administrators to view performance summaries, start and stop the environment, view port usage, get sizing recommendations, set up synchronization and replication with other LDAP instances, and manage security. The Fusion Middleware Control summary screen is displayed in Figure 3-5. Using this screen, administrators can gain a high-level view of the status of OID.

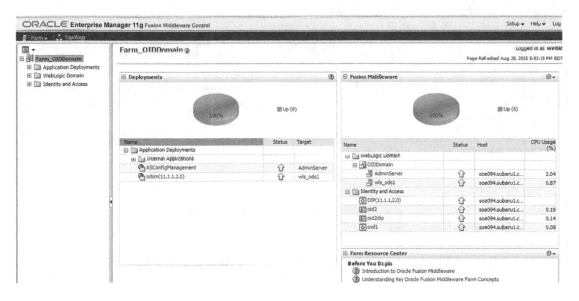

Figure 3-5. *Fusion Middleware Control summary screen*

Once an administrator has accessed the WebLogic Fusion Middlware Control screens, he or she can drill down into individual deployments and applications, as shown in Figure 3-6. In these screens, not only can you see the current statistics and status, but there are also menus that will allow modification and maintenance of the environment.

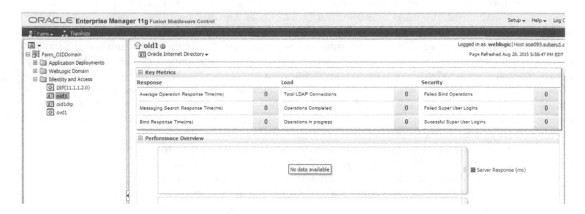

Figure 3-6. *Oracle Internet Directory summary*

Another key administration tool used for OID is the ODSM. From this tool, shown in Figure 3-7, administrators can browse, add, edit, and delete various directory attributes including users, groups, policies, and operational traits.

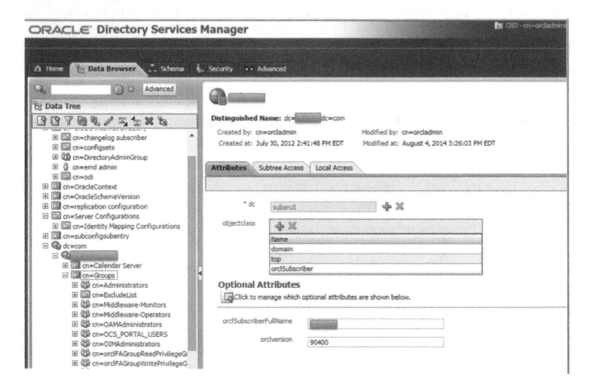

Figure 3-7. *Oracle Directory Services Manager*

Directory Synchronization

For years, OID has been at the core of Oracle's Identity Management solutions and application security within the plethora of Oracle applications and Fusion Middleware products that have been designed around the use of OID for authentication and authorization. Because of this, it is firmly rooted as the de facto standard of security within organizations that have implemented Oracle products. However, few organizations wish to change from their network directory access platforms such as Active Directory. For most, Active Directory provides a high level of network security. OID allows the customization needed for use as an application or general-purpose identity directory. Its synchronization functionality provided by the DIP, is the key capability that allows organizations to keep their investment in Active Directory or other third-party directory systems while leveraging the strengths of OID for their applications.

The DIP enables the organization to keep OID synchronized with disparate directory systems. Profiles can be created for the DIP to connect to and copy the identity data to OID. During this copy, the integration profiles allow the identity data to be transformed to match the structure and attributes necessary for the OID environment or applications using it. DIP can be configured in ways that match the organization's requirements in both performance and directory size. Perhaps the organization has a very large user base spread around the world. It might make sense to reorganize the data structure. Using DIP, the data structure in OID does not necessarily need to match that stored in Active Directory. The DIP supports the synchronization of multiple identity stores into one single OID instance. Because OID supports the storage of multiple contexts, the organization can easily organize and manage users coming from each of the stores. Figure 3-8 shows an example of how the DIP can bring multiple disparate directory sources together into a single source.

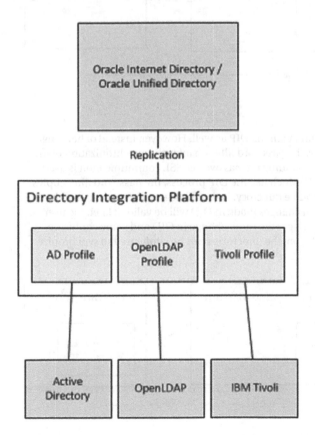

Figure 3-8. *Visualizing the Directory Integration Platform*

Directory synchronization is a valuable resource until inconsistencies are created. These most often come from editing user or group attributes in OID while the source of truth might be another directory system such as Active Directory. A common attribute is the user password. Users do not want to manage multiple passwords for different systems and applications. Requiring them to do so leads to weakened security as users tend to write their passwords down or use easier passwords. Changing a password for a user in OID that was synchronized from Active Directory can cause inconsistencies that might prevent the user from logging into required resources. OID has the ability to use external authentication plug-ins and external password filters to help prevent this from happening.

The external authentication plug-in allows administrators to configure OID to hand off credential verification to the source directory for the given user. Doing this, OID does not maintain the user password for any user that was copied from the source. Instead, user attributes trigger OID to pass the credentials to the source for validation. As such, the valid user must exist in both OID and the source, but password changes in OID will not affect authentication, as the only valid password is stored in the source. Thus, the source of truth remains the source directory, and passwords must be changed there. The DIP handles keeping all attributes synchronized and the plug-in handles authentication, providing a very secure environment without synchronizing passwords. Using external authentication, as shown in Figure 3-9, OID hands off the credential validation to the source directory.

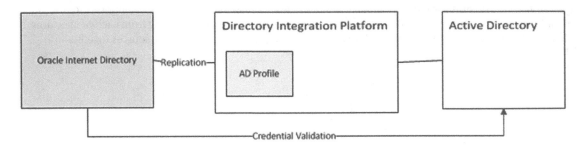

Figure 3-9. *External authentication plug-in*

The external password filter works in conjunction with the DIP as well. However, instead of handing off the credential validation to an external directory, the password filter enables the synchronization of the source password to OID. To ensure data privacy surrounding the passwords, SSL communication is used when the password is copied from the source to OID. Much like the DIP process, the password filter copies password changes to OID as they are made in the source directory. It should be noted, however, that this process can lead to data inconsistencies as password changes made in OID will be valid. If later, the user changes his or her password in the source, this will trigger the same change in OID and some confusion could occur. Instead of handing off credential validation, the directories can be configured to synchronize the passwords as shown in Figure 3-10.

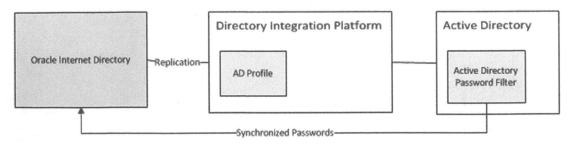

Figure 3-10. *Oracle Internet Directory password filter*

Both the external authentication plug-in and external password filter working with the DIP provide the organization the ability to maintain an application directory that is kept up to date with the enterprise directory system. This leads to a more efficient security setup as administrators only have to maintain enterprise users within the enterprise directory, knowing those additions and updates will filter their way to the OID instance.

Oracle Unified Directory

Oracle has a long-standing history of providing a strong LDAP directory with OID. Recently, this offering has been upgraded to include OUD, a fully Java-implemented LDAP repository that provides many options for scalability while also providing features including synchronization, proxy, and virtualization.

Architecture

OUD is built from the ground up based on the Java EE platform. According to Oracle, this allowed them to leverage the memory management capabilities and tuning provided by using the Java virtual machine (JVM). For data storage, OUD utilizes the Berkeley Database Java Edition from Oracle. This object-oriented database provides a stable platform that is well suited for mapping entries and attributes within the directory. This architecture allows for less I/O latency and platform-independent backup and management capabilities, thus increasing overall performance while making the whole system much less dependent on enterprise architecture decisions.

Much like OID, OUD is very capable of highly available architectures. OUD was designed with high availability as a top priority. It provides the ability to be deployed on multiple nodes in multiple datacenters affording not only local failover, but also disaster recovery. Furthermore, with OUD's referral functionality and transparent rerouting ability, outages can be instantly failed over to other datacenters, thus providing 99.99 percent uptime.

Scalability

Extremely high availability is provided by the OUD architecture and its ability to support multiple nodes and datacenters. Coupled with high availability, scalability provides the enterprise the ability to start the directory large enough to support its current requirements without the need to size the environment to support future needs as well. Oracle states that OUD can be scaled to billions of users on commodity servers. This is achieved through the proxy capabilities and distributing the identity data across partitions deployed on a series of servers. Distribution of partitions allows the work to be spread among multiple servers, thus reducing the workload and I/O operations typically seen in environments where the load can only be balanced across one or two servers in a datacenter.

To add the greatest value to the scalability of OUD, global indexing allows OUD to map requests to the correct distribution partition. Data partitioning can be used by OUD to spread data storage across multiple nodes even in multiple datacenters. This can be very useful in not just spreading the workload, but done regionally, it can be leveraged to reduce the effects of network latency. If an enterprise has users spread around the country or even the globe, it is likely it also has datacenters strategically located in different regions. Using OUD's ability to partition data permits regional users to be placed on servers that best suit the region in which they regularly work. The Global Index enables OUD to keep track of where entries are located. If a node receives a request, it is quickly referred to the proper node, no matter its location, to validate the user. This capability can help organizations not only lower costs, but also increase user productivity.

Replication

Like OID, OUD provides a mechanism to replicate data across multiple nodes. This capability is essential to ensuring maximum availability. Replication ensures that data updated on one node of the identity repository is propagated to the other member nodes of the cluster. Extended latency or environments not properly replicated can lead to security concerns, as a user might be able to access resources from which he or she has been removed for a period of time, or password changes might not take effect right away. OUD introduces advanced replication. The advanced replication model uses replication servers to synchronize data changes with other directory servers. By moving the replication work to separate servers, the work of synchronizing changes is offloaded from the directory servers, allowing them to utilize resources focused on directory queries. To ensure security around replication, OUD replication services ensure that identity data requested by a client application is only released after the data has been replicated to other members. Furthermore, identity security is increased by preventing sensitive data from being replicated to servers that could be less secure.

Usability and Manageability

Just like OID, OUD is managed using ODSM and Fusion Middleware Control. Because these were discussed earlier, the discussion is not rehashed here.

Oracle Virtual Directory

Most organizations already have investments in multiple identity stores. These include their network identity store, application-specific identity stores, and perhaps even business-unit-specific LDAP directories. In many cases, the various data stores contain the same users or subsets of the same data. This often leads to confusion, with administrators trying to manage the groups of users and knowing where the various stores are located. Synchronizing these directories into a central repository can lead to other issues such as increased data storage requirements and ensuring the applications are able to leverage the store in a way that is expected. OVD was introduced to resolve these issues. OVD allows organizations to consolidate their identity directory investments into a centralized store without the need to copy data.

OVD is billed as a directory aggregation tool. It provides organizations with the ability to access the various user repositories in use without the need to replicate the data contained within them. In addition, OVD provides data transformation services to allow applications to receive data in the format expected or required. OVD can even provide an LDAP interface from non-LDAP type sources such as database or file-based identity stores.

Architecture

Deployed on WLS, OVD leverages many of the WLS benefits. Within the WLS environment, OVD is able to integrate with the credential store, audit, and logging frameworks as well as be managed using the Fusion Middleware Control interface.

OVD consists of four logical layers or components that work together to provide all of the services, such as data aggregation and transformation. Starting at the first layer, OVD provides listeners that allow external applications to connect to it. The next layer consists of processes that verify the validity of requests and determine which adapter to use to satisfy the request. The request is passed to a joining mechanism that operates with the various adapters to retrieve the data and transform data set. These layers work together in providing what appears to be a single data source to applications. Figure 3-11 shows the main components of OVD.

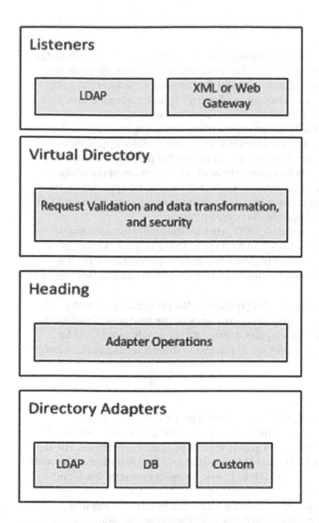

Figure 3-11. *Oracle Virtual Directory components*

Adapters allow OVD to connect to the underlying identity stores whether they be LDAP or database repositories. Adapters are provided to connect to LDAP, database, and local stores. In addition, custom adapters can be configured to handle a variety of other repositories.

OVD, because of its architecture, is extremely fault tolerant. Multiple instances of OVD can be deployed on separate servers or even in different regions with the same configuration. There is no need to replicate data or storage files and no need to provide database high availability options. Each instance of OVD connects to the back-end repositories using its own adapters, so any of the instances can serve requests based on load balancing or outages. Furthermore, the data is guaranteed to be as current as the source repository.

Along with its ability to be deployed across multiple servers to provide its own fault tolerance, OVD adapters can be configured to spread loads across multiple instances of the source directory. For instance, if there are two Active Directory instances using replication, the OVD adapter can be configured to reference both, thereby providing automatic failover if one of the instances fails.

Aggregation

OVD does not store the identity data that it presents. Instead, through the use of the adapters mentioned in the previous section, OVD serves as a proxy for multiple back-end directories. This reduces the costs and administration effort associated with replicating and synchronizing multiple stores while leveraging the repositories already in use within the organization. It also improves efficiency by decreasing the time and effort taken during development as new directories or interfaces do not need to be built.

Most companies have a couple, if not several different user repositories. These might consist of the network or enterprise directory, business-unit-specific directories, e-mail, LDAP-enabled applications that implement their own directory, and even database sources such as EBS or PeopleSoft. In many of these cases, the data stored in one source cannot easily be adapted to work with the other applications, necessitating the replication of data. Often the individual business units that control the applications have requirements that mandate they retain control of their directories. For whatever reasons multiple data stores must be maintained, OVD can consolidate them and provide that single point.

To facilitate the aggregation of identity store information, OVD provides the ability to transform or map data to formats expected by the application or the back-end data store. These mappings occur in a bidirectional flow. This allows the request to be formatted to match the store requirements while the returned data is then transformed to match the client application requirements. OVD can also be configured to remap attribute names and values.

Acting as a proxy, OVD systematically routes each incoming request to the proper adapter using logic that examines the DN pattern, filters, attributes, and queries to determine the best possible adapters to use to satisfy the request. This reduces the number of adapters queried for the result, tunes OVD for performance, and allows the configuration of more complex environments without affecting performance.

Access Management

Many organizations are working toward providing their users with single sign-on (SSO) capabilities. However, as discussed, these organizations could have multiple user repositories. It was mentioned earlier that OVD provides a single front end for client applications to access various back-end directories. The same goes for access management systems. Products like OAM most times require an LDAP repository to provide authentication and authorization services. Providing that LDAP front end no matter what the back-end repositories look like is what OVD was designed to do.

Another benefit OVD provides to access management systems is an abstraction layer. Over time, changes to the underlying data stores occur. These changes can cause client applications or access management systems to fail. By separating the underlying directory structures from the client applications, OVD protects them from changes by ensuring data continues to be transformed or translated into the correct format required.

Summary

This chapter presented the three main products that make up Oracle Directory Services, providing the foundation of Oracle Identity and Access Management. OID and OUD both provide user management and storage solutions and expose an LDAP interface for client applications and services. OVD helps organizations to consolidate management of multiple directories and provide a single source for applications that require authentication services. The rest of this book concentrates on the installation of OUD as Oracle has indicated the product will be the direction of Oracle Directory Services. However, when OVD provides additional functionality or an alternative solution, it is also discussed.

CHAPTER 4

■ ■ ■

Oracle Directory Services Installation and Configuration

Oracle offers multiple options for Lightweight Directory Access Protocol (LDAP) data storage. Oracle Internet Directory (OID) and Oracle Unified Directory (OUD) both provide storage, and Oracle Virtual Directory (OVD) allows multiple disparate LDAP stores to be presented as a single source. This chapter presents the installation and configuration steps for each product. At the time of this writing, Oracle E-Business Suite is certified for use with OID and not OVD or OUD. The installation process for all three products is presented as a guide for future reference. However, in later chapters, only OID is used.

Preinstallation Tasks

Prior to beginning the actual software installation and laying down binaries on the file system, it should be noted that there are some tasks that must be completed to ensure a successful operation. Care should be taken to create or complete these tasks such as populating operating system (OS) users, setting kernel parameters, and granting the proper permissions. These items are covered in the subsequent sections of this chapter.

Operating System Users

For most Oracle application installs, OS users and groups should be created to perform the installation and configuration tasks. Creating OS groups will allow other OS users to perform certain tasks related to the management of the application environment. The most common OS users and groups related to installing Oracle applications in Linux environments are the oracle user and oinstall or dba groups.

To create the necessary oinstall and dba groups perform the following commands as the root directory:

```
[root@clouddemolab home]# groupadd oinstall
[root@clouddemolab home]# groupadd dba
```

After the groups are created, create the oracle user.

```
[root@clouddemolab home]# useradd -g oinstall -G dba oracle
```

© Kenneth Ramey 2016
K. Ramey, *Pro Oracle Identity and Access Management Suite*, DOI 10.1007/978-1-4842-1521-0_4

■ **Note** -g indicates the primary group to which the user should be added. -G indicates any secondary groups.

To set the password for the user, use the following command as the root user:

```
[root@clouddemolab home]# passwd oracle
```

Operating System Configuration

Prior to installing the Oracle Fusion Middleware infrastructure and Oracle Identity Management software, it is important to ensure the OS meets the minimum requirements and configuration. The following presents the kernel parameters and packages and the file changes that are required.

The following kernel parameters need to be set:

```
kernel.sem  256  32000  100  143
kernel.shmmax 10737418240
```

To set these parameters, edit the sysctl.conf file located in the /etc directory.

```
[root@clouddemolab home]# vi /etc/sysctl.conf
```

Add or edit the following lines in this section of the file:

```
# Controls the maximum number of shared memory segments, in pages
kernel.shmall = 4294967296
kernel.sem = 256 32000 100 142
kernel.shmmax = 10737418240
```

After setting these values in the sysctl.conf file, you must activate and verify the new values are shown using this command:

```
 [root@clouddemolab home]# /sbin/sysctl -p
net.ipv4.ip_forward = 0
net.ipv4.conf.default.rp_filter = 1
net.ipv4.conf.default.accept_source_route = 0
kernel.sysrq = 0
kernel.core_uses_pid = 1
net.ipv4.tcp_syncookies = 1
net.bridge.bridge-nf-call-ip6tables = 0
net.bridge.bridge-nf-call-iptables = 0
net.bridge.bridge-nf-call-arptables = 0
kernel.msgmnb = 65536
kernel.msgmax = 65536
kernel.shmmax = 68719476736
kernel.shmall = 4294967296
kernel.sem = 256 32000 100 142
kernel.shmmax = 10737418240
```

The open file limits must be set to 4096 to support the instance. To do so, edit the `limits.conf` file.

```
[root@clouddemolab home]# vi /etc/security/limits.conf
```

If the environment is to be installed on Oracle Linux or RedHat Linux, you must perform the edit in /etc/security/limits.d/90-nproc.conf as well. If this is missed, the values in this file might override the values in the limits.conf file.

In both of the files just listed, ensure the following lines are added or edited:

```
* soft nofile 4096
* hard nofile 65536
* soft nproc 2047
* hard nproc 16384
```

After editing this file, the server must be rebooted to ensure all the changes take effect.

Operating System Packages

Each Oracle application has its own set of required packages. Depending on the version of Linux you are using, the installation procedure might be different. In the following list, you should note that some packages require both 32-bit and 64-bit versions to be installed on a 64-bit OS. If these packages are not installed, the installation will not complete properly. The Oracle Installer will check these and display errors during the installation.

```
binutils-2.20.51.0.2-5.28.el6
compat-libcap1-1.10-1
compat-libstdc++-33-3.2.3-69.el6 for x86_64
compat-libstdc++-33-3.2.3-69.el6 for i686
gcc-4.4.4-13.el6
gcc-c++-4.4.4-13.el6 glibc-2.12-1.7.el6 for x86_64 glibc-2.12-1.7.el6 for i686 glibc-devel-
2.12-1.7.el6 for i686 libaio-0.3.107-10.el6 libaio-devel-0.3.107-10.el6 libgcc-4.4.4-13.
el6 libstdc++-4.4.4-13.el6 for x86_64 libstdc++-4.4.4-13.el6 for i686 libstdc++-
devel-4.4.4-13.el6 libXext for i686 libXtst for i686 libXext for x86_64 libXtst for x86_64
openmotif-2.2.3 for x86_64 openmotif22-2.2.3 for x86_64 redhat-lsb-core-4.0-7.el6 for x86_64
sysstat-9.0.4-11.el6 xorg-x11-utils* xorg-x11-apps* xorg-x11-xinit* xorg-x11-server-Xorg*
xterm
```

At this point in the procedure, the OS should be fully prepared for the installation to proceed. Performing these operations prior to installing the software will ensure a problem-free installation. In many cases, the installer will provide detailed messages if anything was missed. In the event of errors during the installation process, stop the installation and fix the problems before proceeding.

Database Preparation

Before beginning the installation, prepare the required database schemas. This is done using Oracle's Repository Creation Utility (RCU). The RCU software is available for download from the same location as the Identity Management software. It is very important to ensure that the version of the RCU is exactly the same as the version of the Fusion Middleware software to be installed.

In this case, OID 11.1.1.9 will be installed. Therefore, the RCU version used will be 11.1.1.9. As discussed previously, OID 11.1.1.9 is the latest version certified for use with Oracle E-Business Suite.

After downloading the required software, it is time to begin the repository creation. Unzip the downloaded file to a stage directory. In this case we use /home/oracle/stage/rcu. Once unzipped, a directory called rcuHome will be created. Run the rcu file located in rcuHome/bin as shown in Figure 4-1.

```
oracle@clouddemolab:~/rcu/rcuHome/bin                 _ □ ×

File  Edit  View  Search  Terminal  Help
[oracle@clouddemolab rcuHome]$ cd bin
[oracle@clouddemolab bin]$ ls
adapters              expdp        kgmgr0        oraenv        sqlplus0
adrci                 expdp0       kgpmon        orajaxb       statusnc
adrci0                exp0         lbuilder      orapki        symfind
aqxmlctl              extjob       lcsscan       oraxml        sysresv
aqxmlctl.pl           extjobo      linkshlib     oraxsl        tkprof
bndlchk               extproc32    lmsgen        osh           tkprof0
cfo                   genagtsh     loadjava      owm           tnsping
coraenv               genclntsh    loadpsp       plshprof      tnsping0
dbgeu_run_action.pl   genclntst    loadpsp0      plshprof0     trcasst
dbhome                genezi       lxchknlb      procob32      trcroute
dbshut                genezi0      lxegen        rcu           trcroute0
dbstart               gennfgt      lxinst        rcuJDBCEngine uidrvci
deploync              gennttab     mkstore       relink        umu
dg4pwd                genoccish    ncomp         rman          unzip
dg4pwd0               genorasdksh  netca         rman0         wrap
dgmgrl                gensyslib    netca_deinst.sh rtsora32    wrc
diagsetup             imp          netmgr        schema        wrc0
dropjava              impdp        oerr          sqlldr        xml
echodo                impdp0       ojvmjava      sqlldr0       xmlwf
eusm                  imp0         ojvmtc        sqlplus       zip
exp                   kgmgr        orabase       sqlplus32
[oracle@clouddemolab bin]$ ./rcu█
```

Figure 4-1. *Repository Creation Utility*

Prior to running the RCU, the Database Initialization Parameter, open_cursors should be set to at least 500. The default is usually 300. To change this parameter, perform the following command from an SQLPlusprompt:

```
alter system set open_cursors = 1000 scope = both;
```

The first page of the RCU is a Welcome screen. Clear the Skip this Page Next Time check box to skip the Welcome screen on subsequent runs of the RCU. This is shown in Figure 4-2.

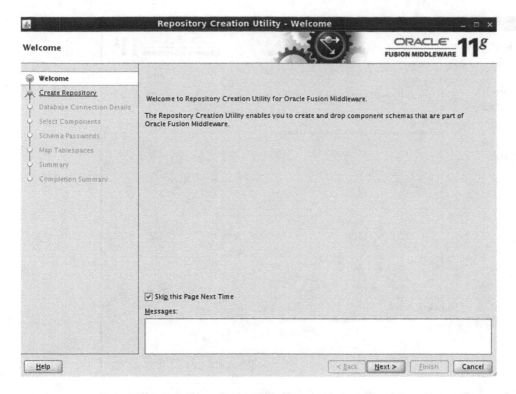

Figure 4-2. *Repository Creation Utility Welcome screen*

Figure 4-3 displays the first decision point in the RCU. At this point you are provided with the option of creating a new metadata repository or deleting an existing one.

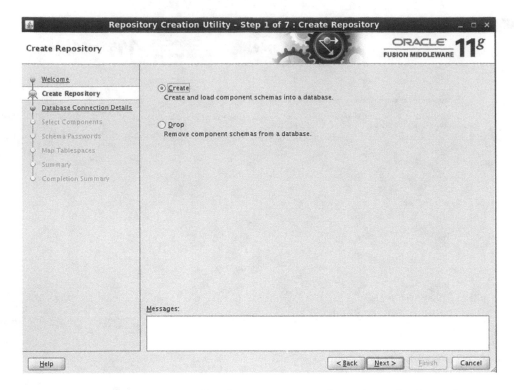

Figure 4-3. *Repository Creation Utility: Create component schemas into a database selection*

The RCU can be used to create the required database schemas or drop schemas as needed. The tool can be run multiple times. Therefore, if a schema was missed or created mistakenly, the RCU can be rerun to create the missed objects or delete entire schemas. Caution should be taken to ensure that the schemas to be deleted are not currently in use. After deciding to create or drop a repository, the RCU will prompt you for the database connection, details as shown in Figure 4-4.

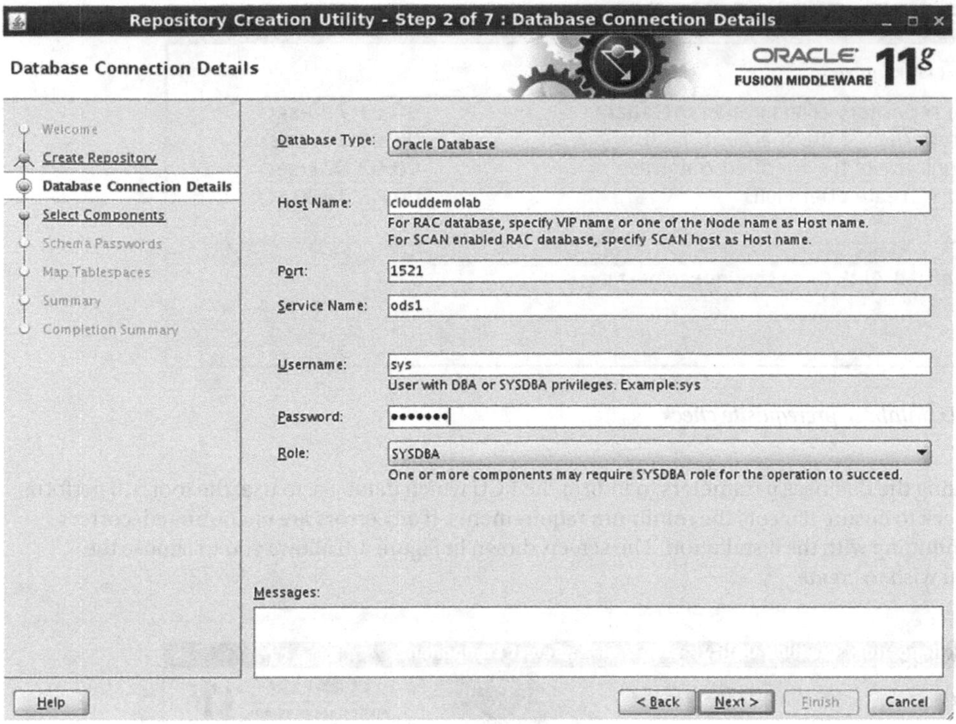

Figure 4-4. Database configuration parameters

It should be noted that the RCU will not support pluggable databases or container databases. If in doubt, discuss this with your database administrator (DBA).

Once the Create or Drop operation is chosen, the RCU tool will prompt for the database connections. Your DBA can provide this information. In this case, the database is actually running on the same host as the Identity Management environment. Although this is possible on a host with enough resources and will support a development instance, it is recommended that the database and Fusion Middleware components be run on separate hosts in production environments. A prerequisite check will be completed as shown in Figure 4-5.

■ **Note**   The RCU should use the SYS account with SYSDBA privileges. However, if this is not possible, the RCU can be configured to generate the schema creation scripts that can be provided to the DBA.

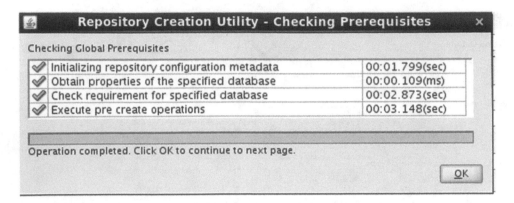

Figure 4-5. *RCU database prerequisite check*

After inputting the database parameters to inform the RCU which database to use, the tool will perform a precursory check to ensure it meets the minimum requirements. If any errors are encountered, correct them before continuing with the installation. The screen shown in Figure 4-6 allows you to choose the components you wish to create.

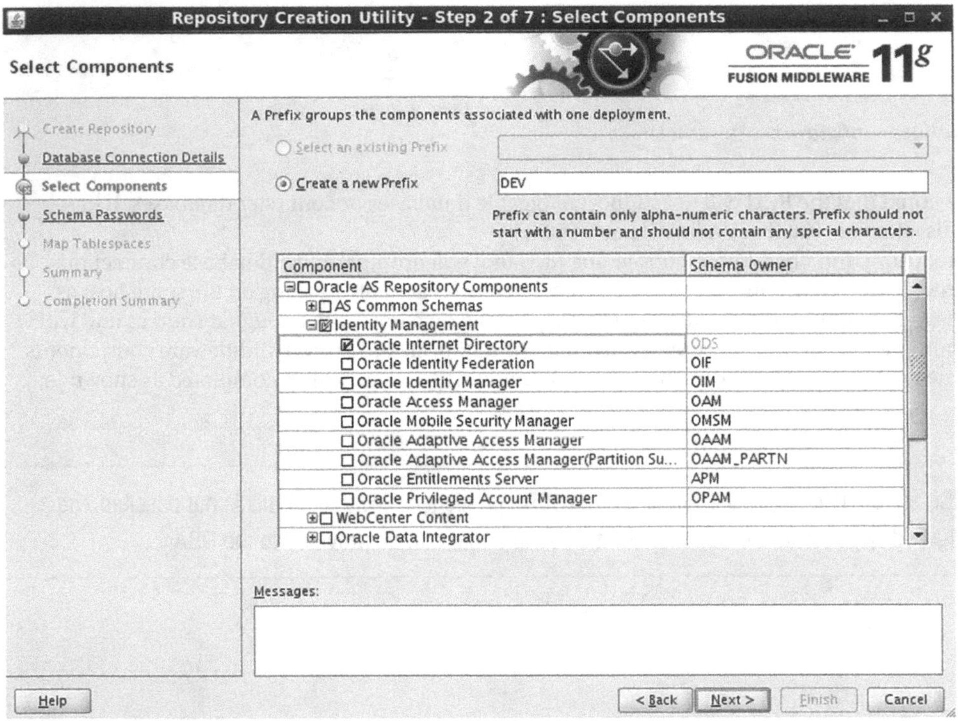

Figure 4-6. *Schema selection screen*

On the Select Components screen, you can select the Fusion Middleware components you plan to install. Although multiple components can be installed within the same database, it is a common practice to separate Identity Management components from other applications such as WebCenter Content or system-oriented architecture (SOA). In this case, only the OID schema Oracle Directory Services will be installed on this database. This is done for convenience for management and maintenance. Patches and upgrades for the database will be isolated to the OID database, and the administrators will not need to worry about affecting the Identity and Access Manager applications. You will be shown the confirmation screen seen in Figure 4-7.

■ **Note**   For most Fusion Middleware products, the database can store multiple instances of the schemas, thus the option to create a prefix in the previous screenshot. However, only one instance of OID is allowed per database. As seen on the Schema Selection screen, no prefix is added to the ODS schema.

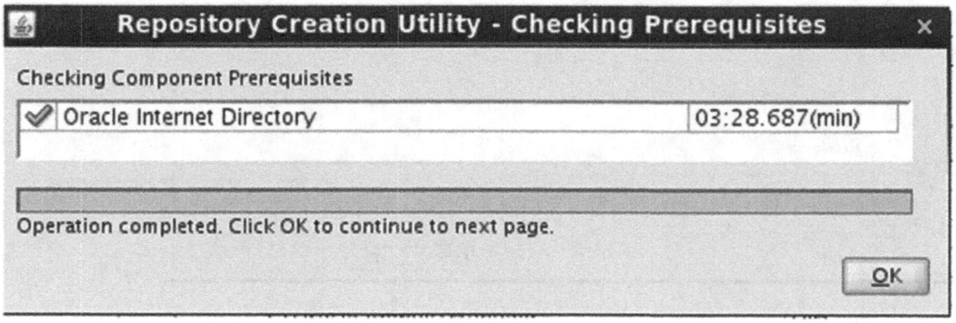

Figure 4-7. *Precheck completed*

After the component selection is made, the RCU will check the database to ensure uniqueness and compliance with prerequisites.

A password must be set for the schemas to be created by the RCU, as shown in Figure 4-8. You can use the same password for all schemas, or different passwords for each. Some environments might require different passwords due to security concerns.

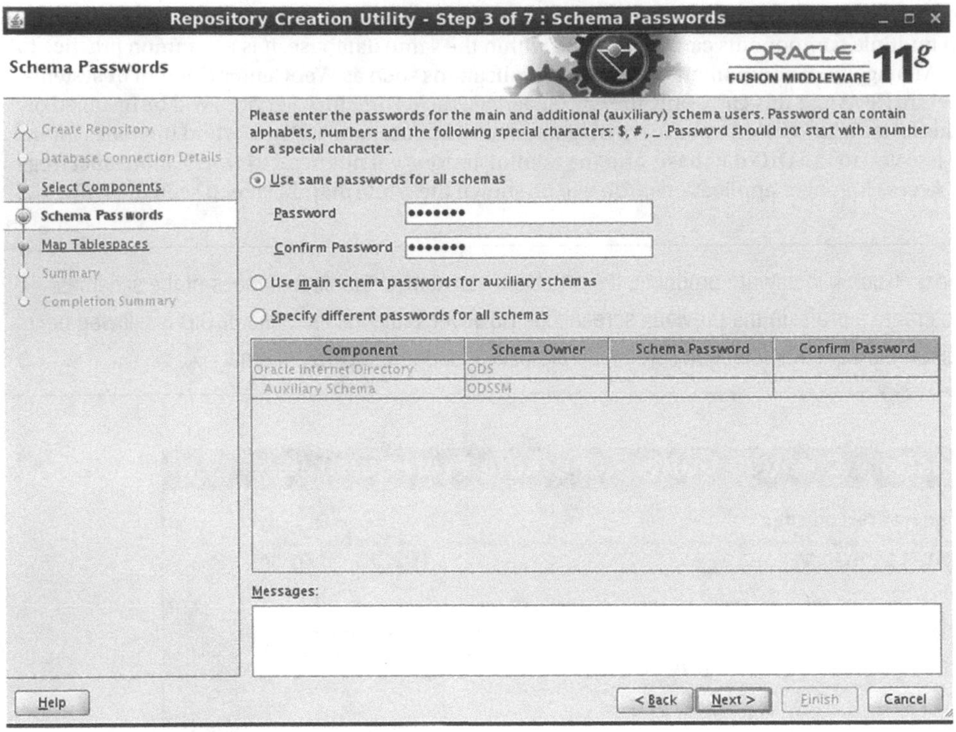

Figure 4-8. *Set schema passwords*

Figure 4-9 displays a summary of the database prerequisite and actions the RCU will follow.

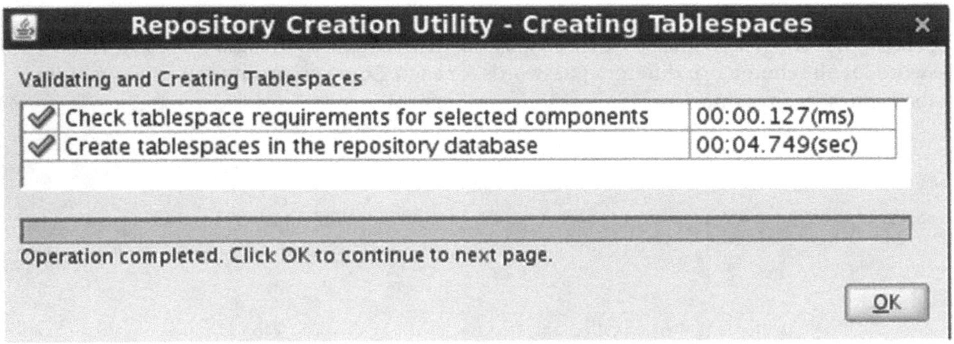

Figure 4-9. *Creation of necessary database objects*

The tablespace mapping screen displays each component to be installed and the tablespaces that will be created. Clicking the Additional Tablespaces button displays a more detailed list. This screen, shown in Figure 4-10, is informational and requires no input.

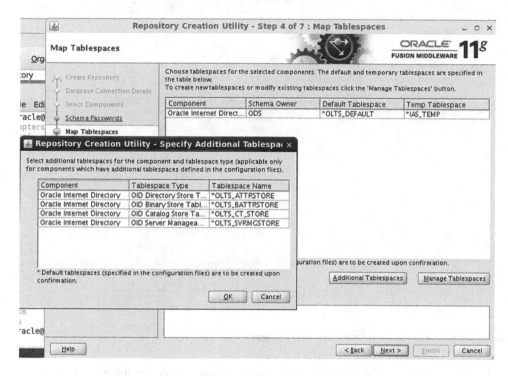

Figure 4-10. *Tablespace mapping*

After clicking Next on this screen, a summary of the inputs is displayed, providing you with a chance to review the configuration before anything is created, as shown in Figure 4-11.

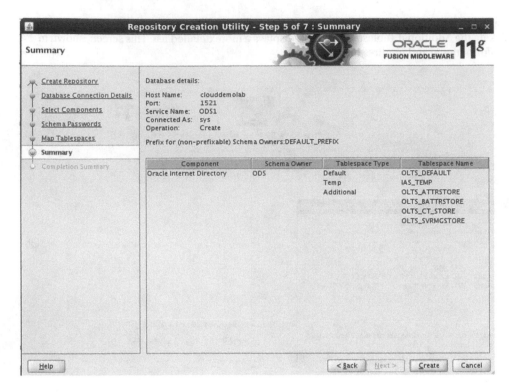

***Figure 4-11.** Repository creation configuration Summary screen*

Figure 4-12 shows the Repository Creation Utility Completion Summary screen. At this point, all of the database schema objects have been created and populated with the necessary data required for OID. The next steps include installation of the WebLogic infrastructure and OID.

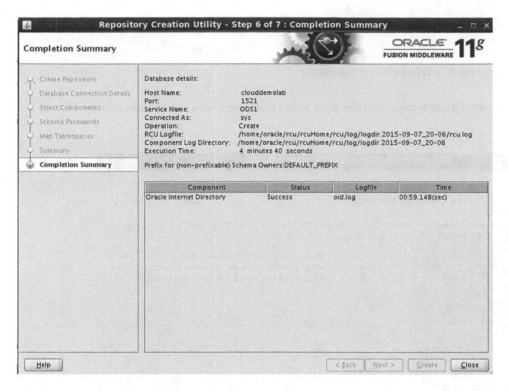

Figure 4-12. *RCU completed*

Fusion Middleware WebLogic Server

Once the prerequisite tasks have been completed, installation of OID can begin with installing the Fusion Middleware WebLogic Server (WLS). As of this writing, OID 11.1.1.9 is certified on WLS 10.3.6. Although it might be possible to utilize a newer version of WLS for this environment, it is highly recommended that you follow the certification matrix provided by Oracle. This will ensure compatability and supportability if problems occur.

The Fusion Middleware environment requires the use of a certified Java Development Kit (JDK). For the purposes of this discussion, JDK 1.6 Update 45 will be used. You can install multiple versions of the JDK on a single machine. However, it is important that the JAVA_HOME and PATH variables are updated to use the proper version during the installation and all management tasks. These can be done using the following commands, or these can be added to profile scripts to avoid retyping the commands.

```
[oracle@clouddemolab ~]$ export JAVA_HOME=/home/oracle/java/jdk1.6.0_45
 [oracle@clouddemolab ~]$ export PATH=$JAVA_HOME/bin:$PATH
```

WLS 11g (version 10.3.6) is currently the latest version of WLS certified with OID 11.1.1.9. Therefore, this section covers the installation of this version. If installing WLS on a 64-bit system, use of the wls10.3.6_ generic.jar file is required. To use this file execute the command as shown in Figure 4-13.

```
[oracle@clouddemolab weblogic]$ java -jar  wls1036_generic.jar
Extracting 0%.......................█
```

Figure 4-13. *Starting the WebLogic Server installation*

Just about every Oracle software installer starts with a Welcome screen, as shown in Figure 4-14; WLS is no different.

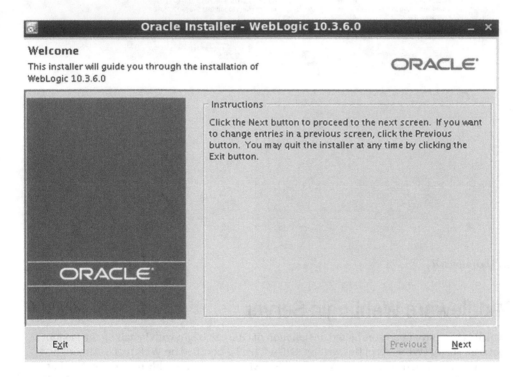

Figure 4-14. *WebLogic Server installation Welcome screen*

The first input required is the location of the new Middleware home directory. Each Fusion Middleware application requires a Middleware Home location. In the case of OID and the Identity and Access Management environments, these will be separate for manageability. For OID, the Middleware Home will be called OIDMiddleware located at /home/oracle/OIDMiddleware. Subsequent to this screen will be a software update screen. You can choose to enter your e-mail address to be notified of updates or skip to the next step. See Figure 4-15 for details.

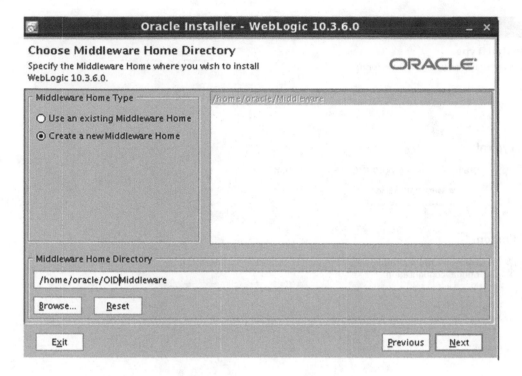

Figure 4-15. *WebLogic Server Middleware Home configuration*

After choosing the ORACLE_HOME you intend to use, you will be presented with the screen shown in Figure 4-16 on which you choose the installation type.

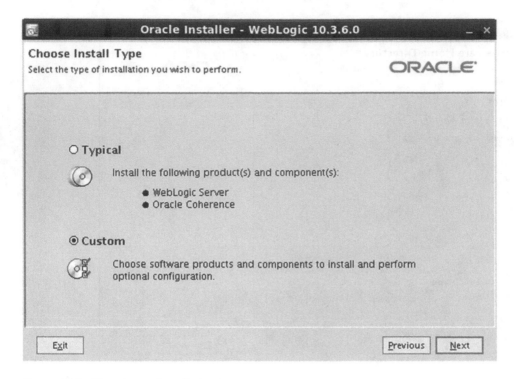

Figure 4-16. *Choosing an installation type*

This step allows you to select a typical or custom installation. A typical installation installs the following components:

- Core Application Server.

- Administration Console.

- Configuration Wizard and Upgrade Utilities.

- Web 2.0 HTTP Pub-Sub Server.

- WebLogic SCA.

- WebLogic JDBC Drivers.

- Third Party JDBC Drivers.

- WebLogic Server Clients.

- WebLogic Web Server Plug-ins.

- UDDI and XQuery Support.

- Evaluation Database.

- Oracle Coherence.

If any of these are not required for the installation, choose Custom and deselect the items not needed, such as the Evaluation Database.

Once an installation type is chosen and you have selected the components you wish to install, the JDK Selection screen, shown in Figure 4-17, displays.

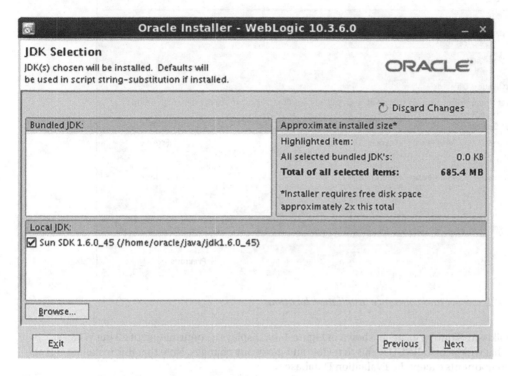

Figure 4-17. *Select the JDK version to be used*

If multiple JDKs are installed on the host, they will be listed in the installer at this step. However, if a JDK was specified when running the wls1036_generic.jar file, this is the JDK that will be listed.

Figure 4-18. *WLS server and coherence installation locations*

The Installation Summary screen, shown in Figure 4-19, displays a confirmation of all the WLS components that will be installed. Use this to review and make any changes. Note that this installation is set to install all components except the Evaluation Database.

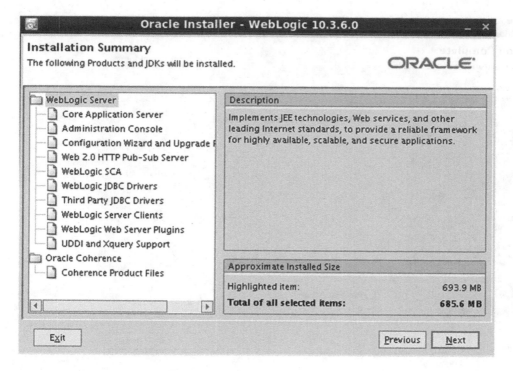

Figure 4-19. *Installation Summary screen*

At the end of the WLS installation, the Installation Complete screen is displayed, as shown in Figure 4-20. You are presented with the Run Quickstart check box. In this scenario, clear this check box. The domain configuration will be performed after installing OID into this Middleware Home.

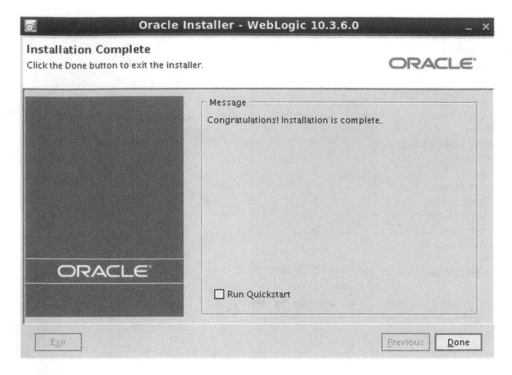

Figure 4-20. *WebLogic Server Installation Complete screen*

You have now installed the binaries required for the OID Middleware Home. The OID application files will be installed into this environment.

Oracle Internet Directory Installation

Before running the Oracle Installer, it is important to ensure that the proper JDK is selected. Just like installing WLS, set the JAVA_HOME directory and ensure the PATH environment variable includes the JAVA_HOME/bin directory.

Run the installer for the Identity Management 11.1.1.9 to install OID as shown in Figure 4-21.

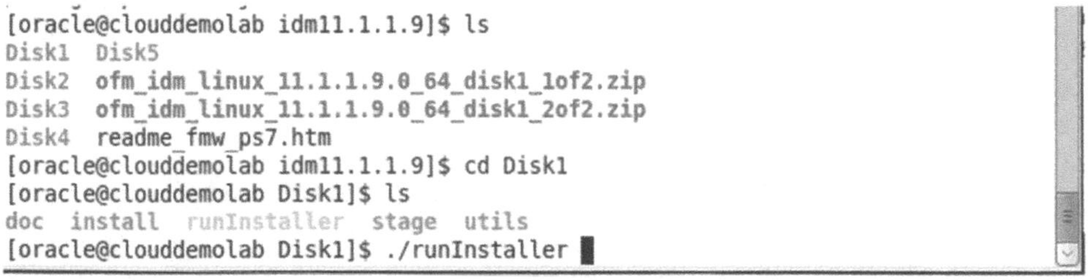

```
[oracle@clouddemolab idm11.1.1.9]$ ls
Disk1   Disk5
Disk2   ofm_idm_linux_11.1.1.9.0_64_disk1_1of2.zip
Disk3   ofm_idm_linux_11.1.1.9.0_64_disk1_2of2.zip
Disk4   readme_fmw_ps7.htm
[oracle@clouddemolab idm11.1.1.9]$ cd Disk1
[oracle@clouddemolab Disk1]$ ls
doc   install   runInstaller   stage   utils
[oracle@clouddemolab Disk1]$ ./runInstaller
```

Figure 4-21. *Directory structure for the Identity Management 11.1.1.9 installation software*

After downloading the Identity Management 11.1.1.9 software from Oracle, unzip the files in a directory called idm11.1.1.9. This creates the Disk1 through Disk5 directories containing all the installation utilities. Within the Disk1 directory, run the file runInstaller. This will open the screen shown in Figure 4-22.

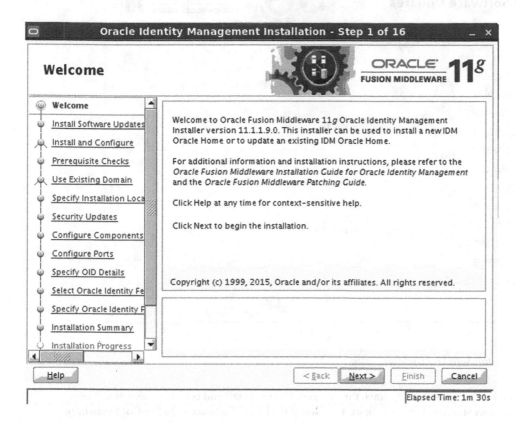

Figure 4-22. *Installation steps listed*

At this point, you can search for updates on Oracle's Support site. However, this is not required. Figure 4-23 shows the screen on which you can search for updates if you choose.

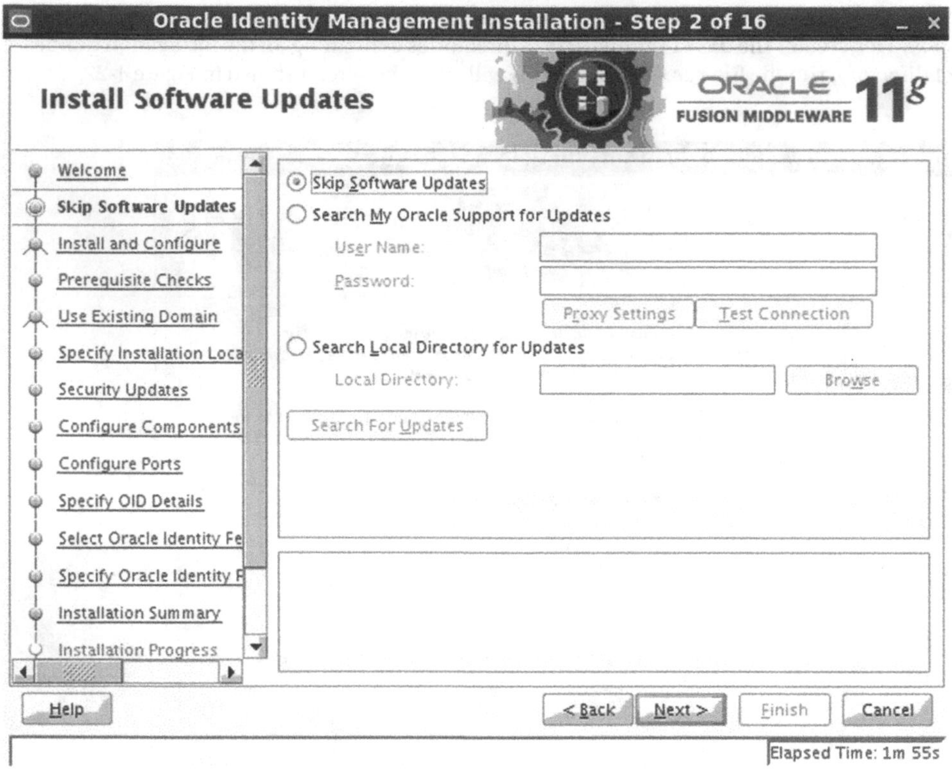

Figure 4-23. Install Software Updates screen

In this section, the plan is to lay down the binaries. Do not install and configure, as this will be completed in a later step. As shown in Figure 4-24, select the Install Software – Do Not Configure option before continuing.

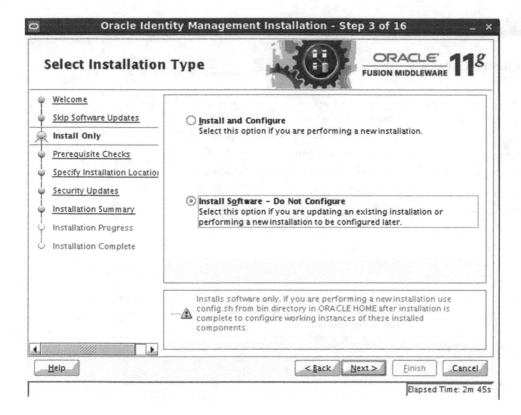

Figure 4-24. *Select Installation Type screen*

The system is checked for required packages and to ensure it meets the minimum requirements. If any of these checks result in errors, they must be corrected before continuing. Warnings should be corrected. Although warnings might not cause installation errors, they could result in future problems. Figure 4-25 shows that all prerequisite checks have completed properly.

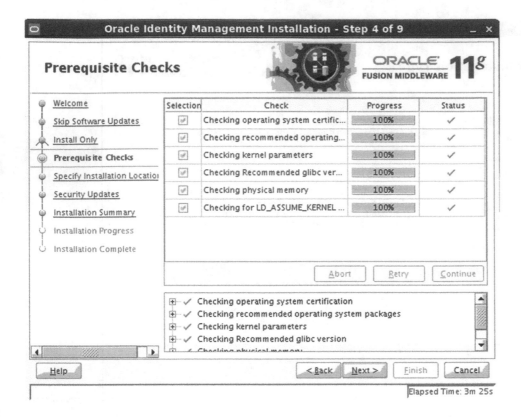

Figure 4-25. *OID Installation Prerequisite Checks screen*

The OID environment will create the Oracle Home structure within the chosen Middleware Home. In this case, the Oracle Home will be located in the /home/oracle/OIDMiddleware/ directory and be called Oracle_IDM1. Figure 4-26 displays the new Oracle Middleware Home.

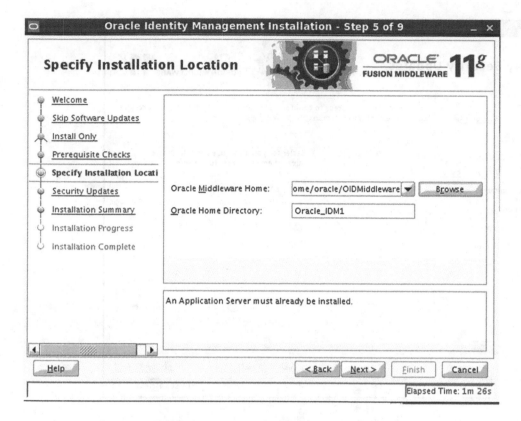

Figure 4-26. *Choose a Middleware Home and Oracle Home location*

The Specify Security Updates screen allows you to enter your e-mail address and be notified of future updates needed by the system. You can continue without filling this information in, but be sure to periodically check Oracle Support for necessary updates to your environments. See Figure 4-27 for details on this step.

Figure 4-27. *Security Updates opt in selection*

There are not many steps that require input during the installation of Oracle Identity Management. Figure 4-28 shows the summary screen.

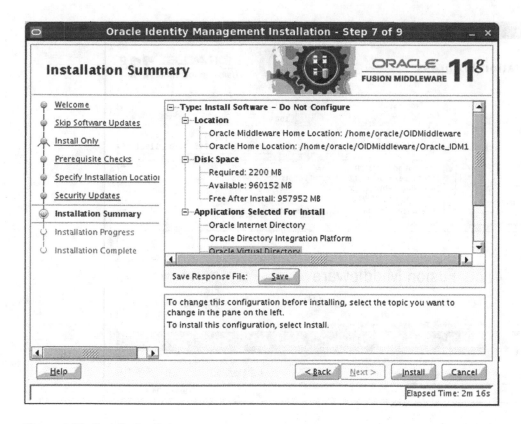

Figure 4-28. Installation Summary screen

After you click Install on the Installation Summary screen, the Universal Installer begins copying files and creating the filesystem. The choices you made during the initial steps provide instruction to the Universal Installer during this phase. Figure 4-29 shows the Installation Progress screen, which shows a continuous progress bar.

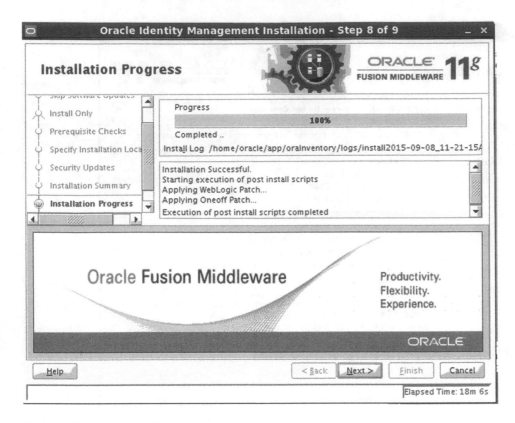

Figure 4-29. *Installation Progress screen*

After the installation completes, there are two scripts that need to be run as the host ROOT user. Log in to a terminal window as the root user and run the specified scripts. The screen shown in Figure 4-30 indicates the necessary scripts. Log in to the server as Root to run these.

```
[root@clouddemolab ~]# cd /home/oracle/OIDMiddleware/
 [root@clouddemolab OIDMiddleware]# cd Oracle_IDM1/
 [root@clouddemolab Oracle_IDM1]# ./oracleRoot.sh
 [root@clouddemolab Oracle_IDM1]#
```

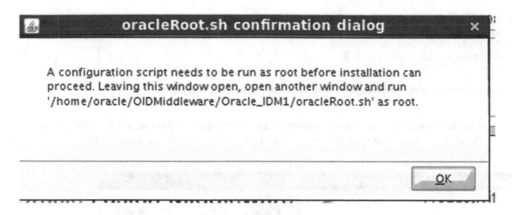

Figure 4-30. *Root scripts*

Before configuring the domain for OID, you should decide if this environment is to be clustered. If your environment is planned with redundancy in mind, repeat the previous steps for installing the WLS and OID software on any additional hosts to be included. The RCU should also be run to create the Oracle Directory Services schema in another database for the additional servers.

Oracle Internet Directory Configuration

In this section, you will be configuring the OID domain within the WLS environment. Before proceeding, you should have an understanding of the configuration scenario to be used:

- OID with Oracle Directory Integration Platform (DIP) and Oracle Directory Service Manager (ODSM) in a new WebLogic domain.

- Fusion Middleware Control and the WebLogic Administration Console will be used to manage the OID environment.

- Directory Integration Platform (DIP) will be utilized to synchronize OID with third-party LDAP sources.

- ODSM will be used to manage the LDAP Directory instance.

- No other WebLogic domain exists within the Oracle Fusion Middleware environment.

Configuration Type

There a number of other scenarios that include installing OID and OVD within a new domain or existing domains. For the purposes of this discussion, it is assumed that these are new domains.

Prior to beginning this step, WLS and Oracle Identity Management software should have been installed but not yet configured. If a Quickstart was run after installing WebLogic and the domain was created, you can extend that domain with OID, which is very similar to the steps presented here.

To begin the domain configuration, run the config.sh file located in the $ORACLE_HOME/bin directory. In this case, ORACLE_HOME is the location where the Oracle Identity Management software was installed, /home/oracle/OIDMiddleware/Oracle_IDM1. This is important, as there are other config.sh files located in other directories found in the Middleware environment. Figure 4-31 shows the location of the configuration file to be used.

```
[oracle@clouddemolab Oracle_IDM1]$ cd bin
[oracle@clouddemolab bin]$ pwd
/home/oracle/OIDMiddleware/Oracle_IDM1/bin
[oracle@clouddemolab bin]$ ./config.sh █
```

Figure 4-31. *Configuration of new WebLogic domain for Oracle Internet Directory*

Just as before, the first screen you are presented with after starting the Configuration file is the Welcome screen, shown in Figure 4-32. No action is necessary here. Just click Next to begin configuring OID.

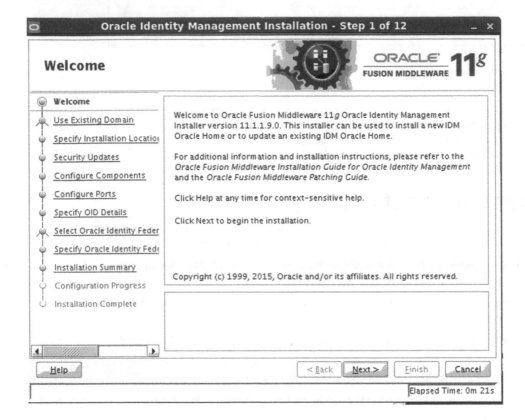

Figure 4-32. *Domain configuration steps*

The screen shown in Figure 4-33 allows you to choose whether to create a new domain, extend an existing one, or expand a cluster. Because this is a new installation, choose Create New Domain. If you ran the Quickstart earlier in the process, select Extend Existing Domain.

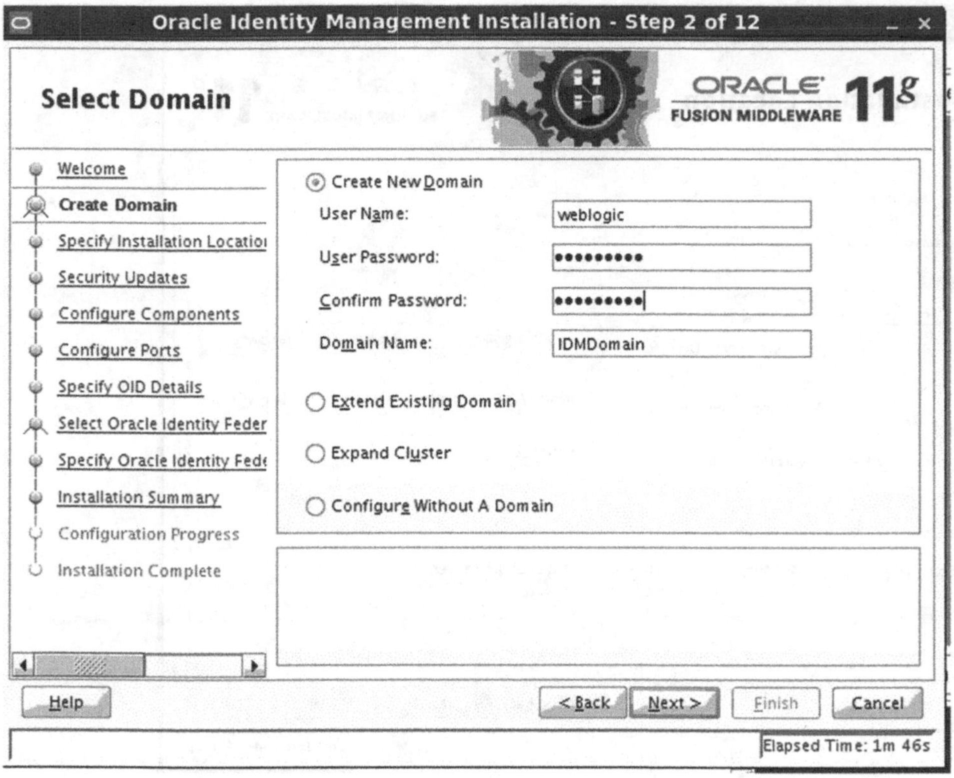

Figure 4-33. *Create a new domain*

Enter the name of the administration user, normally weblogic, and the desired password and the name you wish to use for the domain.

Because you are creating a new OID domain, you will be prompted for the details of the new domain. Figure 4-34 shows the screen where you can enter values for the domain location, OID instance name, and instance location. It should be noted that you can create new OID instances at a later time.

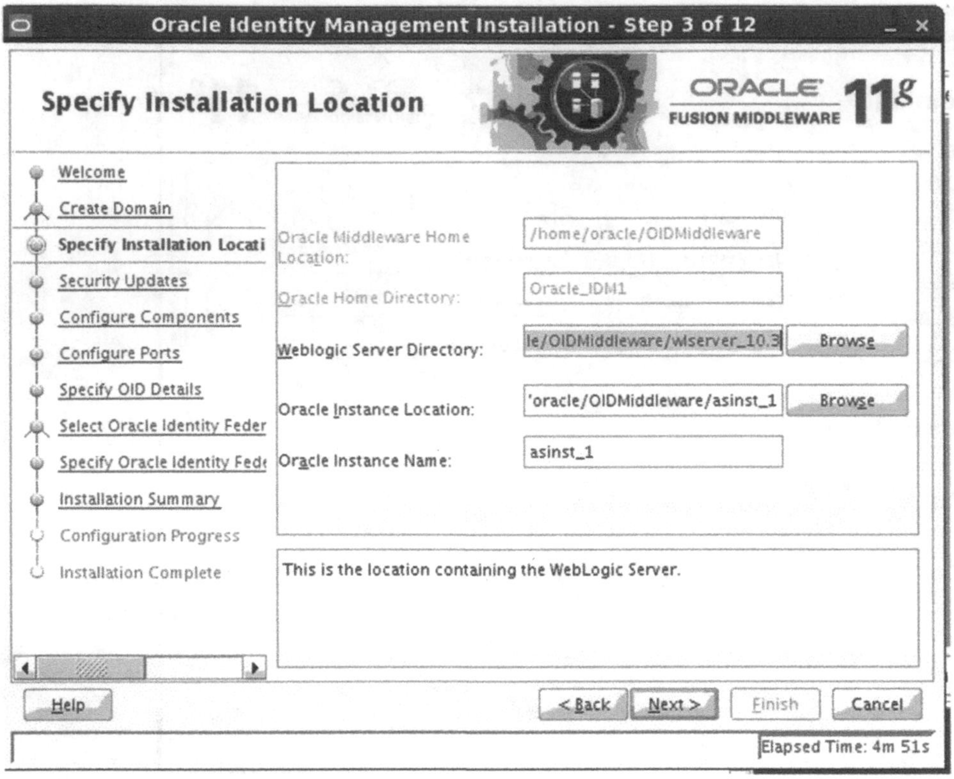

Figure 4-34. *Configure the instance location and WebLogic Home directories*

On the Configure Components screen, shown in Figure 4-35, choose the Identity Management components you wish to deploy.

Figure 4-35. *Component selection for the new domain*

In this case, OID, OVD, and the DIP will all be installed in the Identity Management domain. As selections are made, the tool will automatically select any of the required components necessary to support the installation. It is recommended that you not change any of the preselected components.

After instructing the configuration tool where to install the new OID domain, you will have the option to configure the ports OID will use, as shown in Figure 4-36.

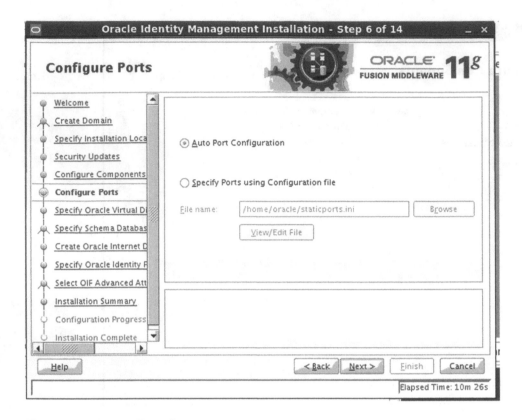

Figure 4-36. *Port configuration*

It is possible to use the default ports on a new installation. If any of the ports are already in use, create a `staticports.ini` file and specify its location on this screen.

___

■ **Note**   There is a sample `staticports.ini` file located in the installation media. It is located in `Disk1/stage/Response`. You can copy this file and edit it as necessary to specify the ports to be used during the installation.

___

If you have chosen to use OVD in addition to OID, the OVD information screen shown in Figure 4-37 prompts you for the required information.

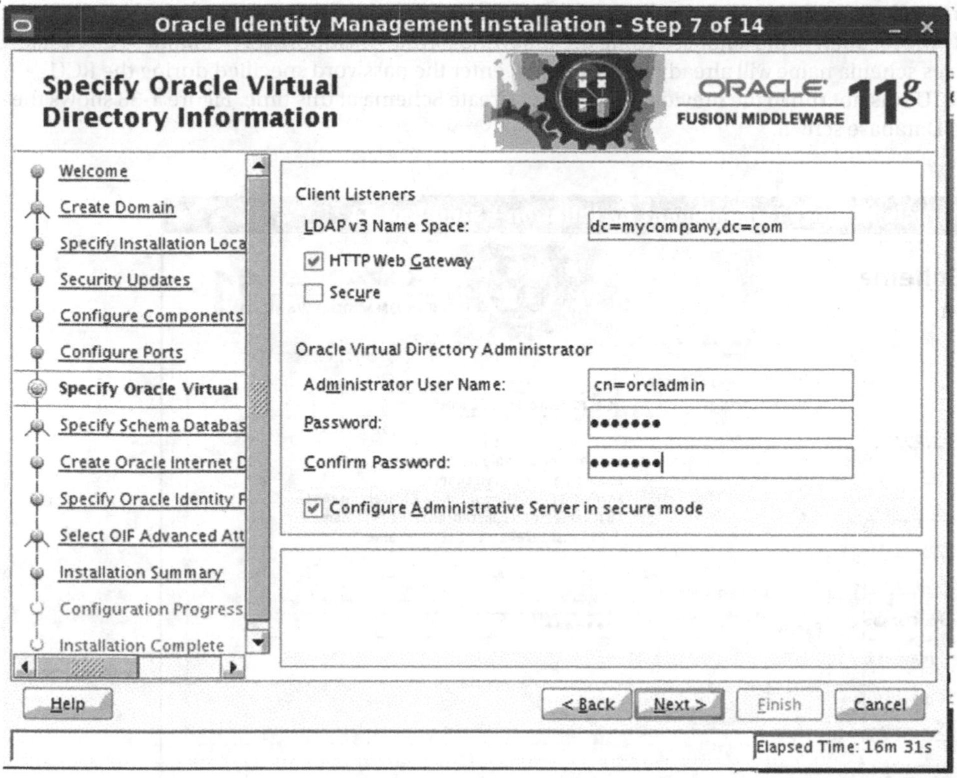

Figure 4-37. Configure the Oracle Virtual Directory realm and adminstrator password

The account cn=orcladmin is the standard administration account used for OID. Set the password for this, and keep close track of it. Without it, you will be unable to perform some management functions.

■ **Note**   There is a script that can be run to reset the orcladmin password. To run it, you must know the Oracle Directory Services schema connection information. The utility is called oidpasswd and it is located within the $ORACLE_INSTANCE/bin directory.

Before starting the installation process, the RCU was used to create the necessary schema objects. In this step, specify the location of the database using the following format: host:port:servicename. The Oracle Directory Services schema name will already be populated; enter the password specified during the RCU process. If the RCU was not run in the previous step, select Create Schema at this time. Figure 4-38 shows the Specify Schema Database screen.

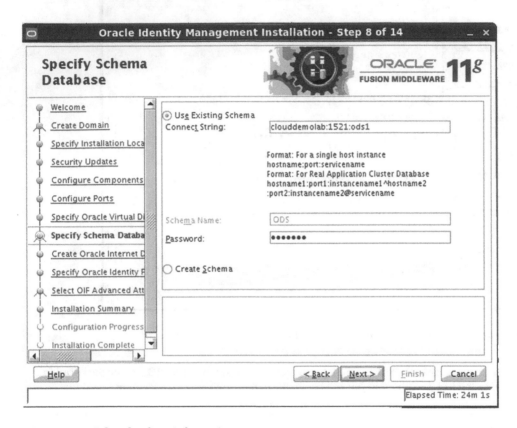

Figure 4-38. *Select database information*

Much like the step to configure the OVD information, enter the same data. This information will be used by the OID configuration. Note that OID and OVD are two different products. Figure 4-39 shows the start of the new OID setup.

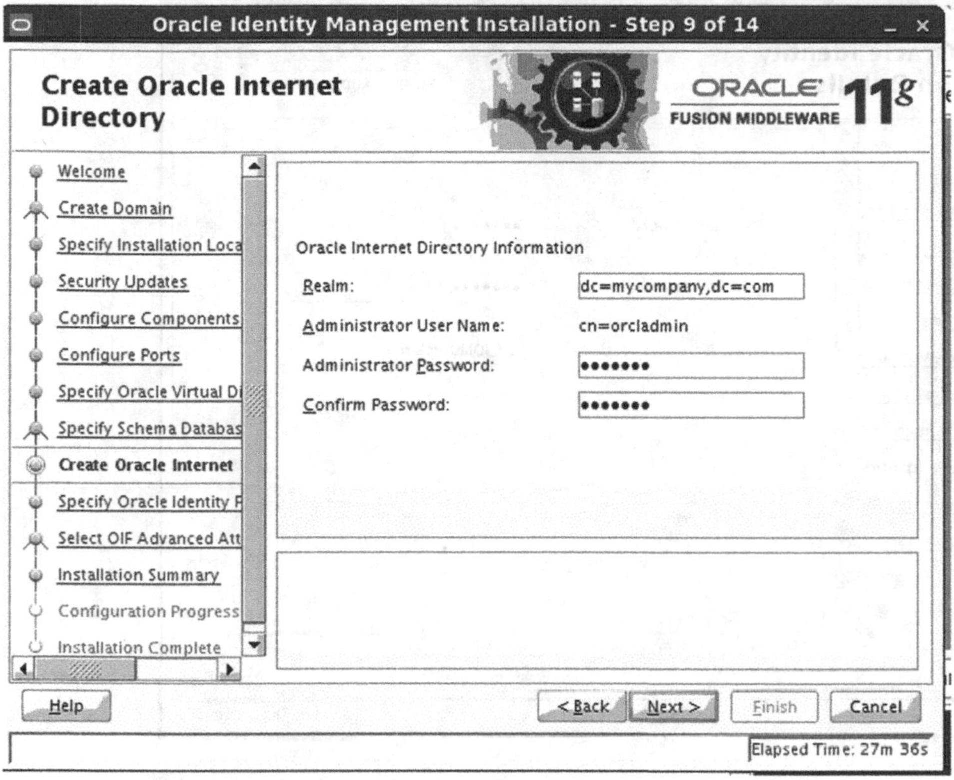

Figure 4-39. *Specify the Oracle Internet Directory Realm information*

The domain configuration will prompt for Oracle Identity Federation information. This will be used to generate signing and encryption keystores as seen in Figure 4-40.

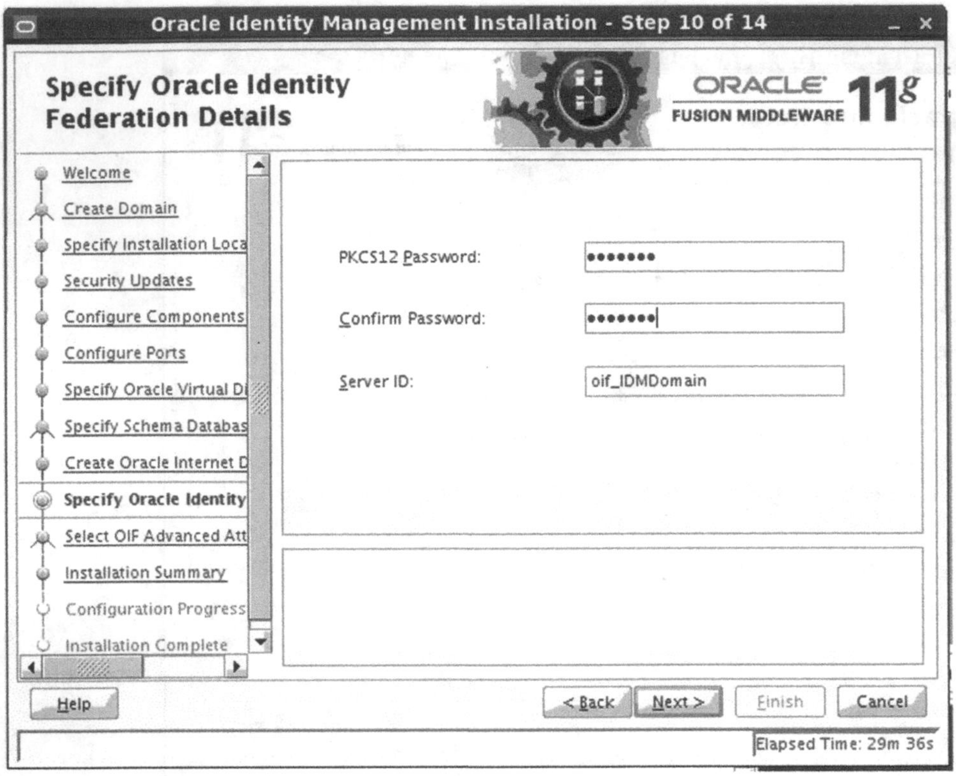

Figure 4-40. *Oracle Identity Federation configuration*

The default values can be left at this stage. These determine how Identity Management stores session information and how it retrieved its data. These values can be changed postinstallation if needed. See Figure 4-41 for the default values.

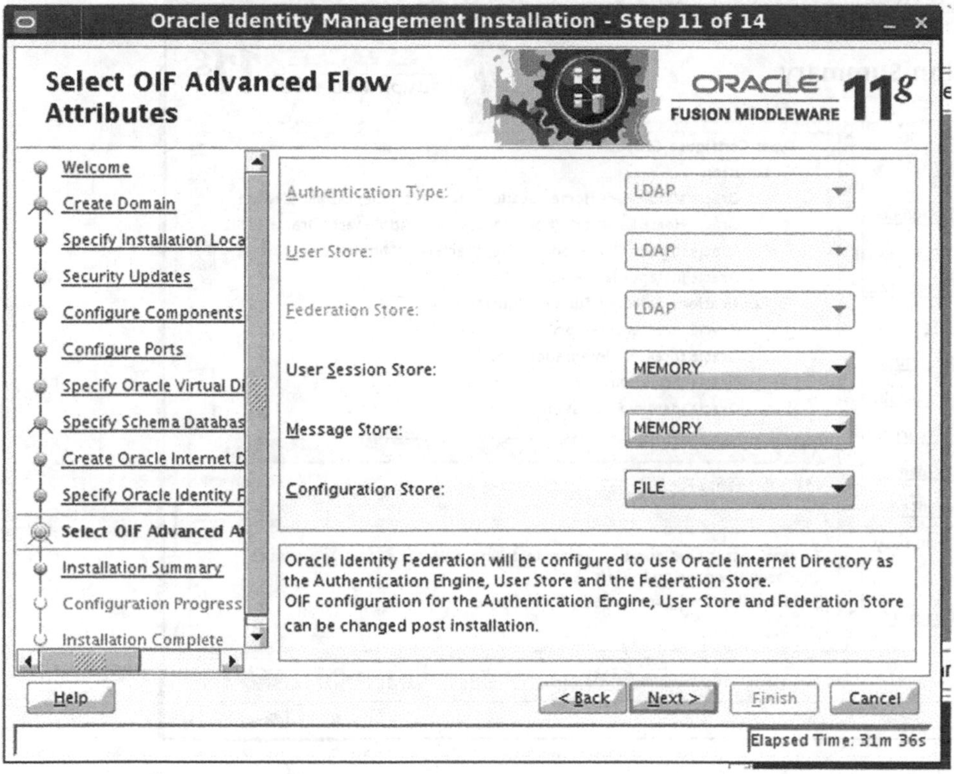

Figure 4-41. Configure the Identity Federation attributes

After reviewing the data provided, click Continue to create the Oracle Identity Management domain. Note that this process can take significant time to complete. An example of this can be seen in Figure 4-42.

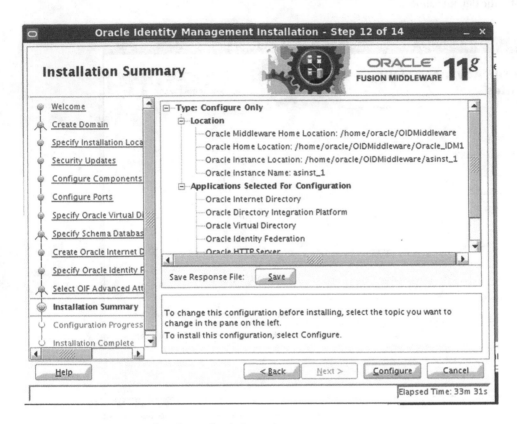

Figure 4-42. Summary of configuration information

At this point, you have entered all the instructions needed by the configuration utility to create the new OID and OVD domains. Figure 4-43 shows the Configuration Progress screen. This process can be quite time consuming. Some steps can seem like they have hung, whereas others will be quite fast. Ensure that each step runs properly before continuing. Check the logs indicated on this screen if there are any issues reported.

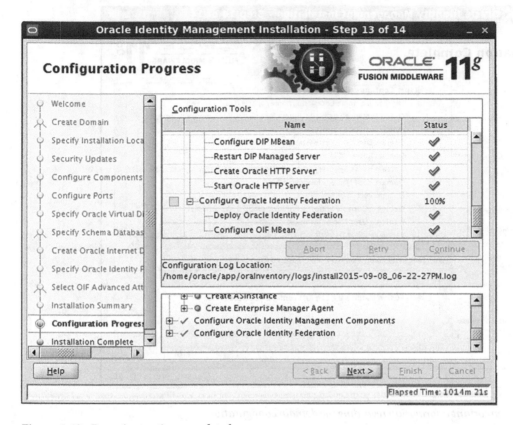

Figure 4-43. Domain creation completed

Once the configuration is complete, you will be presented with a summary screen that displays many important data points, including port numbers, administration URLs, and directory locations. Figure 4-44 shows the configuration summary after all steps have completed.

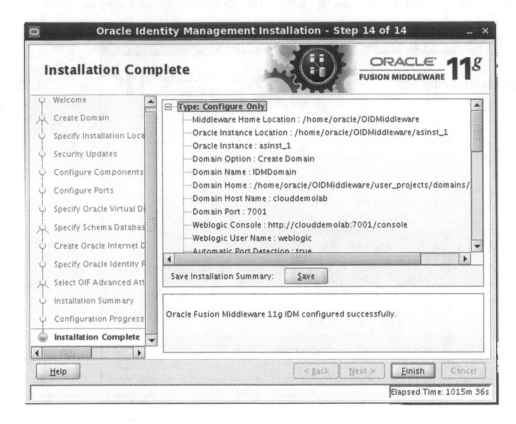

Figure 4-44. *Important information regarding the domain configuration*

Figure 4-45 displays a closer look at the Installation Complete screen that shows the result of all of the configuration parameters.

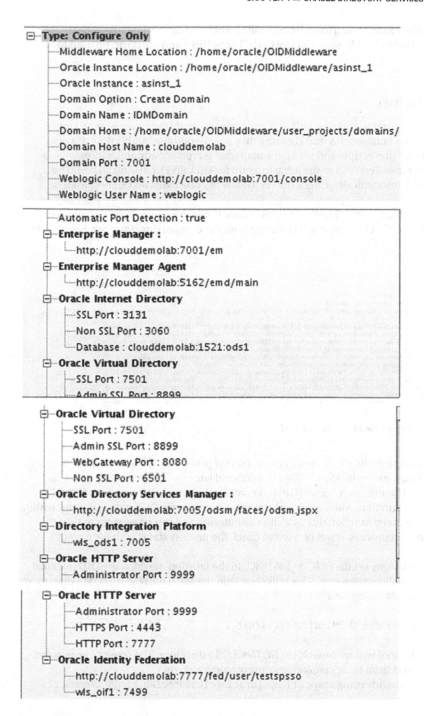

Type: Configure Only
- Middleware Home Location : /home/oracle/OIDMiddleware
- Oracle Instance Location : /home/oracle/OIDMiddleware/asinst_1
- Oracle Instance : asinst_1
- Domain Option : Create Domain
- Domain Name : IDMDomain
- Domain Home : /home/oracle/OIDMiddleware/user_projects/domains/
- Domain Host Name : clouddemolab
- Domain Port : 7001
- Weblogic Console : http://clouddemolab:7001/console
- Weblogic User Name : weblogic

- Automatic Port Detection : true
- **Enterprise Manager :**
  - http://clouddemolab:7001/em
- **Enterprise Manager Agent**
  - http://clouddemolab:5162/emd/main
- **Oracle Internet Directory**
  - SSL Port : 3131
  - Non SSL Port : 3060
  - Database : clouddemolab:1521:ods1
- **Oracle Virtual Directory**
  - SSL Port : 7501
  - Admin SSL Port : 8899

- **Oracle Virtual Directory**
  - SSL Port : 7501
  - Admin SSL Port : 8899
  - WebGateway Port : 8080
  - Non SSL Port : 6501
- **Oracle Directory Services Manager :**
  - http://clouddemolab:7005/odsm/faces/odsm.jspx
- **Directory Integration Platform**
  - wls_ods1 : 7005
- **Oracle HTTP Server**
  - Administrator Port : 9999

- **Oracle HTTP Server**
  - Administrator Port : 9999
  - HTTPS Port : 4443
  - HTTP Port : 7777
- **Oracle Identity Federation**
  - http://clouddemolab:7777/fed/user/testspsso
  - wls_oif1 : 7499

Figure 4-45. *Pertinent information about the new OID domain*

It is important to record this information. However, you will be able to view this later using the Administration Console or the Fusion Middleware Control tools. These URLs and ports can be used to manage the environment.

Verifying the Installation

After all the installation and configuration tasks for OID, it is important to verify the environment. Doing so involves logging into the various components and ensuring they are operational. At this time it is also suggested that you verify start and stop scripts and set up the managed servers for administration.

In the previous section, you installed WLS as the infrastructure for OID, OVD, DIP and ODSM. The components should have started automatically. Check the OS to view the processes that were started to support OID.

Open a console and log into the host machine as the oracle user. Using the name of the domain created previously, use the command ps to check for processes running from the domain directory. See Figure 4-46 for a look at this process.

```
[oracle@clouddemolab domains]$ ls
IDMDomain
[oracle@clouddemolab domains]$ ps -ef | grep IDMDomain
oracle   28989  28838  0 12:08 pts/3    00:00:00 grep IDMDomain
oracle   71222      1  0 Sep08 pts/2    00:00:00 /bin/sh /home/oracle/OIDMiddleware/user_projects/domains/IDMDomain/bin/sta
rtWebLogic.sh
oracle   71270  71222  0 Sep08 pts/2    00:14:20 /home/oracle/java/jdk1.6.0_45/bin/java -server -Xms256m -Xmx512m -XX:MaxPe
rmSize=512m -Dweblogic.Name=AdminServer -Djava.security.policy=/home/oracle/OIDMiddleware/wlserver_10.3/server/lib/weblogic.
policy -Dweblogic.ProductionModeEnabled=true -da -Dplatform.home=/home/oracle/OIDMiddleware/wlserver_10.3 -Dwls.home=/home/o
racle/OIDMiddleware/wlserver_10.3/server -Dweblogic.home=/home/oracle/OIDMiddleware/wlserver_10.3/server -XX:PermSize=256m -
XX:MaxPermSize=512m -Dweblogic.ssl.JSSEEnabled=true -Dcommon.components.home=/home/oracle/OIDMiddleware/oracle_common -Djrf.
version=11.1.1 -Dorg.apache.commons.logging.Log=org.apache.commons.logging.impl.Jdk14Logger -Ddomain.home=/home/oracle/OIDMi
ddleware/user_projects/domains/IDMDomain -Djrockit.optfile=/home/oracle/OIDMiddleware/oracle_common/modules/oracle.jrf_11.1.
1/jrocket_optfile.txt -Doracle.server.config.dir=/home/oracle/OIDMiddleware/user_projects/domains/IDMDomain/config/fmwconfig
/servers/AdminServer -Doracle.domain.config.dir=/home/oracle/OIDMiddleware/user_projects/domains/IDMDomain/config/fmwconfig
-Digf.arisidbeans.carmlloc=/home/oracle/OIDMiddleware/user_projects/domains/IDMDomain/config/fmwconfig/carml -Digf.arisidsta
ck.home=/home/oracle/OIDMiddleware/user_projects/domains/IDMDomain/config/fmwconfig/arisidprovider -Doracle.security.jps.con
```

Figure 4-46. *Verify running processes for WLS and ODSM*

This will provide information regarding WLS, and managed server processes. If this does not return any information, the environment will need to be started. This is discussed later.

Oracle Process Manager and Notification Server (OPMN) controls the actual OID instance. OPMN is installed during the domain configuration. Although it is the process manager for OID, it does not run within WLS. It provides startup and shutdown functionality as well as monitoring and restart services to the OID environment. During the validation process, it will be used to check the process status with the opmnctl command.

Within the same console as before, set the ORACLE_INSTANCE to the location in which the OID instance was created during the domain configuration step. This is likely within the MIDDLEWARE_HOME directory; for example, /home/oracle/OIDMiddleware/asinst_1.

```
export ORACLE_INSTANCE=/home/oracle/OIDMiddleware/asinst_1
```

The opmnctl command is located within the ORACLE_INSTANCE/bin directory. The opmnctl command can accept a number of commands from basic status checks to complete restarts.

You can retrieve a list of commands using opmnctl help. [oracle@clouddemolab bin]$ ./opmnctl help

```
[oracle@clouddemolab bin]$ ./opmnctl help usage: opmnctl [verbose] [<scope>]
<command> [<options>] verbose: print detailed execution message if available Permitted
<scope>/<command>/<options> combinations are:
scope      command      options
-------    ---------    ---------
           start                               - Start opmn
           startall                            - Start opmn & all managed processes
           stopall                             - Stop opmn & all managed processes
           shutdown                            - Shutdown opmn & all managed processes
[<scope>]  startproc    [<attr>=<val> ..]      - Start opmn managed processes
[<scope>]  restartproc  [<attr>=<val> ..]      - Restart opmn managed processes
[<scope>]  stopproc     [<attr>=<val> ..]      - Stop opmn managed processes
[<scope>]  reload                              - Trigger opmn to reread opmn.xml
[<scope>]  status       [<options>]            - Get managed process status
[<scope>]  metric       [<attr>=<val> ..]      - Get DMS metrics for managed processes
[<scope>]  dmsdump      [<dmsargs>]            - Get DMS metrics for opmn
[<scope>]  debug        [<attr>=<val> ..]      - Display opmn server debug information
[<scope>]  set          [<attr>=<val> ..]      - Set opmn log parameters
[<scope>]  query        [<attr>=<val>]         - Query opmn log parameters
           launch       [<attr>=<val> ..]      - Launch a configured target process
           phantom      [<attr>=<val> ..]      - Register phantom processes
           ping         [<max-retry>]          - Ping local opmn
           validate     [<filename>]           - Validate the given opmn xml file
           setlocale    [<host>]               - Set or query the instance locale
           help                                - Print brief usage description
           usage        [<command>]            - Print detailed usage description
           createinstance                      - Create an Oracle Instance
           createcomponent                     - Create a specified component
           deleteinstance                      - Delete an instance and components
           deletecomponent                     - Delete a specified component
           registerinstance                    - Register with admin server
           redeploy                            - Redeploy the admin server application
           unregisterinstance                  - Unregister with admin server
           updateinstanceregistration          - Update instance registration
           updatecomponentregistration         - Update component registration
```

To check the OID process use the basic opmnctl status command:

```
[oracle@clouddemolab bin]$ ./opmnctl status

Processes in Instance: asinst_1
---------------------------------+--------------------+---------+---------
ias-component                    | process-type       |     pid | status
---------------------------------+--------------------+---------+---------
ohs1                             | OHS                |   73204 | Alive
ovd1                             | OVD                |   72408 | Alive
oid1                             | oidldapd           |   72284 | Alive
oid1                             | oidldapd           |   72288 | Alive
oid1                             | oidmon             |   72276 | Alive
EMAGENT                          | EMAGENT            |   72559 | Alive
```

■ **Note**　Set the ORACLE_HOME, ORACLE_INSTANCE, and PATH environment variables to better interact with the environment.

After checking the process status, you can move on to using the Adminstration Console, Fusion Middleware Control, and ODSM to further check the environment and get familiar with the administration tools.

The WebLogic Administration Console provides the overall environment status and control. The managed servers' status can be checked on the Environment ➤ Servers screen. Figure 4-47 shows the Server Status screen for the WebLogic components of the OID domain.

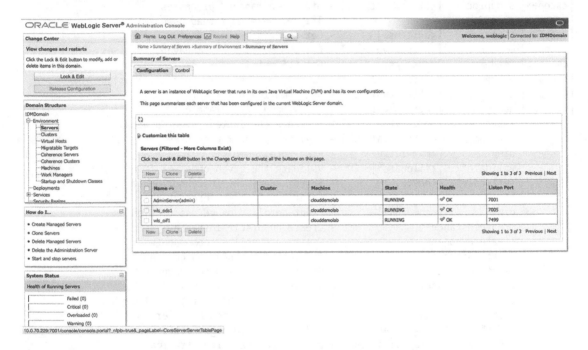

Figure 4-47. *Server Administration Console screen*

This screen provides the overall status of the managed servers, but drilling down on each one can provide some configuration details, including ports, machine information, JDK information, and so on. See Figure 4-48 for a more detailed look at the managed server configuration.

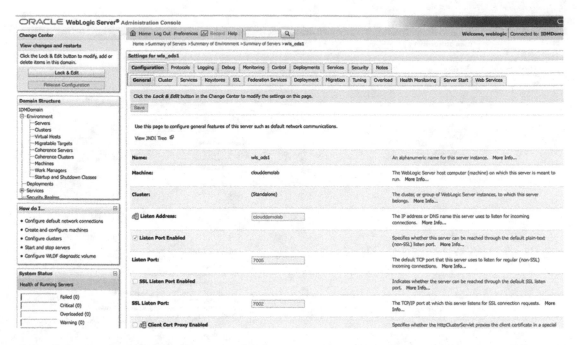

Figure 4-48. *Managed server configuration details*

The Administration Console screens presented here provide just the tip of the iceberg of the information and configuration options available. At this point, however, you are just looking for validation that the managed servers are running.

The Fusion Middleware Control screen, shown in Figure 4-49, provides much more detail regarding the status and health of the overall system.

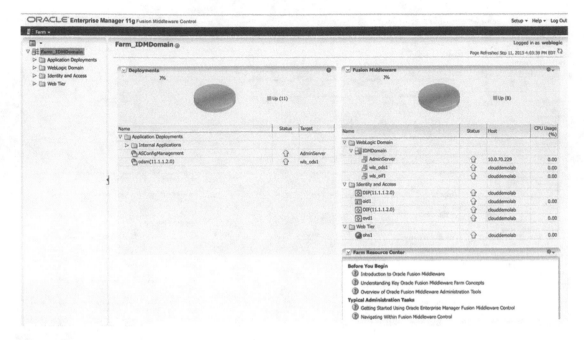

Figure 4-49. *Fusion Middleware Control home screen*

At a glance, the home screen provides the overall health of the system. Even the status of each component within the Fusion Middleware component such as OID, DIP, and OVD is displayed on the home page. It easy to verify that everything is running and operating properly. Drilling down the components in the left side menu provides more information. More information is provided in later chapters where the administration is covered in depth.

Figure 4-50 shows the status page of the OID instance. This screen is a quick view of the operational statistics. You can use this to drill down into the details.

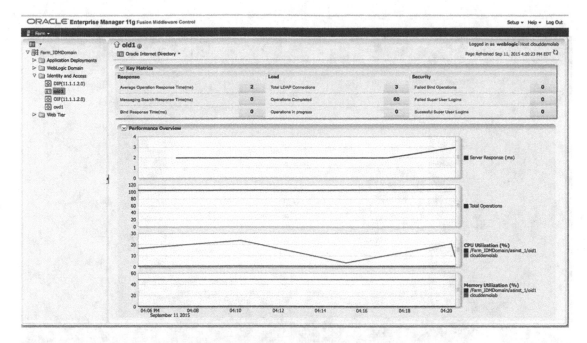

Figure 4-50. *Individual identity component status screen*

After validating the overall status of the OID servers, you can access the ODSM to check the LDAP directory created during the domain configuration. Figure 4-51 shows the login of ODSM. This is a tool that can be used to browse, edit, and manage users, groups, and instance settings.

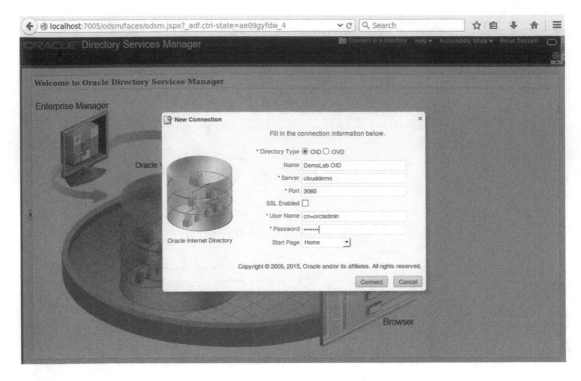

Figure 4-51. *Creating a connection using ODSM*

After these steps, you have a fully installed OID and have verified it. In the next chapters, you will be presented with more detail of the management screens as the subsequent component installations continue.

Summary

This chapter covered the installation and initial configuration of OID. This forms the foundation of a successful Identity Management implementation. From this point, you can start managing application users and attributes within Oracle's generic LDAP directory. Applications, both Oracle and third party, can connect to OID to validate user credentials as an LDAP identity store. The identity store can also be used by databases for authentication. Although OID provides basic LDAP authentication and a data store for identity-based systems, the environment maintains only single authentication to single applications. Oracle Access Manager can provide a better user experience where users log in once and have access to applications that have been incorporated into the environment. Oracle Identity Manager will provide user self-service and management services. These additional components depend on a solid LDAP implementation and are presented in future chapters.

CHAPTER 5

■ ■ ■

Directory Synchronization and Virtualization

Oracle Internet Directory (OID), Oracle Virtual Directory (OVD), and the Directory Integration Platform (DIP) provide Oracle Directory Services with the ability to consolidate user management and integrate with other applications. These concepts were presented in earlier chapters. This chapter covers using the DIP to replicate users into the OID instance from Active Directory in preparation for the rest of the integration with EBS and Oracle Identity and Access Manager.

The Directory Integration Platform

The key to synchronizing OID and Active Directory is the DIP. The use of Oracle DIP enables IT departments to replicate Lightweight Directory Access Protocol (LDAP) information from multiple sources including Active Directory, OpenLDAP, and other LDAP or database stores into a centralized directory that can be used in conjunction with Oracle products and applications.

Data synchronization is accomplished using profiles that can be created in the DIP system to map and transform external directory identity information to match the requirements of the Oracle systems. These profiles are used when the DIP executes and queries LDAP sources to insert or modify data in OID. In the following sections, you are presented with a basic profile to synchronize OID with a single Active Directory instance. DIP can support multiple profiles and multiple sources. This can be helpful if you are required to synchronize different Active Directory organizational units (OUs) into different namespaces within OID or need to synchronize users from varying sources.

Creating a Synchronization Profile

The Fusion Middleware Control interface will be used to create the DIP Profile. More detailed information regarding the Fusion Middleware Control interface is presented in Chapter 8. Navigating to http://hostname:port/em opens the Fusion Middleware Control welcome screen shown in Figure 5-1.

© Kenneth Ramey 2016

K. Ramey, *Pro Oracle Identity and Access Management Suite*, DOI 10.1007/978-1-4842-1521-0_5

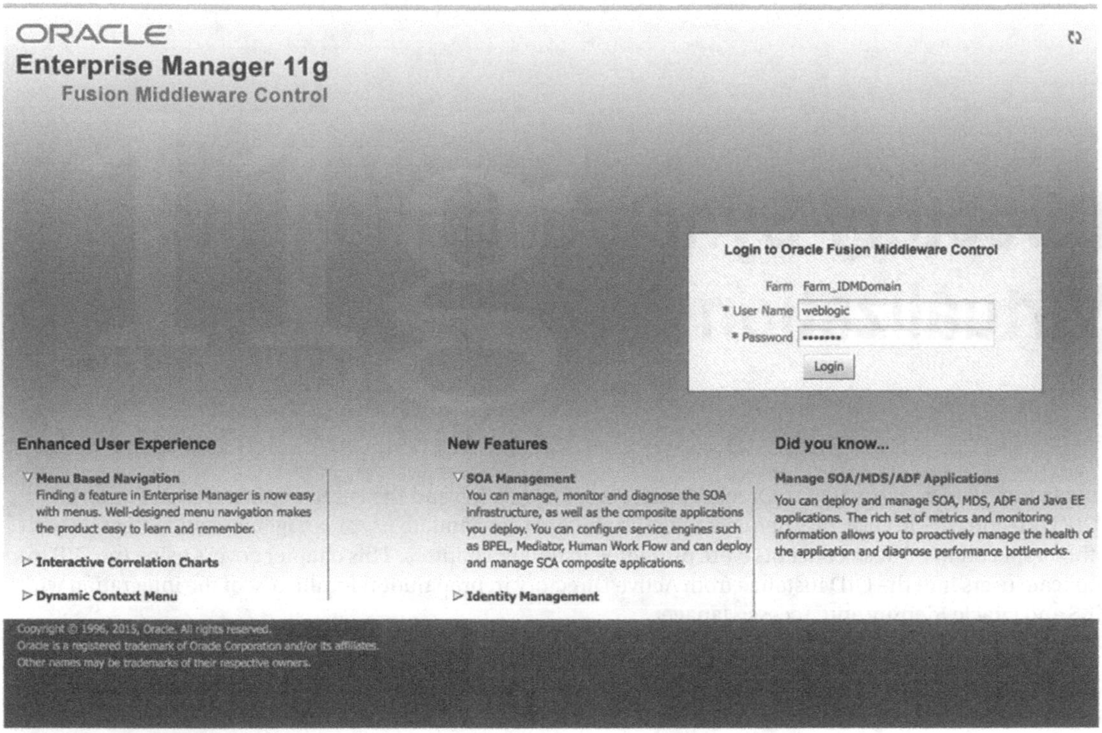

Figure 5-1. *Fusion Middleware Control login screen*

The OID Fusion Middleware Control can be accessed using a browser and navigating to
http://<host>:<port>/em. The port used should be the WebLogic Admin Server port selected during the
domain configuration. In this case, it is 7001. After logging in to the Fusion Middleware Control interface,
use the menu structure located on the left side of the screen to locate the DIP(11.1.2) instance located under
Identity and Access.

After selecting DIP(11.1.2), you are presented with the current status of the server processes as shown in
Figure 5-2. Note that the execution summary is blank because there is not yet a profile to be executed. This
screen is a quick reference. After profile(s) have been created, the summary of each will be displayed in this
section.

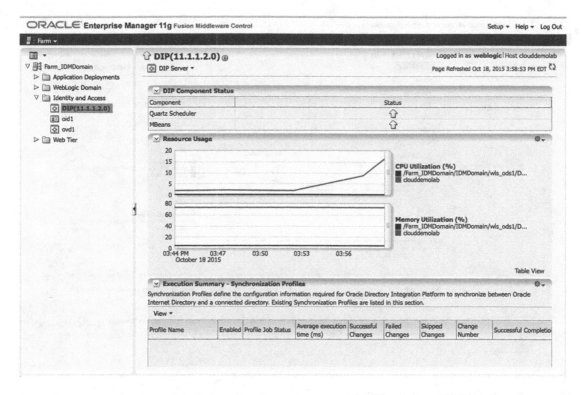

Figure 5-2. *Directory Integration Platform home screen*

On the DIP home screen, use the DIP Server drop-down menu to navigate to Administration ➤ Synchronization Profiles. Synchronization profiles are different from provisioning profiles. The latter are discussed later in this book when EBS integration is presented. Figure 5-3 depicts the status screen and menu options.

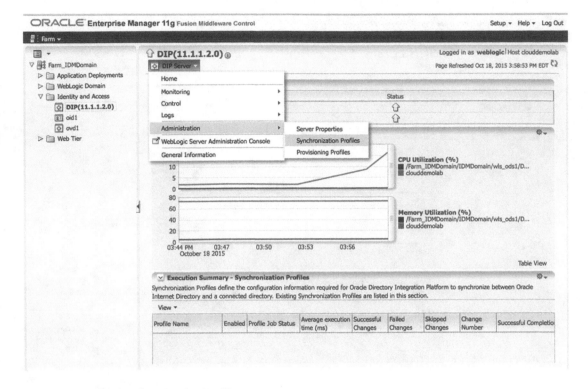

Figure 5-3. *Select Synchronization Profiles*

On the Manage Synchronization Profiles page, shown in Figure 5-4, all existing profiles are listed. From here, you can create, delete, and edit profiles as needed. Enabled profiles are those that are currently being executed by the DIP scheduler. They each run at the interval configured for them.

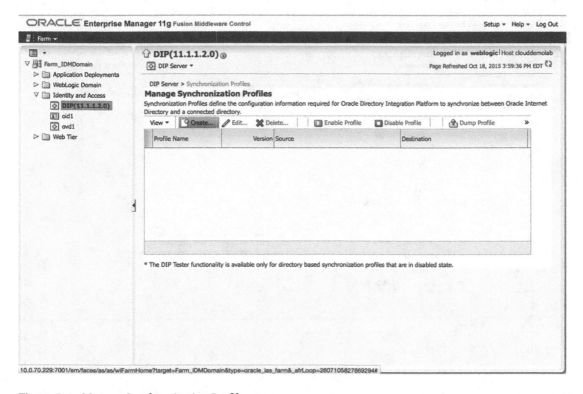

Figure 5-4. *Manage Synchronization Profiles screen*

OID with the DIP installs with a number of preconfigured profiles to support directory sources such as Active Directory, IBM Tivoli, Sun Directory Server, and Novell eDirectory, as well as database and LDIF sources. These are basic templates that include common attribute mappings. The individual needs of the organization will dictate how much customization these profiles will require. However, they are a good starting point to avoid creating something from scratch. Note that directory sources other than the included templates will require a completely custom profile.

Because this is the first profile in the system, select Create in the window. You will be prompted for information regarding the type of profile and source server configuration. Be sure to have the source server information available before starting this process. You will need the host, port, and an account with at least read access in the directory.

The first step in creating a synchronization profile is to provide a name and connection details regarding the source identity store. The creation screen is shown in Figure 5-5.

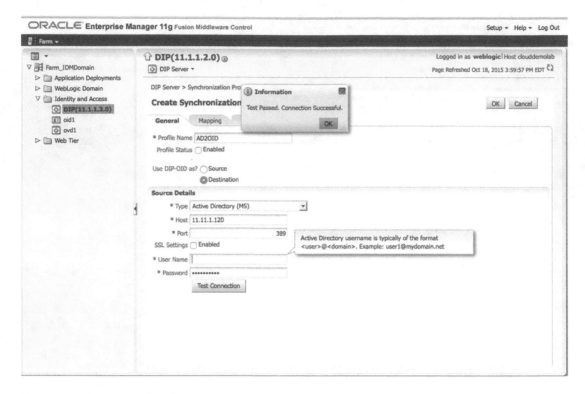

Figure 5-5. *Connection details*

Provide a name for the profile you are creating. If you plan to have only one profile for a given directory, it can be something generic such as AD2OID. However, if you anticipate having multiple profiles for the same source, you might wish to provide a more specific name such as AD_Region2OID. This example could be used if your organization requires users in different Active Directory OUs to be placed in different OID namespaces or handled differently. A good naming convention can help administrators easily manage profiles.

After providing a name for the profile, enter the connection details gathered previously for the source directory. Because this example is an Active Directory server, the Active Directory (MS) option is selected for type. Ensure that you select the proper server type for your profile so that the DIP can create the profile template accordingly. You must enter host and port for the source directory and provide a username/ password pair for an account that has, at least, read access on the users and groups to be synchronized. Any information that this account does not have access to will not be synchronized. This could lead to missing data in OID.

For a one-way synchronization from Active Directory to OID, read access is all that is required. When this type of synchronization is configured, changes in Active Directory are written to OID. However, nothing is written back to Active Directory. This maintains Active Directory as the source of truth for all users in the environment. OID serves as the application identity store. Note that the DIP profiles do not synchronize passwords from Active Directory to OID. Password handling is performed either by the external authentication plug-in or the Active Directory password filter. These options are discussed later in this chapter.

Properly synchronizing two disparate identity stores requires that the source object attributes be correctly mapped to the destination. For example, Active Directory might use an attribute such as SAMAccountName for user login whereas the OID instance might use UID. This must be accounted for in the DIP profile. Figure 5-6 displays the mapping screen.

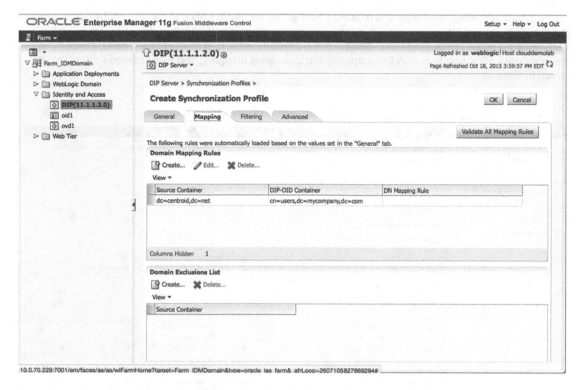

Figure 5-6. *Synchronization profile mapping*

After the source directory connection details are entered and pass the connection test, it is time to configure the mapping details. The Profile Mapping page provides inputs for Source Container/Destination Rules, Exclusion Rules, and Attribute Mapping Rules. Each of these sections are configurable to meet the requirements of the organization.

In the Domain Mapping Rules section, you are able to configure one or more source containers, and where they map to within OID. This is extremely useful if the source directory structure consists of multiple domains or containers that are destined for different OID containers. It should be noted here that the exclusion and mapping rules set forth in a single profile will apply to all of the containers defined in this Domain Mapping Rules section. If different exclusions or mapping rules are required for each container, you should consider creating multiple profiles to handle each container.

In many cases, organizations have a single domain within the source directory that must be mapped to a single domain in OID. In this case, Figure 5-6 shows the source container being the base distinguished name (DN) and the destination container is the OID domain primary users container. For the purposes of this example, this mapping is sufficient.

It should be noted that the DIP primarily synchronizes new accounts and modification to existing accounts. However, each directory source handles object deletion differently and special care is required to ensure that objects deleted from the source are deleted from the destination directory. This might include steps such as granting the synchronization account domain admin privileges so that it can properly view the tombstone records of deleted accounts, or granting permissions to the domain units storing deleted or inactivated accounts. Refer to the source directory documentation or administrator to determine what is needed.

Attribute mapping rules allow you to specify how to convert entries from the source to the destination. The Oracle back-end directory must either be the source or the destination. When converting the entries, there are three types of mapping rules: domain rules, attribute rules, and reconciliation rules. These mapping rules allow you to specify DN mapping, attribute-level mapping, and reconciliation rules. This is shown in Figure 5-7.

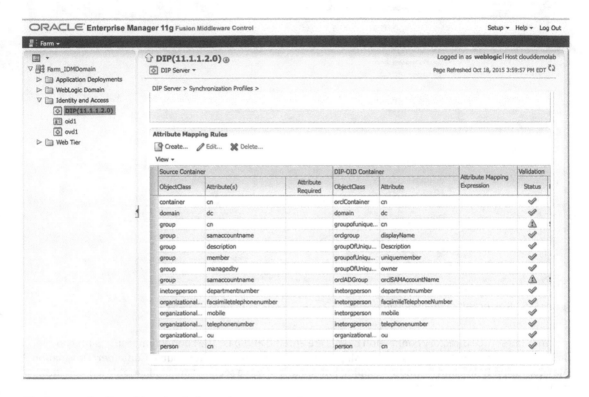

Figure 5-7. *Attribute Mapping Rules settings*

When creating attribute mapping rules, the source `ObjectClass` and `Attribute` are mapped either directly or transformed to populate destination attributes. It is important that you keep some considerations in mind during the creation of the mapping rules. All fields that are required in OID should be based on a required field in the source directory. If building a transformation, ensure that the elements used in the mapping are populated in the source. If they are not, the data entered into OID could be malformed. If the source contains binary values, then it is important to specify the attribute type as binary.

Figure 5-8 displays an example of attribute mapping rules used when synchronizing OID from Active Directory. Although you can create these manually, when using one of the out-of-the-box templates, the rules are precreated and only need modification if your environment uses additional attributes or has one-off requirements.

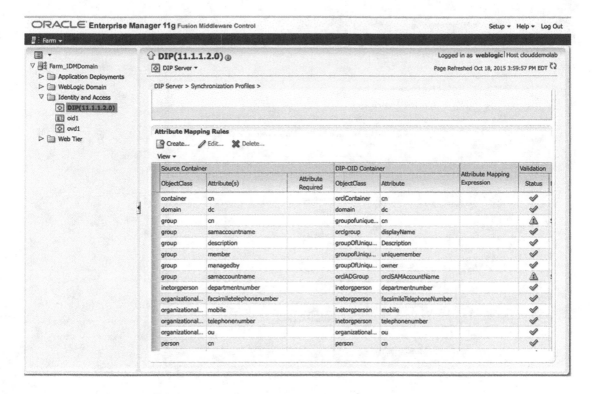

Figure 5-8. *DIP mapping rules*

An example of editing a mapping rule is presented in Figure 5-9. An often used mapping rule is a rule to transform the source `userPrincipalName` and `sAMAccountname` into a format that can be used to populate the `orclSAMAccountname` field in OID using the following rule:

```
toupper(truncl(userPrincipalName,'@'))+"$"+sAMAccountname
```

It should be noted that your environment might have different requirements.

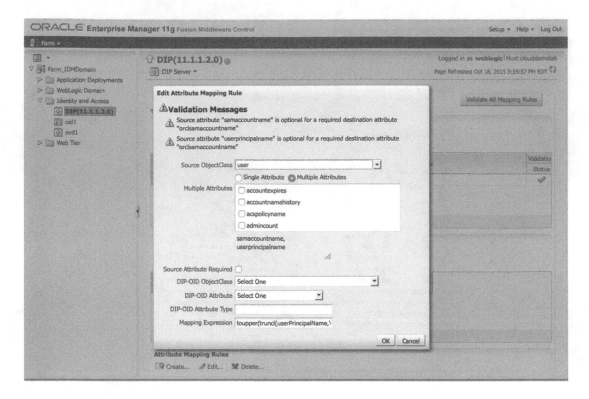

Figure 5-9. *Editing a mapping rule*

Filtering rules can be used to reduce the population of synchronized objects. You can use the rules to exclude Active Directory OUs or objects that do not meet certain criteria. The Filtering tab is shown in Figure 5-10.

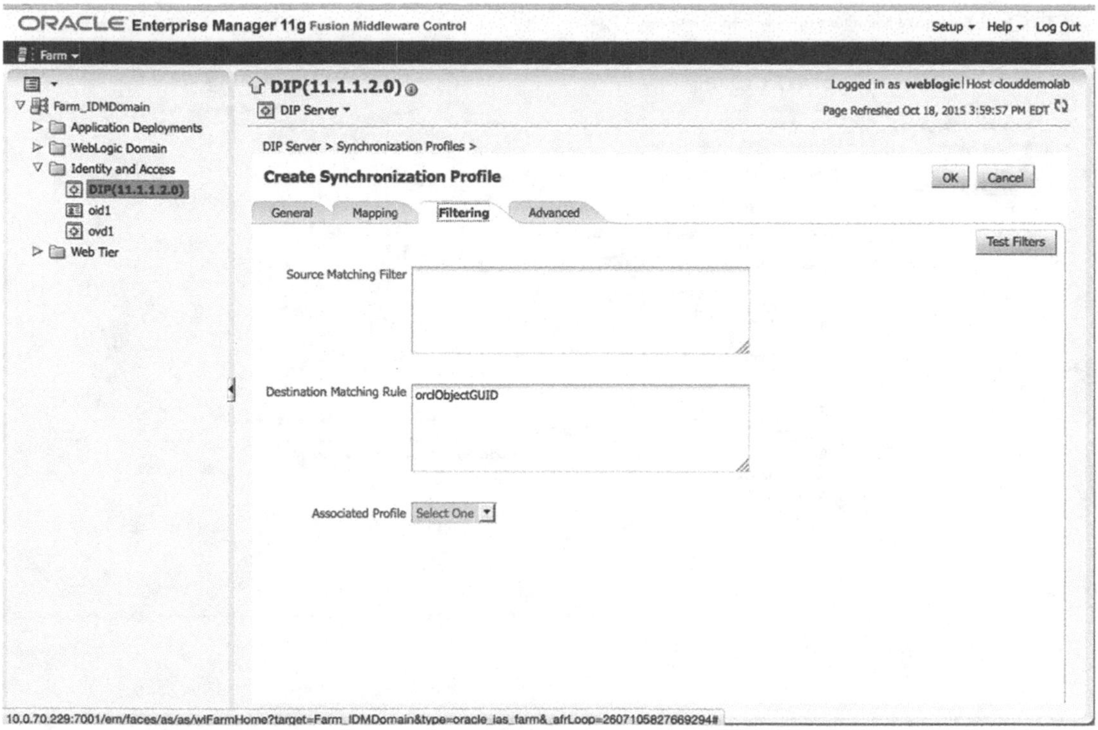

Figure 5-10. *Filtering rules*

Complex filters should be enclosed in double quotes. In some versions of OID, testing a complex filter not enclosed in quotes will cause this screen to lock up and the OID instance will eventually crash. A complex filter is any filter that has more than one single criteria and uses operators such as AND and OR.

Figure 5-11 shows the advanced settings for the new DIP profile. This Advancced tab allows you to set the scheduling interval for running the synchronization profile and update other attributes of the platform. The Last Change Number field can be updated to rerun recent changes. However, careful consideration should be given before updating the value.

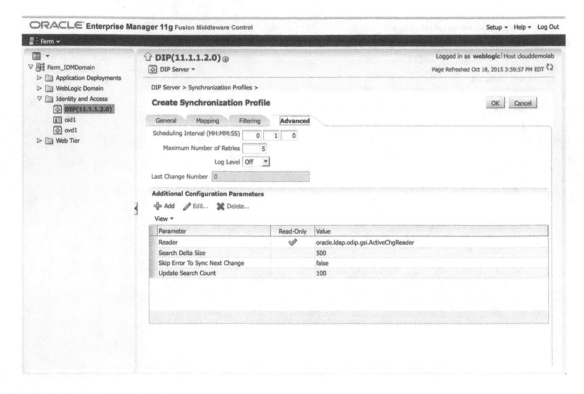

Figure 5-11. *Advanced options*

After you create a profile, it will be listed on the Manage Synchronization Profiles screen seen in Figure 5-12. Here you can enable, disable, edit, delete, and test your profiles as needed. As an administrator, you can create as many profiles as necessary for your requirements. Editing a profile will return you to the pages previously presented.

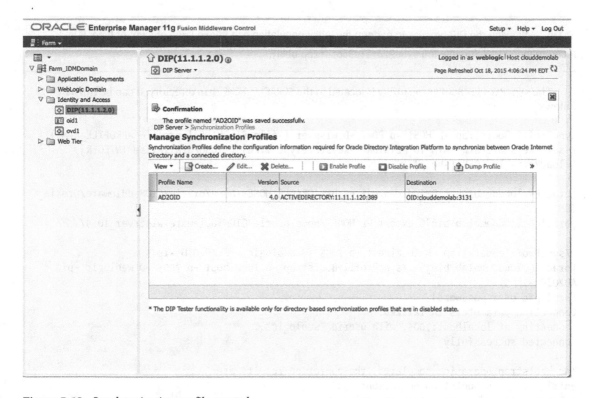

Figure 5-12. *Synchronization profile created*

It is recommended that you test a profile prior to enabling it. Only disabled profiles can be tested using the DIP Tester. It should also be noted that only LDAP source to LDAP destination profiles can be tested using this method. To test a profile, first ensure it is disabled and click the DIP Tester button. On the first test screen, you can dump the profile and see the mappings created during the creation step. Click the Launch Tester button.

The DIP Tester provides two options for testing; Basic and Advanced. Basic will run the test using preconfigured settings. It will run and log messages to the Fusion Middleware Control. This can be useful if you are troubleshooting a synchronization error or looking for a failed synchronization. The Advanced mode allows you to configure the test settings such as Change Number to search for and synchronize a specific change in the source directory.

■ **Note**   Although it is possible to create and manage synchronization profiles using the `manageSyncProfiles` utility, it is recommended that you use the Fusion Middleware Control.

After creating a synchronization profile and prior to enabling it, use the `syncProfileBootstrap` utility to immediately populate the destination directory with data from the source.

To use `syncProfileBootstrap`, first make sure that the `WLS_HOME` and `ORACLE_HOME` environment variables are set to the proper values. `WLS_HOME` should be set to the `<Middleware Directory>/wls10.3.6`. `ORACLE_HOME` should be set to the directory where you installed OID. This is typically `<Middleware Directory>/Oracle_OID`. You should also be prepared with the WebLogic Admin Server host and port along with the WLS password.

■ **Tip**   Allowing the DIP process to perform the initial population can take a large amount of time. It is recommended that you use the `syncProfileBootstrap` utility.

The `syncProfileBootstrap` utility is located in the `$ORACLE_HOME/bin` directory. It can be run as follows:

```
syncProfileBootstrap -h HOST -p PORT -D wlsuser {-file FILENAME |-profile -PROFILE_NAME}
[-ssl -keystorePath PATH_TO_KEYSTORE -keystoreType TYPE] [-loadParallelism INTEGER]
[-loadRetry INTEGER][-help]

[oracle@clouddemolab OIDMiddleware]$ export ORACLE_HOME=/home/oracle/OIDMiddleware/Oracle_
IDM1
[oracle@clouddemolab bin]$ export WL_HOME=/home/oracle/OIDMiddleware/wlserver_10.3/

./syncProfileBootstrap -h localhost -p 7005 -D weblogic -pf AD2OID -lp 5
[oracle@clouddemolab bin]$ ./syncProfileBootstrap -h localhost -p 7005 -D weblogic -pf
AD2OID -lp 5
[Weblogic user password]
Connection parameters intialized.
Connecting at localhost:7005, with userid "weblogic"..
Connected successfully

The bootstrap operation completed, the operation results are:
entries read in bootstrap operation: 433
entries filtered in bootstrap operation: 0
entries ignored in bootstrap operation: 0
Entries processed in bootstap operation: 346
Entries failed in bootstrap operation: 87
```

■ **Note**   If the source directory from which you are loading data contains a large number of entries, the quickest and easiest method to bootstrap the target directory is by using an LDIF file. Bootstrapping with an integration profile is not recommended in this case because connection errors could occur when reading and writing between the source and target directories. Using an LDIF file is also recommended if the DNs contain special characters, which might not be escaped properly when bootstrapping with an integration profile.

After the directory has been bootstrapped, you can enable the profile and allow OID to be synchronized with values from the source Active Directory. Return to the Fusion Middleware Control screens and enable the synchronization profile as shown in Figure 5-13.

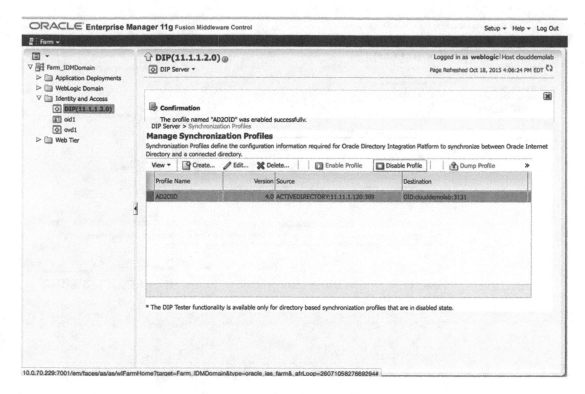

Figure 5-13. *Enabling a synchronization profile*

Once a profile has been enabled, you are able to view the statistics and status of the synchronization profile on the DIP server home screen shown in Figure 5-14. At a glance, you will see the number of changes, number of errors, number of skipped objects, last completed date, and the last run status. To view more in-depth information, you can view log messages.

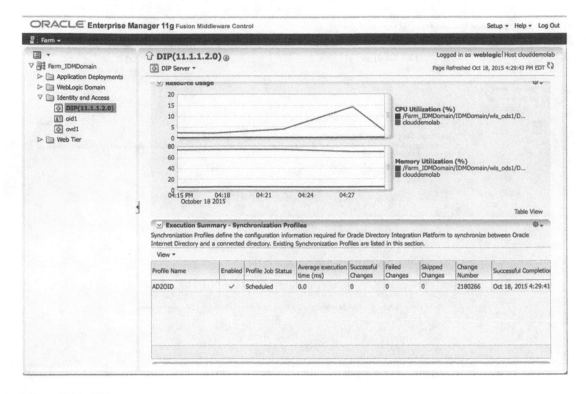

Figure 5-14. *DIP status*

During the synchronization process, it is possible that a single object can cause the process to stop. By default, DIP will not continue if it encounters an error. You can check the DIP logs to view the object that caused the synchronization to stop. This log screen is shown in Figure 5-15.

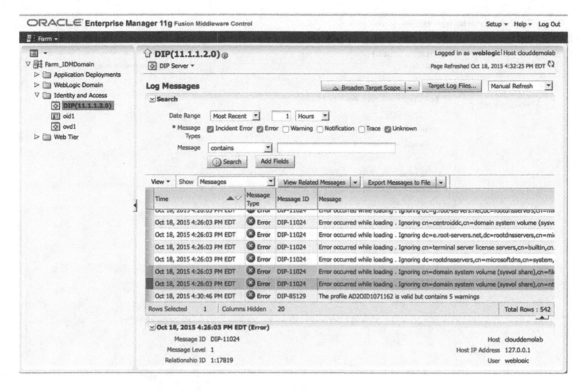

Figure 5-15. *Synchronization profile log messages*

Many times, errors are caused by missing mandatory attributes. After identifying the problem, it might be as simple as fixing the problem in the source Active Directory account.

Other times, the problem might seem more complex. It is possible that a new Active Directory OU was created and populated with users. The DIP synchronization might try to create the users prior to the new OU, which will result in an error.

You can configure DIP to skip errors and continue to prevent the overall process from failing. In the latter example just presented, this can allow the OU to get created and the next synchronization will pick up the missed objects. The Advanced tab shown in Figure 5-16 can be used to tweak DIP options for a particular profile.

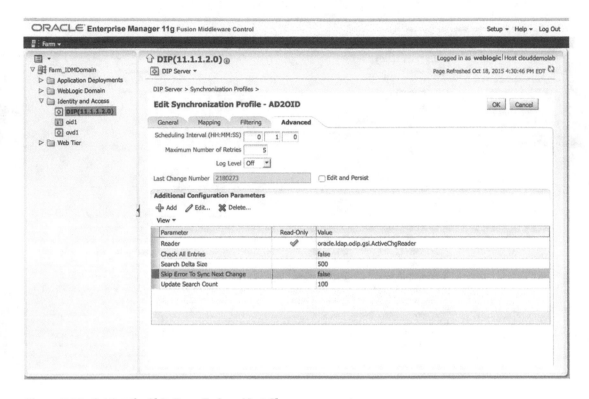

Figure 5-16. *Setting the Skip Error To Sync Next Change parameter*

Another troubleshooting option is to edit the profile exclusion rules. This option allows you to configure the synchronization to skip objects if they do not meet a certain criteria. You might find this useful if your environment contains a number of LDAP objects that you do not wish to synchronize. Use the Mapping tab shown in Figure 5-17 to add or edit exclusion rules.

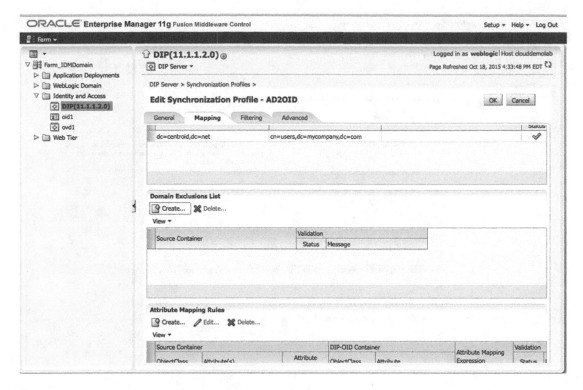

Figure 5-17. *Edit domain exclusion rules and filtering*

If the DIP server has been down or you need to run the sync to catch information that was missed due to error, you might need to run the process with an earlier change number. Select the Edit and Persist check box and update the Last Change Number field. Doing this will allow the DIP process to run all changes since the new Last Change Number entered. You will need to query the source directory to get the change number to which you wish to return. Again the Advanced tab can be used for this. Figure 5-18 shows the Edit and Persist check box necessary for modifying this field.

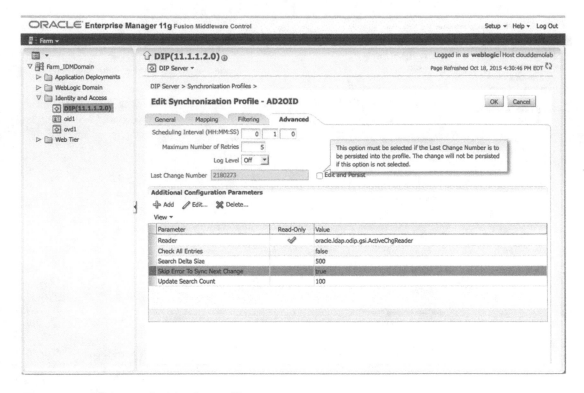

Figure 5-18. *Editing synchronization profile*

At the end of this chapter, you should have a fully synchronized OID. The data stored in this directory should match your Active Directory source according to the attribute mapping rules configured. Using this chapter, you should be able to edit user attribute mappings and troubleshoot profiles.

Summary

Many organizations have a need to keep identity directories in sync with each other. Perhaps OID is used as the application authentication directory and Active Directory is used by the network for authentication. Users must be in both places to access network resources and their requred applications. The DIP provides a mechanism to replicate data stored in one source to be replicated to the other. Although this could be accomplished manually, the DIP is an automated process that is provided by Oracle. Using the information in this chapter will assist you in creating the necessary components to keep disparate identity stores synchronized.

CHAPTER 6

■ ■ ■

Oracle Access Manager Installation

Oracle Internet Directory (OID) has been installed, and is populated with users from Active Directory. You have configured a synchronization process to ensure account information changes in Active Directory are populated to OID. The benefit to this is that all applications that use OID for authentication and role information continually have the latest user information. Fusion Middleware applications and other Lightweight Directory Access Protocol (LDAP) compatible applications can be configured to authenticate using OID. However, many organizations wish to build on this capability by providing a single sign-on (SSO) environment. Oracle introduced Oracle Access Manager (OAM) to give organizations exactly this ability. This chapter covers how to install the OAM tools in preparation for implementing SSO for the EBS and WebCenter environments.

In a previous chapter, OID was installed and configured. If OID is not already present in your environment, or has not been validated, refer to Chapter 4 for instructions.

Preinstallation Tasks

Operating System Users

For most Oracle application installs, operating system (OS) users and groups should be created to perform the installation and configuration tasks. Creating OS groups will allow other OS users to perform certain tasks related to the management of the application environment. The most common OS users and groups related to installing Oracle applications in Linux environments are the oracle user and oinstall or dba groups.

To create the necessary oinstall and dba groups, perform the following commands as the root directory:

```
[root@clouddemolab home]# groupadd oinstall
[root@clouddemolab home]# groupadd osdba
```

After the groups are created, create the oracle user.

```
[root@clouddemolab home]# useradd  -g oinstall -G osdba oracle
```

■ **Note**   -g indicates the primary group to which the user should be added. -G indicates any secondary groups.

© Kenneth Ramey 2016   123
K. Ramey, *Pro Oracle Identity and Access Management Suite*, DOI 10.1007/978-1-4842-1521-0_6

To set the password for the user, use the following command as the root user:

```
[root@clouddemolab home]# passwd oracle
```

Operating System Configuration

Prior to installing the Oracle Fusion Middleware infrastructure and Oracle Identity Management software, it is important to ensure the OS meets the minimum requirements and configuration. The following presents the kernel parameters and packages and the file changes that are required.

The following kernel parameters need to be set:

```
kernel.sem  256  32000  100  143
kernel.shmmax 10737418240
```

To set these parameters, edit the sysctl.conf file located in the /etc directory.

```
[root@clouddemolab home]# vi /etc/sysctl.conf
```

Add or edit the following lines in this section of the file:

```
# Controls the maximum number of shared memory segments, in pages
kernel.shmall = 4294967296
kernel.sem = 256 32000 100 142
kernel.shmmax = 10737418240
```

After setting these values in the sysctl.conf file, you must activate and verify the new values are shown using this command:

```
[root@clouddemolab home]# /sbin/sysctl -p
net.ipv4.ip_forward = 0
net.ipv4.conf.default.rp_filter = 1
net.ipv4.conf.default.accept_source_route = 0
kernel.sysrq = 0
kernel.core_uses_pid = 1
net.ipv4.tcp_syncookies = 1
net.bridge.bridge-nf-call-ip6tables = 0
net.bridge.bridge-nf-call-iptables = 0
net.bridge.bridge-nf-call-arptables = 0
kernel.msgmnb = 65536
kernel.msgmax = 65536
kernel.shmmax = 68719476736
kernel.shmall = 4294967296
kernel.sem = 256 32000 100 142
kernel.shmmax = 10737418240
```

The open file limits must be set to 4096 to support the instance. To do so, edit the limits.conf file:

```
[root@clouddemolab home]# vi /etc/security/limits.conf
```

If the environment is to be installed on Oracle Linux or RedHat Linux, you must perform the edit in /etc/security/limits.d/90-nproc.conf as well. If this is missed, the values in this file could override the values in the limits.conf file.

In both of the files listed, ensure the following lines are added or edited:

```
* soft nofile 4096
* hard nofile 65536
* soft nproc 2047
* hard nproc 16384
```

After editing this file, the server must be rebooted to ensure all the changes take effect.

Operating System Packages

Each Oracle application has its own set of required packages. Depending on the version of Linux you are using, the installation procedure might be different. In the following list, you should note that some packages require both 32-bit and 64-bit versions to be installed on a 64-bit OS. If these packages are not installed, the installation will not complete properly. The Oracle Installer will check these and display errors during the installation.

```
binutils-2.20.51.0.2-5.28.el6
compat-libcap1-1.10-1
compat-libstdc++-33-3.2.3-69.el6 for x86_64
compat-libstdc++-33-3.2.3-69.el6 for i686
gcc-4.4.4-13.el6 gcc-c++-4.4.4-13.el6
glibc-2.12-1.7.el6 for x86_64
glibc-2.12-1.7.el6 for i686
glibc-devel-2.12-1.7.el6 for i686
libaio-0.3.107-10.el6
libaio-devel-0.3.107-10.el6
libgcc-4.4.4-13.el6
libstdc++-4.4.4-13.el6 for x86_64
libstdc++-4.4.4-13.el6 for i686
libstdc++-devel-4.4.4-13.el6
libXext for i686
libXtst for i686
libXext for x86_64
libXtst for x86_64
openmotif-2.2.3 for x86_64
openmotif22-2.2.3 for x86_64
redhat-lsb-core-4.0-7.el6 for x86_64
sysstat-9.0.4-11.el6
xorg-x11-utils*
xorg-x11-apps*
xorg-x11-xinit*
xorg-x11-server-Xorg*
xterm
pdksh-5.2.14
```

At this point in the procedure, the OS should be fully prepared for the installation to proceed. Performing the preceding operations prior to installing the software will ensure a problem-free installation. In many cases, the installer will provide detailed messages if anything was missed. In the event of errors during the installation process, stop the installation and fix any problems before proceeding.

Database Preparation

Just like OID, the installation of OAM requires specific database objects to be created. This includes a number of tables, views, and packages created in various database schemas. This is done using the Repository Creation Utility (RCU). Although the database objects can be created within the same database, it is often recommended that the Oracle Identity and Access Management repository be created in a separate instance. This simplifies database administration tasks and future maintenance. The RCU Create Repository screen is shown in Figure 6-1. Take care to download and run the RCU that is designated for the version of Oracle Identity and Access Management you are installing. Unzip the download and run the rcu.sh found in the <RCU_HOME>/rcu/bin directory.

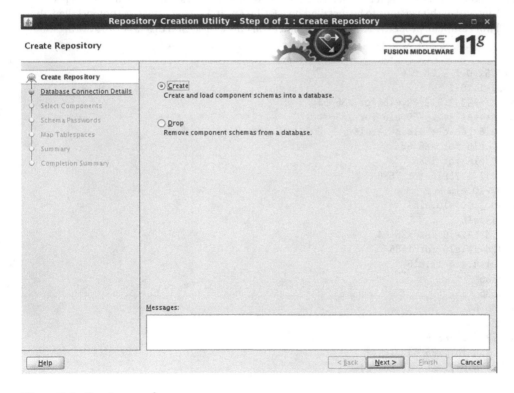

Figure 6-1. *Create new schema*

The same process is undertaken to create the database repository objects as for OID. The RCU is started and Create is selected.

Oracle database details are entered. The details in the screen in Figure 6-1 point to the same database server as Oracle Directory Services. However, the database instance was created specifically for Oracle Identity and Access Manager to keep the two systems separated. Figure 6-2 shows the database details entered on screen.

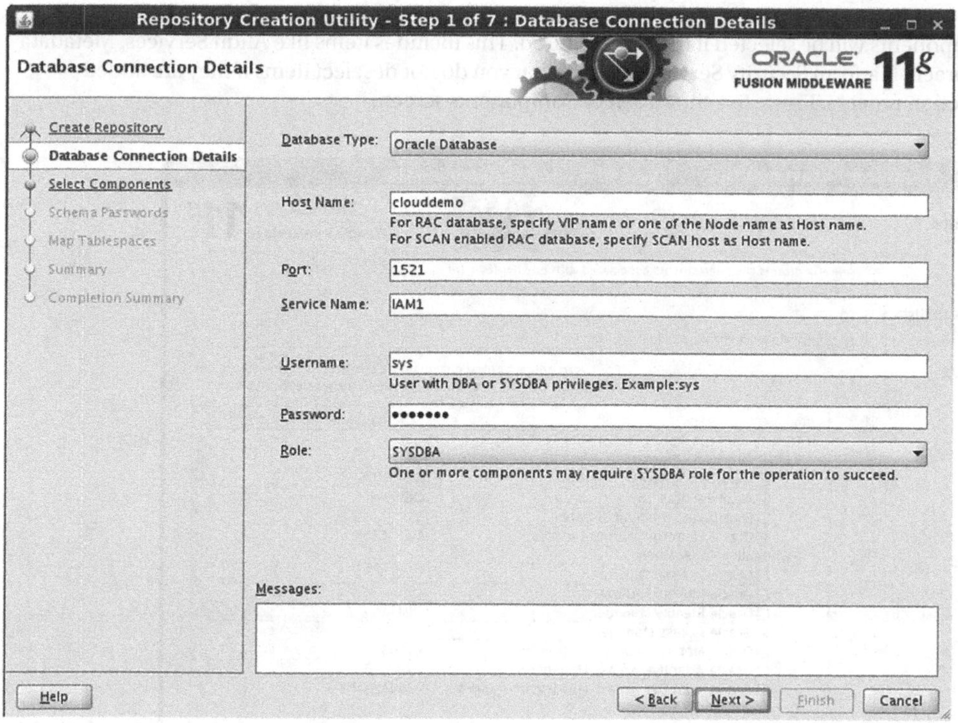

Figure 6-2. *Enter database connection details*

As shown in Figure 6-3, the RCU will check to ensure the database meets the minimum prerequisites. If there are any failures, these must be corrected before moving forward in the process.

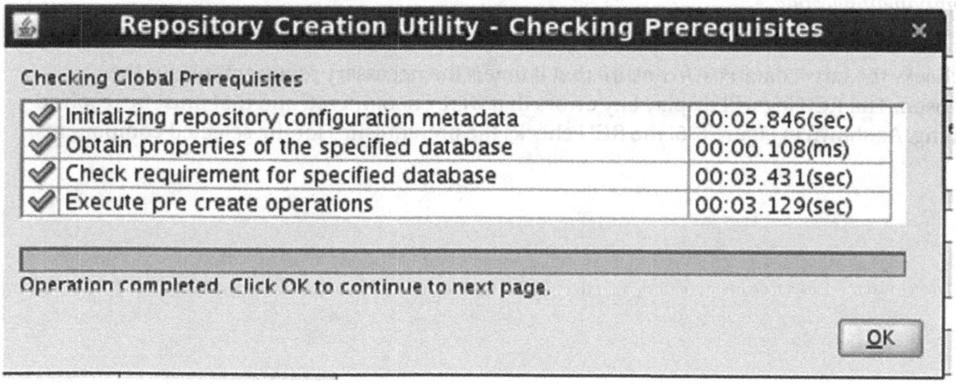

Figure 6-3. *Database prechecks completed*

On the Select Components screen of the RCU, select Oracle Access Manager, as shown in Figure 6-4. Additional components will be selected if they are required. This includes items like Audit Services, Metadata Services, and Oracle Platform Security Services. Ensure that you do not deselect items if they are added during the selection process. Figure 6-4 shows Select Components screen.

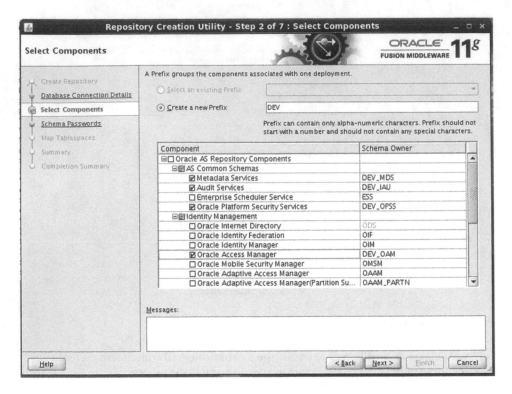

Figure 6-4. *Component selection*

The RCU checks the target database to ensure that it meets the necessary requirements for the components chosen. The RCU log will display any errors that were encountered and that must be resolved prior to continuing. As shown in Figure 6-5, the RCU checks the prerequisites for the selected components.

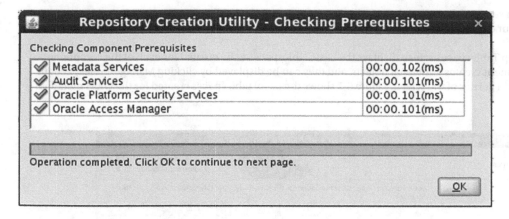

Figure 6-5. *Database prerequisite checking*

After the RCU verifies the prerequisites, you will be prompted for a password to be used by the new database schemas, as shown in Figure 6-6.

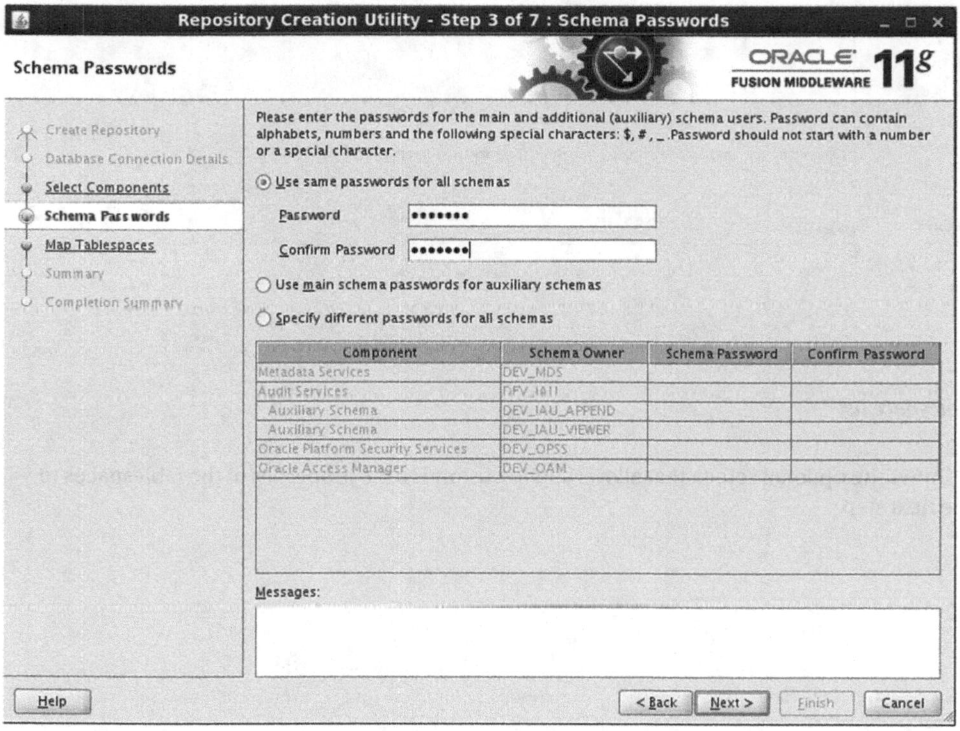

Figure 6-6. *Schema passwords*

You can set all of the schemas to use the same password or set different passwords for each component. Although your organization might require different passwords, it is often sufficient to use the same password.

The Map Tablespaces screen displays the basic tablespaces to be created for each of the components. Each component creates additional objects, and they can be displayed by clicking Manage Tablespaces in the lower right corner of the screen. Figure 6-7 shows the list of tablespaces created for the OAM metadata repository.

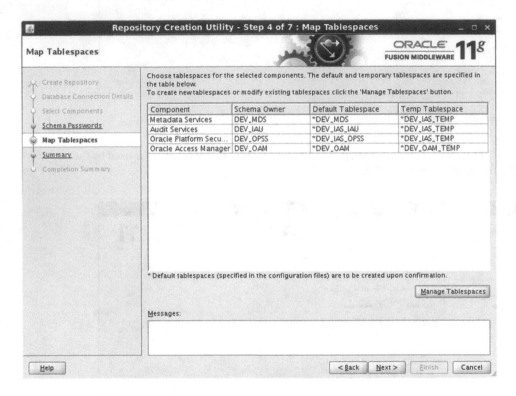

Figure 6-7. *Tablespace list*

Figure 6-8 shows the optional screen that allows you to customize the properties of the tablespaces to be created in the next step.

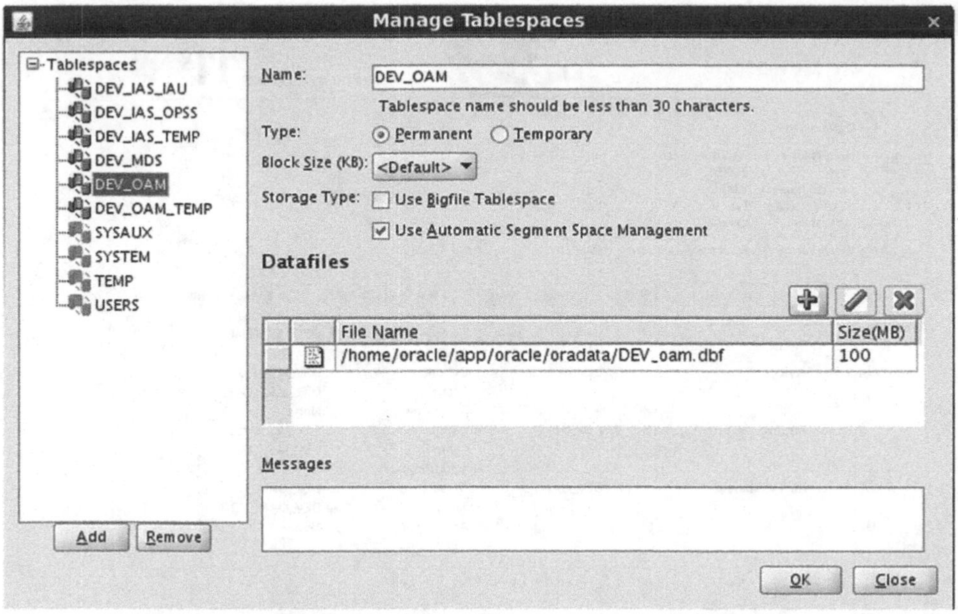

Figure 6-8. *Manage Tablespaces screen*

Unless working closely with a database administrator (DBA), you should avoid modifying the default values provided during the RCU. However, your DBAs might have suggestions or requirements to improve performance.

Figure 6-9 provides a look at the Summary screen. This screen gives you a chance to see all of the objects that will be created based on your inputs on previous screens. If anything looks out of place, this is a last chance to make any tweaks before the database objects are created.

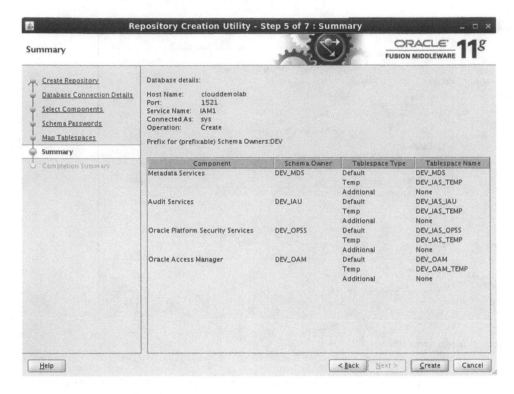

Figure 6-9. *Creation Summary screen*

As the RCU creates the objects required for the metadata repository, a progress screen, shown in Figure 6-10, is displayed. Allow this process to complete without interuption. If, for any reason, this process is stopped, you should restart the RCU to drop all components from this run and restart the creation from scratch.

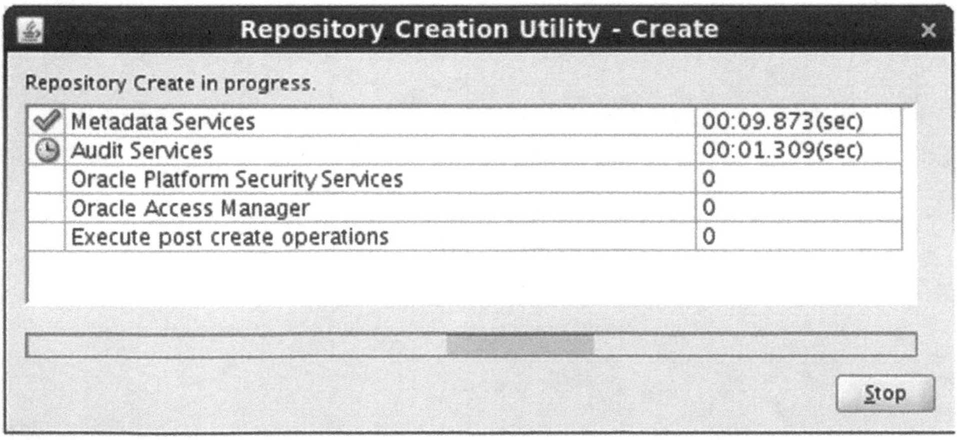

Figure 6-10. *RCU completion*

The RCU has completed and all of the database schema objects have been created to support OAM. Now that the database has been prepared, the OAM software can be installed, and the domain configured.

Access Manager Software Installation

Oracle software installs using the Universal Installer. The tool works as a guide that walks through ensuring the proper software binaries are installed in the correct places. The runInstaller tool requires that the Java Runtime Environment be specified at runtime. Do this by using the –jreLoc parameter.

In Linux this this is run as follows:

```
[oracle@clouddemolab Disk1]$ ./runInstaller -jreLoc /home/oracle/jdk1.6.0.45/jre
```

Figure 6-11 shows the Welcome screen of the Oracle Universal Installer. The version information for Oracle Identity and Access Management should be seen in the text, in this case, 11.1.2.3. If this does not match the version you are installing, find the correct installer software. The RCU run in the previous section is only compatible with 11.1.2.3.

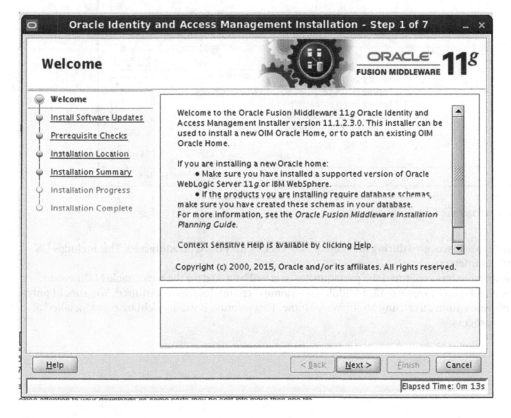

Figure 6-11. *Welcome screen*

As with other Oracle products, the installer first verifies that the target host meets the minimum requirements and that all necessary OS packages are installed. See the prerequisites list at the beginning of this chapter for details. Figure 6-12 shows the prerequisite checks successfully completed.

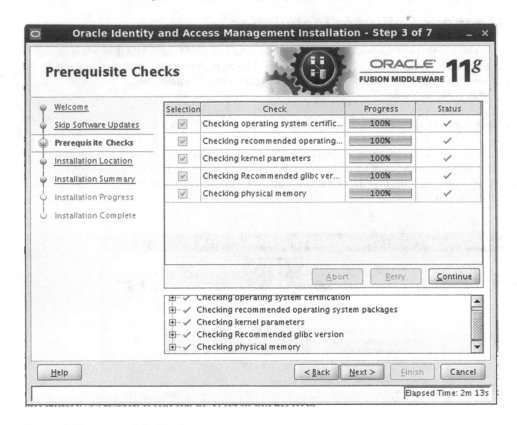

Figure 6-12. *Prerequisite Checks screen*

If any issues are discovered during the prerequisite checks, they must be addressed. This includes OS packages and parameters.

After the installer has confirmed the prerequisites, you will be asked for the new Oracle Middleware Home directory. As seen in Figure 6-13, a Middleware Home directory location is required. You should only install this software within an existing Middleware Home. This location is where WebLogic was installed at the start of this process.

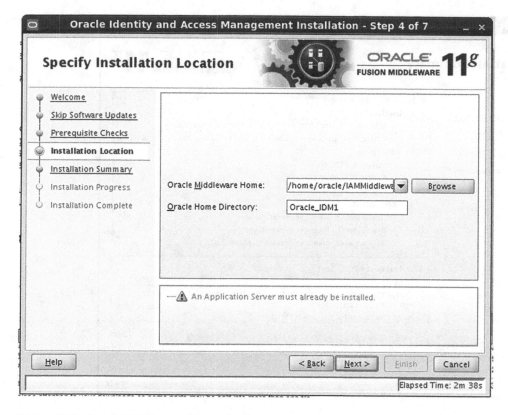

Figure 6-13. *Oracle Middleware Home selection screen*

The OAM software must be installed into an existing Fusion Middleware Home. Installing WLS creates the Fusion Middleware home. Instructions to install WLS can be found in Chapter 4. Follow those instructions and create a home within a directory called IAMMiddleware. This ensures the OAM environment is separated from the OID middleware directory structure.

The Oracle Identity and Access Manager Installer is only used to install Oracle Access Manager and Oracle Identity Manager. As such, it will not prompt you for the components to be installed. As seen in Figure 6-14, you are provided with a summary of the planned installation.

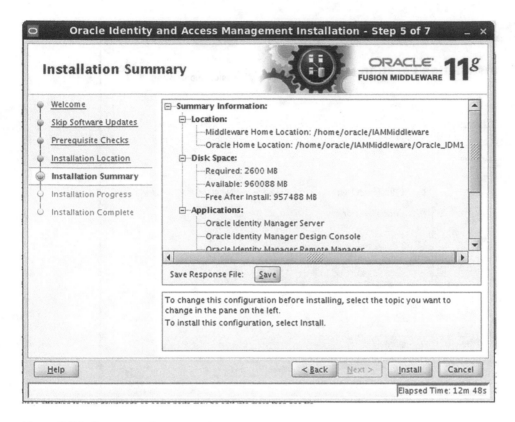

Figure 6-14. *Summary of components*

Prior to the completion, the Universal Installer displays a summary of the components that wil be installed into the Middleware Home. Click Install to lay down the binaries.

The progress bar shown in Figure 6-15 will display 100 percent when the proecss is complete. Be patient, as there are times when this progress bar might not appear to be moving. Check the install log at the location shown on the screen if there are any issues.

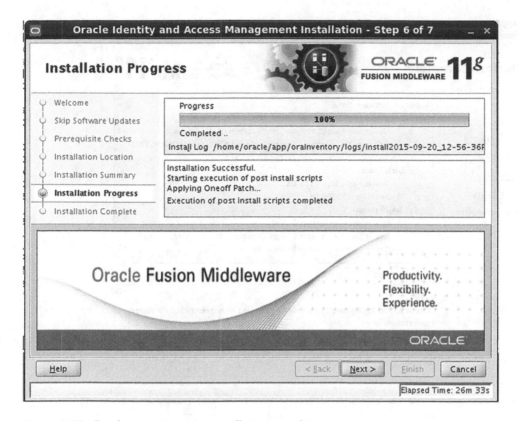

Figure 6-15. *Oracle Access Manager installation completion*

On completion, the installer will provide a summary of the components installed and the location of the files. Make a note of the information shown in the completion data. An example of this completion summary is shown in Figure 6-16.

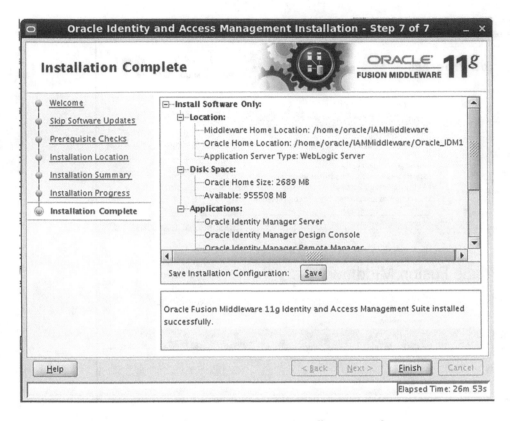

Figure 6-16. *Oracle Identity and Access Management installation complete*

The Oracle Identity and Access Management software installation is now complete. As discussed previously, the environment can be implemented in a split or combined domain. In a split domain, OAM is installed in a separate Middleware Home or even a separate physical server. Combined domains place both components within the same Middleware Home. For the purposes of this book, a split domain will be used. The rest of this chapter focuses on creating the OAM domain.

Creating the Access Manager Domain

After the installation of the OAM, a new domain can be configured. This is accomplished by running the `config.sh` script located in the `IDM_HOME/common/bin` directory. It should be noted that there are multiple locations of `config.sh`. To configure the OAM domain, the specified configuration script must be used.

This is run from the `<MIDDLEWARE_HOM>/Oracle_IDM1/common/bin` directory.

```
[oracle@clouddemolab bin]$ pwd
/home/oracle/IAMMiddleware/Oracle_IDM1/common/bin
[oracle@clouddemolab bin]$ ./config.sh
```

Running the configuration utility from the `ORACLE_HOME/common/bin` directory will launch the Access Manager domain configuration wizard. You will first be welcomed by the screen shown in Figure 6-17.

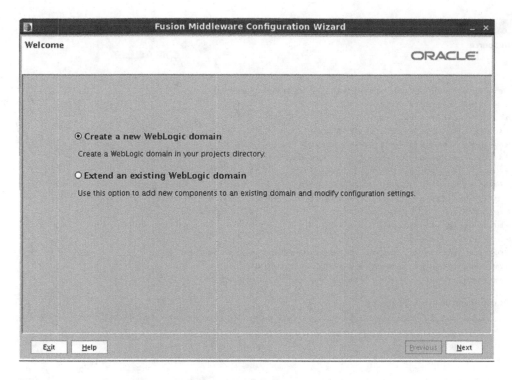

Figure 6-17. *Welcome screen to create a new domain*

Fusion Middleware software is deployed within a domain in the WLS environment. To start, select the Create a New WebLogic Domain option.

After selecting the configuration type, you will be presented with a list of Identity Management components that can be configured within the new domain. This selection screen is shown in Figure 6-18. The domain configuration process involves selecting the software components that will be deployed into the domain as it is created. This list is based on the software installed during the previous step. During the selection process, required components are preselected as needed. For this step, Oracle Access Management and Mobile Security Suite 11.1.2.3.0 is selected, and the Oracle Enterprise Manager component is also preselected.

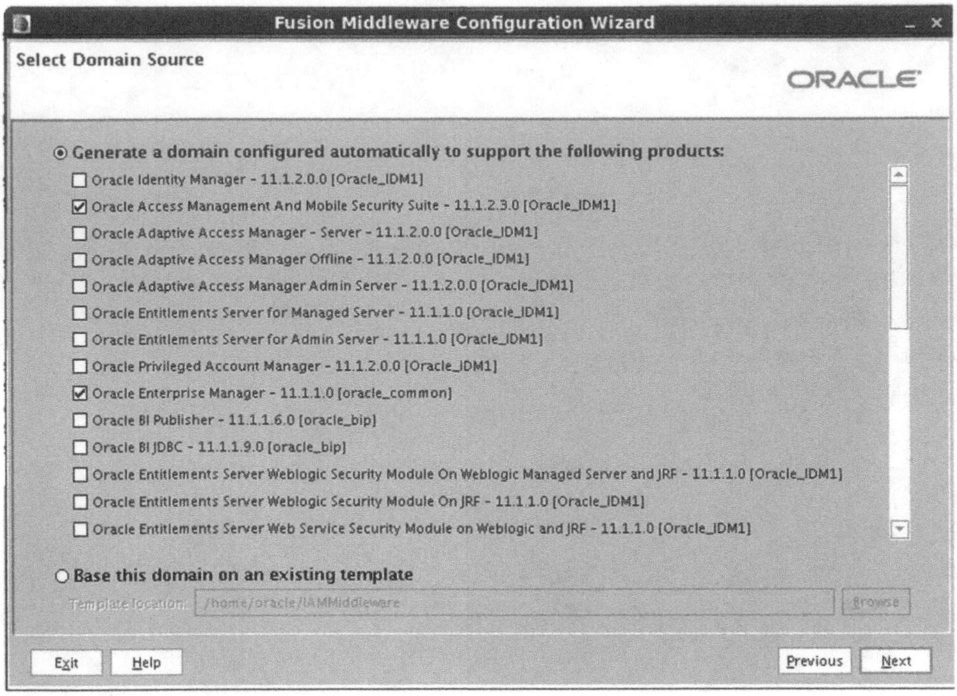

Figure 6-18. *Select components for the domain*

During this step, you provide a name for the domain and specify the file system location. Depending on the file system requirements and high availability, these files might need to be deployed in different locations. These are discussed in the high availability section of this book. Figure 6-19 shows an example of this step.

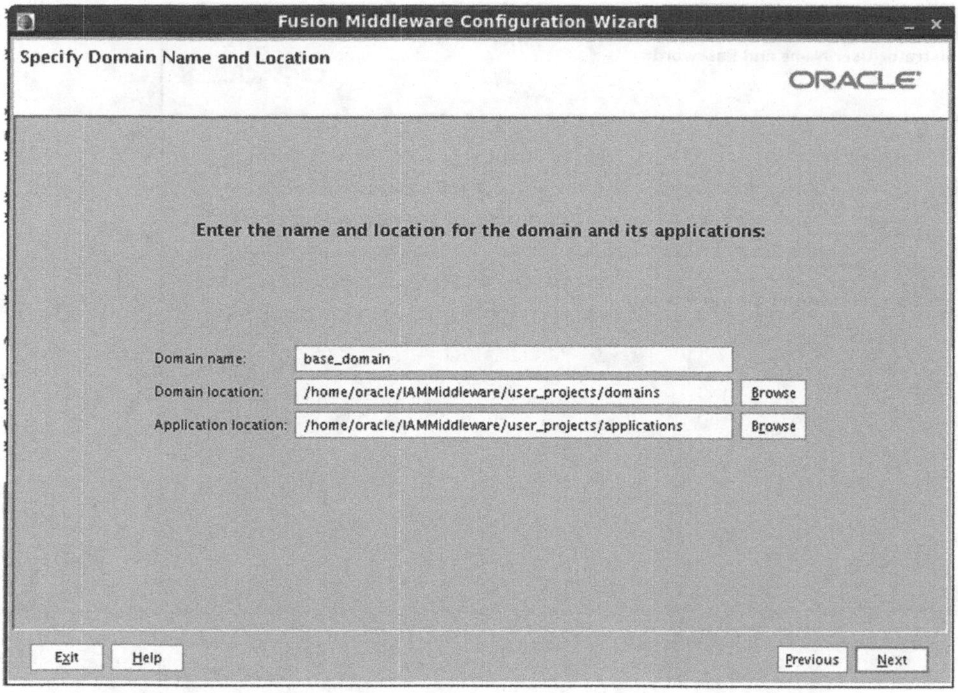

Figure 6-19. *Specifying a domain location*

Provide a password for the weblogic user, as shown in Figure 6-20. Although you can specify a different username at this stage, it is common to use weblogic. At a later time you can create other users who will have access to the administration utilities. The weblogic user password should be set to something standard for your environment. This password will be used for starting and stopping managed servers as well as logging into the WebLogic Admin Console and Fusion Middleware Control.

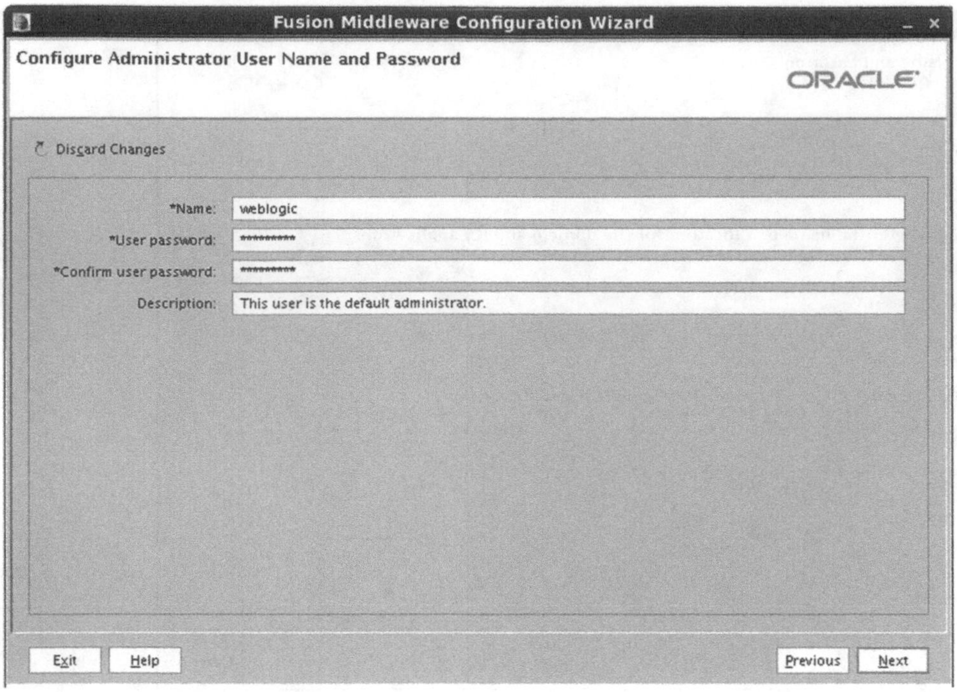

Figure 6-20. *Set administration user password*

Figure 6-21 shows the Start Mode selection screen.

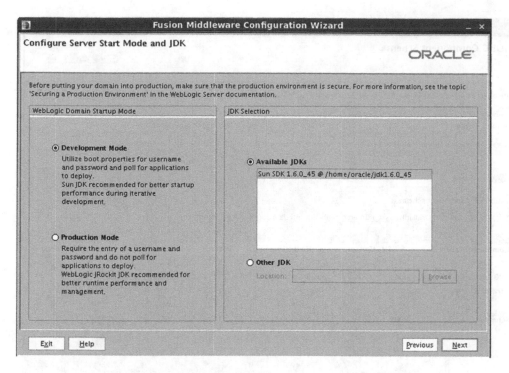

Figure 6-21. Domain Startup Mode configuration

The Startup Mode determines how the managed servers are started. In Development Mode, the managed servers can be started and stopped from the command line without a password. Also configuration changes can be made and activated within the WebLogic Console without locking the environment. Configuring the Startup Mode to Production Mode locks the environment down to ensure no changes are made without locking the console for edits. Command-line tools will also require a password.

■ **Note** Locking the Administration Console prevents multiple administrators from making changes and overwriting each other.

The database connection screen, shown in Figure 6-22, requires the entry of database connection details for each of the components to be configured in the WebLogic domain. The database schemas displayed are prepopulated and should have been created using the RCU.

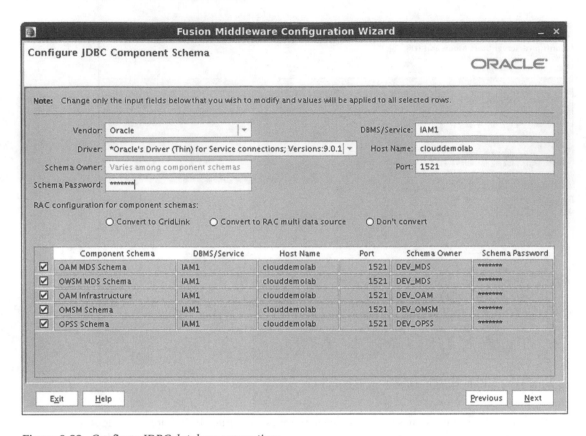

Figure 6-22. *Configure JDBC database connections*

Enter the database details such as host, port and service name. The password for each of the schemas must be entered. This step creates the Java database connectivity (JDBC) data sources within the WebLogic domain.

■ **Note**   Selecting the check box next to all of the schemas on this screen will allow the entries to be duplicated without being required to enter the data multiple times.

After the JDBC connection details are entered, the information is validated by the configuration tool. Any errors will be shown. If a schema was not able to be validated, revisit the previous step to ensure the schema name and details are correct. If the database schema does not exist, rerun the RCU to create it. Figure 6-23 displays the database repository verification completed.

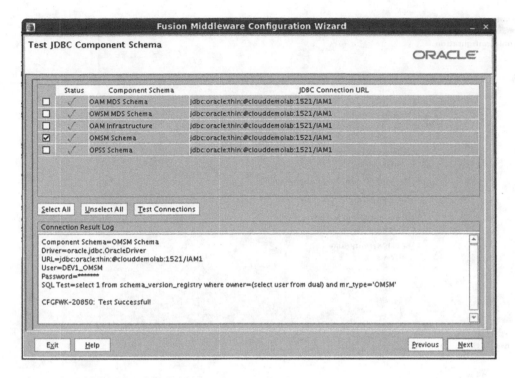

Figure 6-23. *Checking the schemas*

For the purposes of this chapter, you will be creating the Administration Server, Managed Servers, Clusters and Machines, as shown in Figure 6-24. If at this point your environment requires Deployments and Services or the RDBMS Security Store, select them now. The items selected on this screen dictate the following screens. Only those required by the selections will be seen.

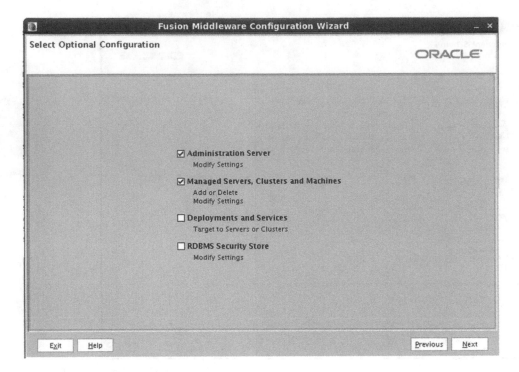

Figure 6-24. *Optional configurations*

In the following steps, the Administration Server, Managed Servers, Clusters and Machines will be configured. Figure 6-25 shows the Configure the Administration Server screen.

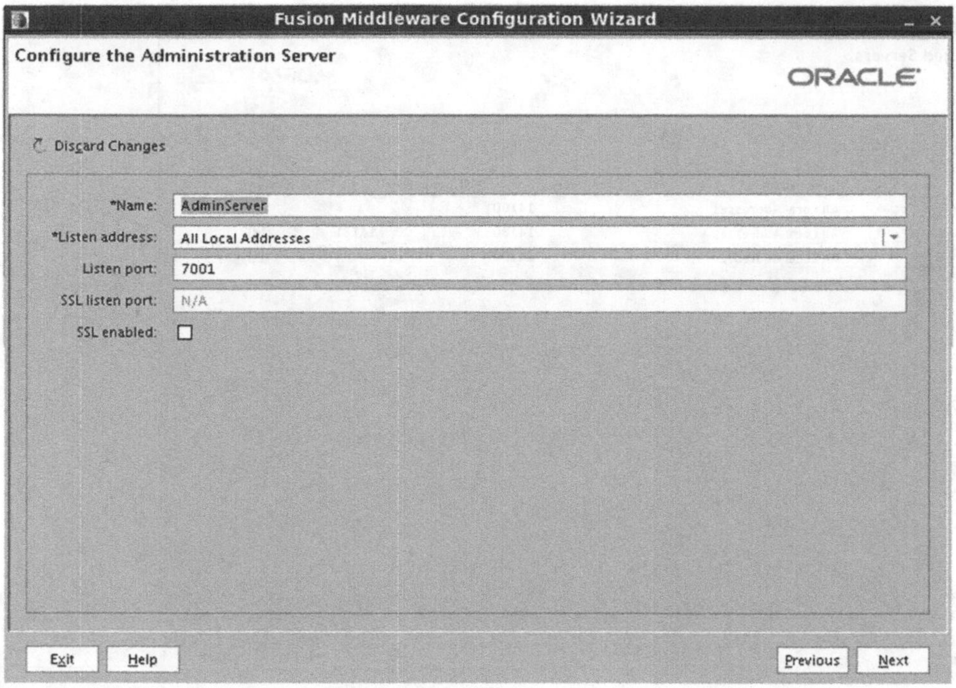

Figure 6-25. *Administration Server configuration*

One Administration Server per domain can be running at a time. Using the configuration tool, one Administration Server can be specified. In clustered environments, a backup Administration Server can be configured on the secondary nodes in case the primary is lost. During this step, ensure the port specified is available on the physical host.

After entering the Adminstration Server details, you will be presented with the Configure Managed Servers screen seen in Figure 6-26. The managed servers will be prepopulated based on the components selected earlier.

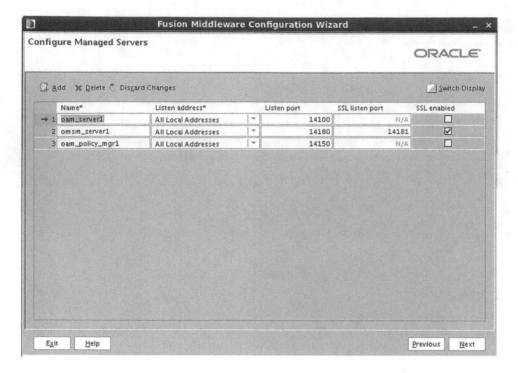

Figure 6-26. *Managed servers configuration*

During the domain configuration, the selected products will be deployed in managed servers. Figure 6-26 displays the managed servers to be created. You should ensure the ports entered on this screen are available.

If you are planning to install multiple instances of OAM to provide the environment with failover or load balancing capabilities, the Configure Clusters screen shown in Figure 6-27 allows this configuration.

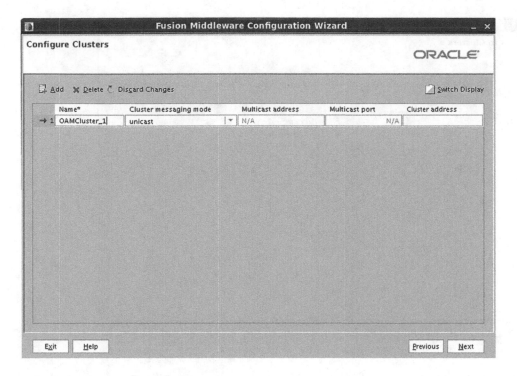

Figure 6-27. *Cluster configuration*

Clustering allows multiple instances of applications to be deployed and work together to provide a highly available environment or better performance. The Configure Clusters screen permits the configuration tool to define a cluster during this stage. Go ahead and configure the OAM cluster. Clusters can be created later using the Administration Console.

After designating the names of the cluster(s), you will need to assign managed servers to each of the clusters as seen in Figure 6-28.

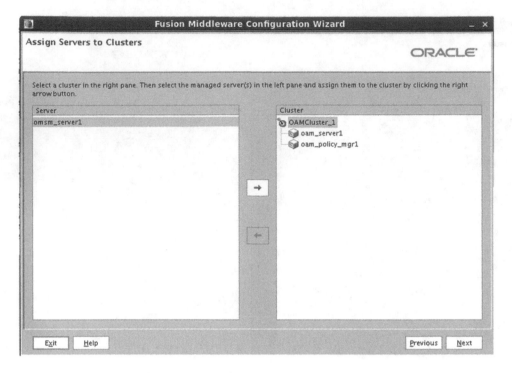

Figure 6-28. *Assign managed servers to clusters*

Managed servers can be assigned to the clusters defined on the previous screens. Depending on the products deployed within the given environment, you might wish to spread the managed servers across different clusters. These can be reassigned later using the Administration Console.

Machines define a host that manages processes within managed servers. You can create multiple machines on a given host or spread machines across multiple hosts. Figure 6-29 displays the Configure Machines screen.

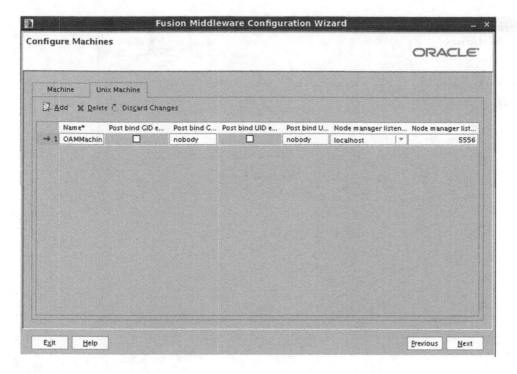

Figure 6-29. *Machine configuration*

It is important that a UNIX machine is created if the host is Linux or UNIX based. The machine configuration tells the WebLogic environment how to contact the node manager to control the managed servers.

After the machine(s) have been configured, it is time to assign the managed servers to be created to the proper machines, as shown in Figure 6-30. Usually, in a clustered environment, multiple machines exist, each with one node of the managed servers. This is what enables a single Administration Server to contact and control managed servers on different hosts or within different Middleware Homes

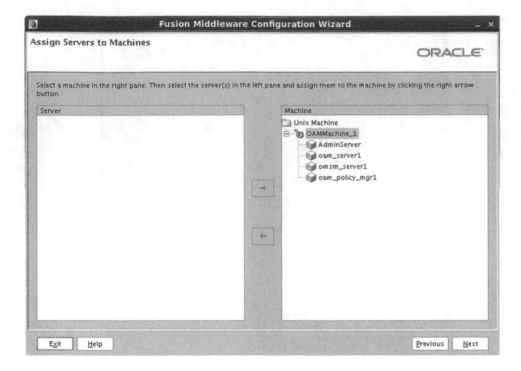

Figure 6-30. *Assigning managed servers to machines*

The Configuration Summary screen, displayed in Figure 6-31, provides a last look at all of the configuration parameters prior to performing the configuration. If anything at this point looks incorrect, go back and make any necessary fixes before continuing.

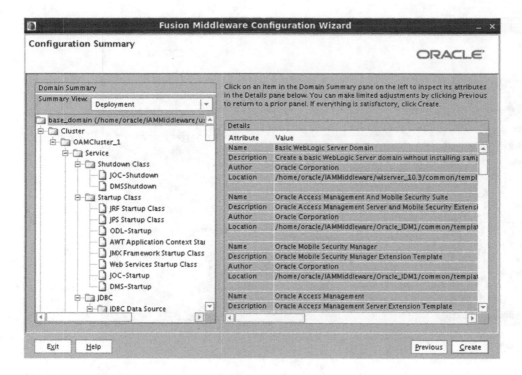

Figure 6-31. Configuration Summary screen

After inspecting the Configuration Summary screen, click Create to start the configuration process. Figure 6-32 shows the completed configuration.

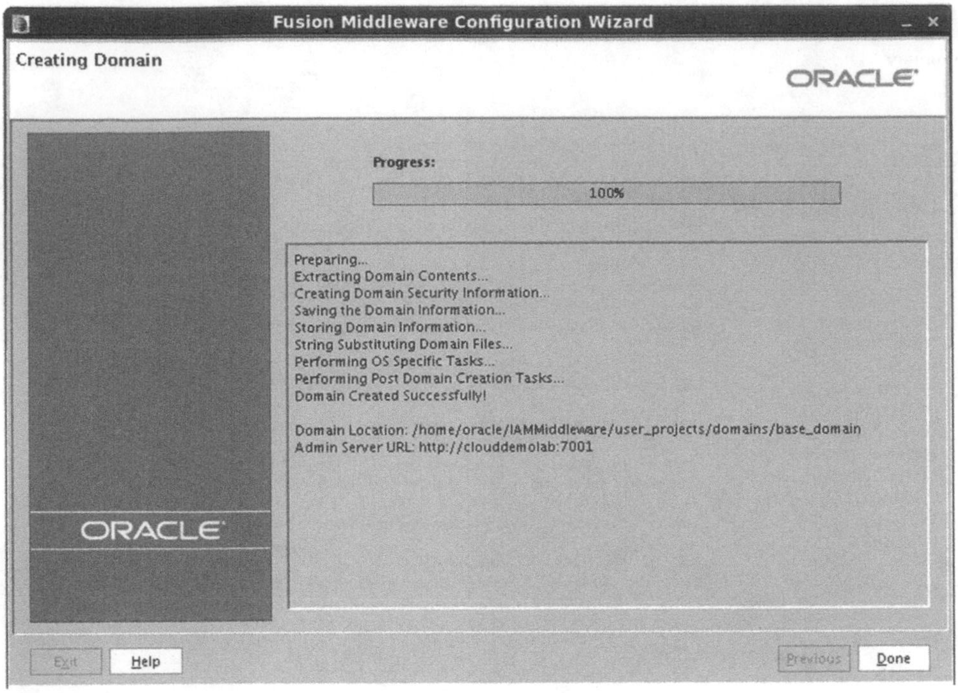

Figure 6-32. *Domain configuration complete*

The OAM domain configuration is complete. Before starting it, there are several more required steps. The next chapter covers the installation and configuration of the Identity Manager components. Subsequently, the overall Identity and Access Manager environment is configured to work together.

Summary

This chapter was a walk-through of the installation of OAM. After the installation of the software files, you were shown the configuration of the OAM domain. At this point, all of the necessary files have been copied and the file system is ready. If your implementation only requires SSO, you can skip the next chapter on Identity Manager installation.

## CHAPTER 7

Identity Manager Installation

In the previous two chapters, you were provided with the instructions for installing and configuring Oracle Internet Directory (OID) and Oracle Access Manager (OAM). These two components set the foundation of Identity Storage and single sign–on (SSO). Identity Manager adds additional elements such as user self-service and governance to the environment, thereby completing the end-to-end identity life cycle management implementation. This chapter focuses on the installation and initial domain configuration of Oracle Identity Manager (OIM).

Preinstallation Tasks

Operating System Users

For most Oracle application installs, operating system (OS) users and groups should be created to perform the installation and configuration tasks. Creating OS groups will allow other OS users to perform certain tasks related to the management of the application environment. The most common OS users and groups related to installing Oracle applications in Linux environments are the oracle user and oinstall or dba groups.

To create the necessary oinstall and dba groups, perform the following commands as the root directory:

```
[root@clouddemolab home]# groupadd oinstall
[root@clouddemolab home]# groupadd dba
```

After the groups are created, create the oracle user:

```
[root@clouddemolab home]# useradd  -g oinstall -G dba oracle
```

■ **Note**   -g indicates the primary group to which the user should be added. -G indicates any secondary groups.

To set the password for the user, utilize the following command as the root user.

```
[root@clouddemolab home]# passwd oracle
```

Operating System Configuration

Prior to installing the Oracle Fusion Middleware infrastructure and Oracle Identity Management software, it is important to ensure the OS meets the minimum requirements and configuration. The following presents the kernel parameters and packages and the file changes that are required.

The following kernel parameters need to be set:

```
kernel.sem  256  32000  100  143
kernel.shmmax 10737418240
```

To set these parameters, edit the `sysctl.conf` file located in the `/etc` directory.

```
[root@clouddemolab home]# vi /etc/sysctl.conf
```

Add or edit the following lines in this section of the file:

```
# Controls the maximum number of shared memory segments, in pages
kernel.shmall = 4294967296
kernel.sem = 256 32000 100 142
kernel.shmmax = 10737418240
```

After setting these values in the `sysctl.conf` file, you must activate and verify the new values are shown using this command:

```
 [root@clouddemolab home]# /sbin/sysctl -p
net.ipv4.ip_forward = 0
net.ipv4.conf.default.rp_filter = 1
net.ipv4.conf.default.accept_source_route = 0
kernel.sysrq = 0
kernel.core_uses_pid = 1
net.ipv4.tcp_syncookies = 1
net.bridge.bridge-nf-call-ip6tables = 0
net.bridge.bridge-nf-call-iptables = 0
net.bridge.bridge-nf-call-arptables = 0
kernel.msgmnb = 65536
kernel.msgmax = 65536
kernel.shmmax = 68719476736
kernel.shmall = 4294967296
kernel.sem = 256 32000 100 142
kernel.shmmax = 10737418240
```

The open file limits must be set to 4096 to support the instance. To do so, edit the `limits.conf` file.

```
[root@clouddemolab home]# vi /etc/security/limits.conf
```

If the environment is to be installed on Oracle Linux or RedHat Linux, you must perform the edit in /etc/security/limits.d/90-nproc.conf as well. If this is missed, the values in this file could override the values in the `limits.conf` file.

In both of these files, ensure the following lines are added or edited:

```
* soft nofile 4096
* hard nofile 65536
* soft nproc 2047
* hard nproc 16384
```

After editing this file, the server must be rebooted to ensure all the changes take effect.

Operating System Packages

Each Oracle application has its own set of required packages. Depending on the version of Linux you are using, the installation procedure might be different. In the following list, you should note that some packages require both 32-bit and 64-bit versions to be installed on a 64-bit OS. If these packages are not installed, the installation will not complete properly. The Oracle Installer will check these and display errors during the installation.

```
binutils-2.20.51.0.2-5.28.el6
compat-libcap1-1.10-1
compat-libstdc++-33-3.2.3-69.el6 for x86_64
compat-libstdc++-33-3.2.3-69.el6 for i686
gcc-4.4.4-13.el6 gcc-c++-4.4.4-13.el6
glibc-2.12-1.7.el6 for x86_64
glibc-2.12-1.7.el6 for i686
glibc-devel-2.12-1.7.el6 for i686
libaio-0.3.107-10.el6
libaio-devel-0.3.107-10.el6
libgcc-4.4.4-13.el6
libstdc++-4.4.4-13.el6 for x86_64
libstdc++-4.4.4-13.el6 for i686
libstdc++-devel-4.4.4-13.el6
libXext for i686
libXtst for i686
libXext for x86_64
libXtst for x86_64
openmotif-2.2.3 for x86_64
openmotif22-2.2.3 for x86_64
redhat-lsb-core-4.0-7.el6 for x86_64
sysstat-9.0.4-11.el6
xorg-x11-utils*
xorg-x11-apps*
xorg-x11-xinit*
xorg-x11-server-Xorg*
xterm
pdksh-5.2.14
```

At this point in the procedure, the OS should be fully prepared for the installation to proceed. Performing these operations prior to installing the software will ensure a problem-free installation. In many cases, the installer will provide detailed messages if anything is missed. In the event of errors during the installation process, stop the installation and fix any problems problem before proceeding.

Database Preparation

Just like the OID, the installation of OIM requires specific database objects to be created. This includes a number of tables, views, and packages created in various database schemas. This is done using the Repository Creation Utility (RCU). Although the database objects can be created within the OID database, it is often recommended that the Oracle Identity and Access Management repository be created in a separate instance. This simplifies database administration tasks and future maintenance. To prevent issues with installation, it is important to ensure the RCU version used matches the version of the Fusion Middleware product to be installed. Mismatches found during the domain configuration will prevent the process from continuing. Unzip the download and run rcu.sh found in the <RCU_HOME>/rcu/bin directory. You will first see the Create Repository screen shown in Figure 7-1.

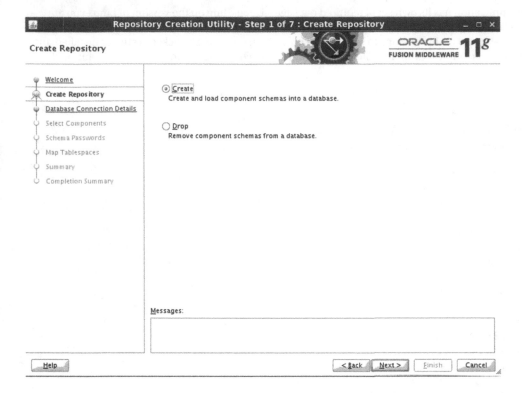

Figure 7-1. *Create or Drop schema*

Because this is the first time installing OIM, select the Create option on this screen. This will start the RCU in creation mode.

After choosing to create the schemas, you must enter the database connection details for the target system on the screen shown in Figure 7-2. You can choose to create the Identity Manager schema within the same database as the OID. However, to keep database administration simpler, the Identity Manager schema is often installed within a different database. This instance can be the same as the OAM.

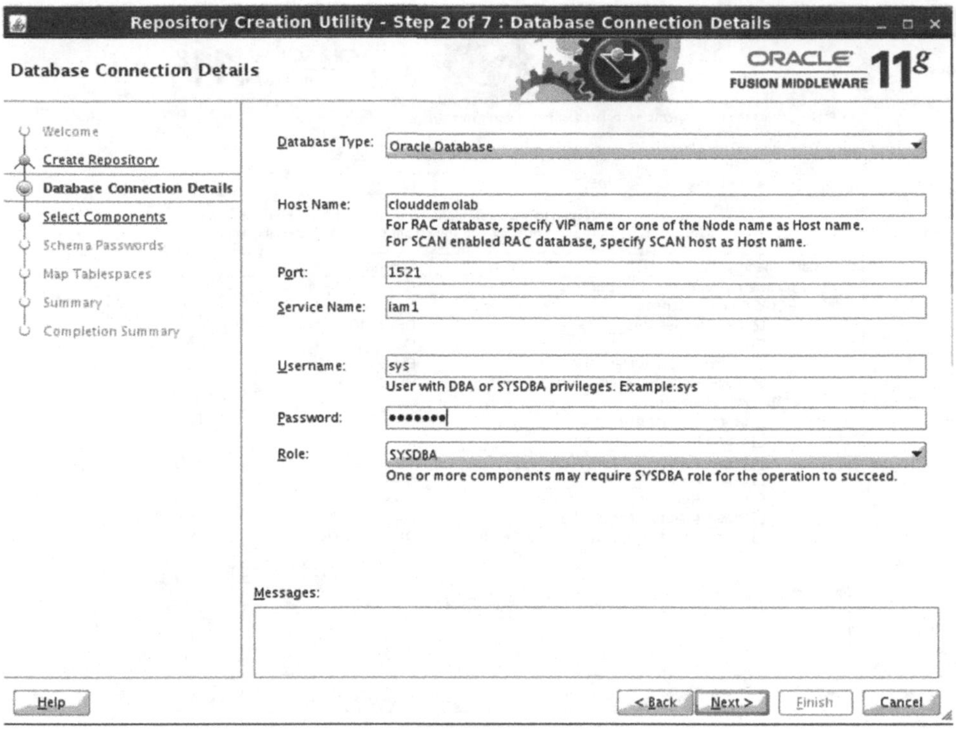

Figure 7-2. *Database Connection Details screen*

■ **Note** $ORACLE_HOME/rdbms/admin/xaview.sql must be run to enable the XA transactions views and synonyms before the OIM schemas can be created.

After the RCU verifies the connection details, it will prompt you to select the components to be installed within the new repository. This screen is shown in Figure 7-3.

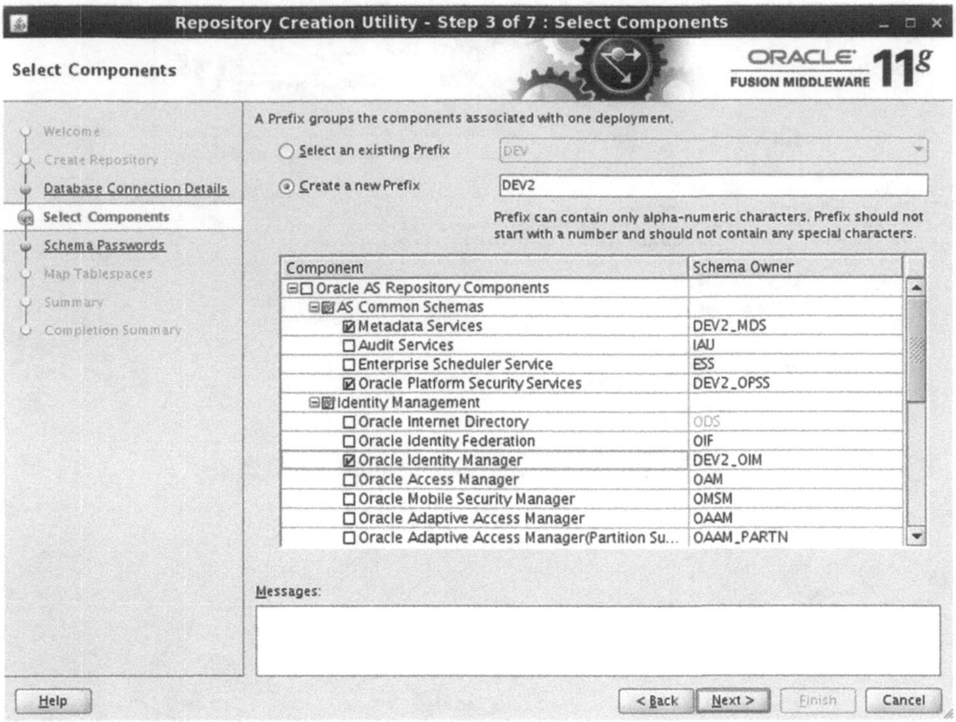

Figure 7-3. *Select Components screen*

During this step of the RCU, you must select the components to be installed. Note that as you select the OIM component, other required items will be preselected. Do not deselect these, as they will be validated during the domain configuration step. The RCU will then validate that the database meets the prerequisites necessary for the components selected as seen in Figure 7-4.

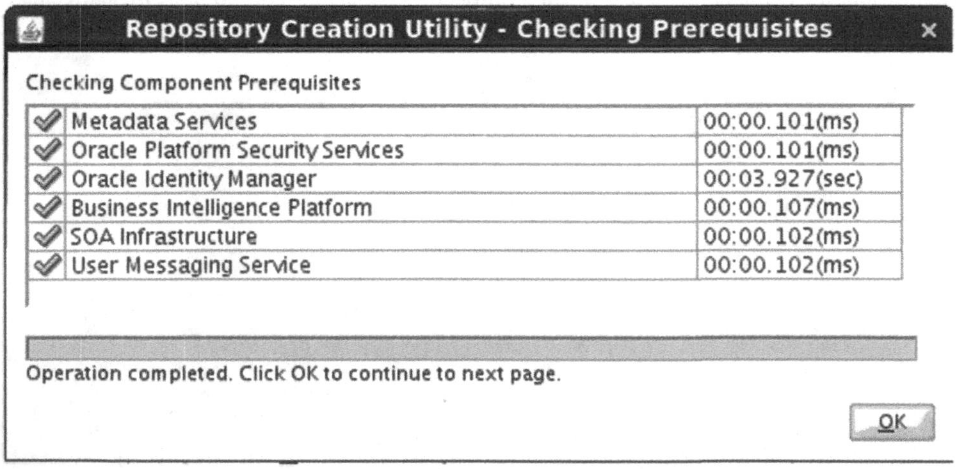

Figure 7.4. *Checking prerequisites*

Each of the Fusion Middleware components has database requirements, such as maximum connections or open processes. The RCU will check these prerequisites prior to creating the database schemas and objects.

Provided the database meets the minimum requirements, the next step is to enter passwords to be used by the new database schemas, as shown in Figure 7-5.

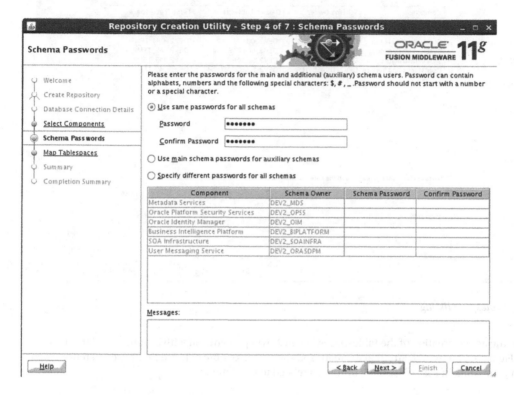

Figure 7-5. *Schema Passwords screen*

During this step, indicate the value you wish to use for the password. You can elect to use the same password for all schemas or use a different password for each. Make the decision based on security requirements and ease of management.

Figure 7-6 displays the tablespace review screen, which shows the new database tablespaces that will be created for the selected Identity Management components. You can click Next to continue or choose to customize the new tablespaces.

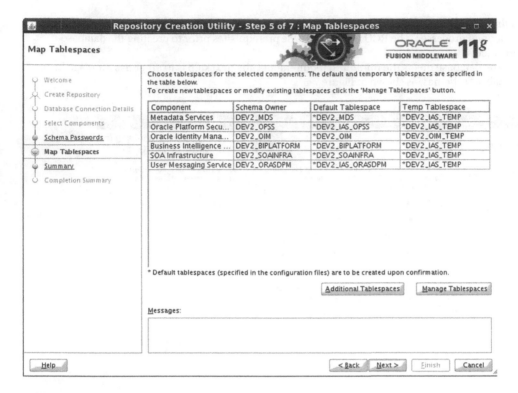

Figure 7-6. *Tablespace listing*

Prior to the actual creation of the tablespaces, the RCU will present you with a summary of the actions it will take. Figure 7-7 shows the Summary screen. You should make note of these for future reference when talking with your DBAs in case of runtime problems related to the database.

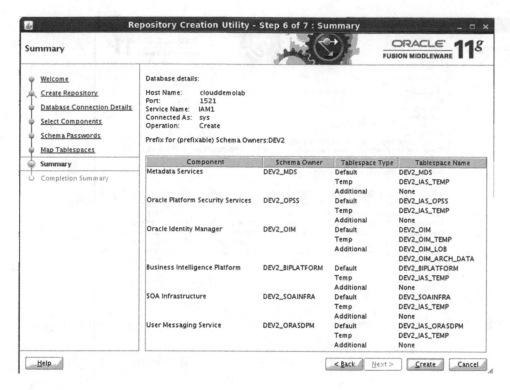

Figure 7-7. Creation Summary screen

After all database objects have been created, you will be provided with the Completion Summary screen, shown in Figure 7-8. Click Close to complete the process.

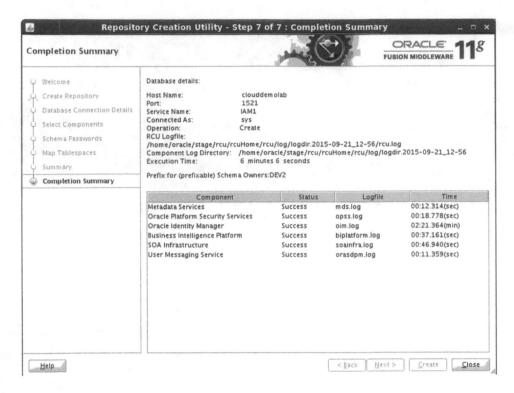

Figure 7-8. *Completion Summary screen*

This completes the repository creation process for OIM. The necessary database schemas and objects for Identity Manager and its required components have been installed within the target database. It is now possible to continue with the installation process.

Identity Manager Software Installation

In the previous section, you were taken through the steps to create the OIM database schemas and objects. The following sections discuss the installation of the Identity Manager software. This process creates the necessary file system structure and lays down the binaries needed by the Fusion Middleware products presented.

OIM must be installed within a WLS home. In Chapter 6, you were presented with the steps to install OAM in a separate WLS home. You can choose to install the Identity Manager software in the same home as Access Manager, or you can create a completely separate home specifically for it. It is common to separate Access Manager from Identity Manager on different tiers of the network, or on different physical hosts. If this is required for your environment, follow the WLS installation steps in Chapter 4.

Service-Oriented Architecture Installation

OIM requires Oracle Service-Oriented Architecture (SOA) to run properly. This installation is separate from the OIM process, but can be installed within the same WebLogic home. After the SOA installation, you can install OIM and configure the domain for both products at the same time. This is the recommended process for the two products.

Just like many other Fusion Middleware products, the SOA installation tool is started using the runInstaller command to start the Oracle Universal Installer. This is found on Disk 1 of the installation media. When running the tool, you must indicate the location of the Java Runtime Environment. This is done as shown in Figure 7-9.

```
runInstaller -jreLoc /home/oracle/jdk1.6.0_45/jre
```

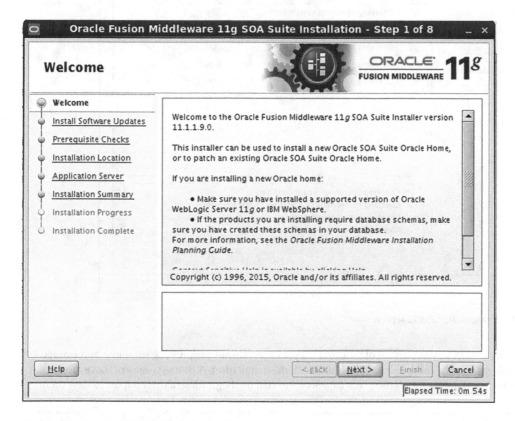

Figure 7-9. *Starting the Universal Installer*

OIM requires SOA 11.1.1.9. This version will be installed using this tool. The starting screen displays information pertinent to the planned installation and a reminder to run the RCU. Much like other iterations of the Universal Installer, Oracle checks the OS to ensure it meets the minimum requirements. A completed prerequisite check is shown in Figure 7-10.

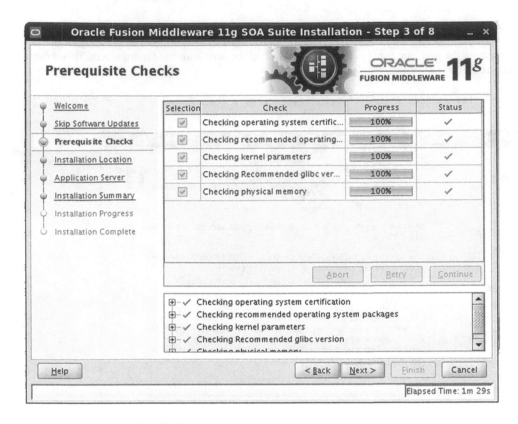

Figure 7-10. Prerequisite Checks screen

As with OAM, SOA has its own set of required OS packages, kernel parameters, memory, and storage allowances. These must be met prior to continuing with the installation. Although many of these are the same as the Access Manager installation, it is important to visit the beginning of this chapter to view them.

■ **Note**   Prerequisite failures will be shown with a red X on the Universal Installer screen. You can open a terminal window logged in as root to correct any problems and retry the prerequisite checks until all issues have been resolved.

In the next step, you must select the Middleware Home location for this installation. Because this environment consists of separate WLS for each Access Manager and Identity Manager, it is important to install SOA in the correct Middleware Home. In this case, Identity Manager will be installed in the IDMMiddleware directory. See Figure 7-11 for more details.

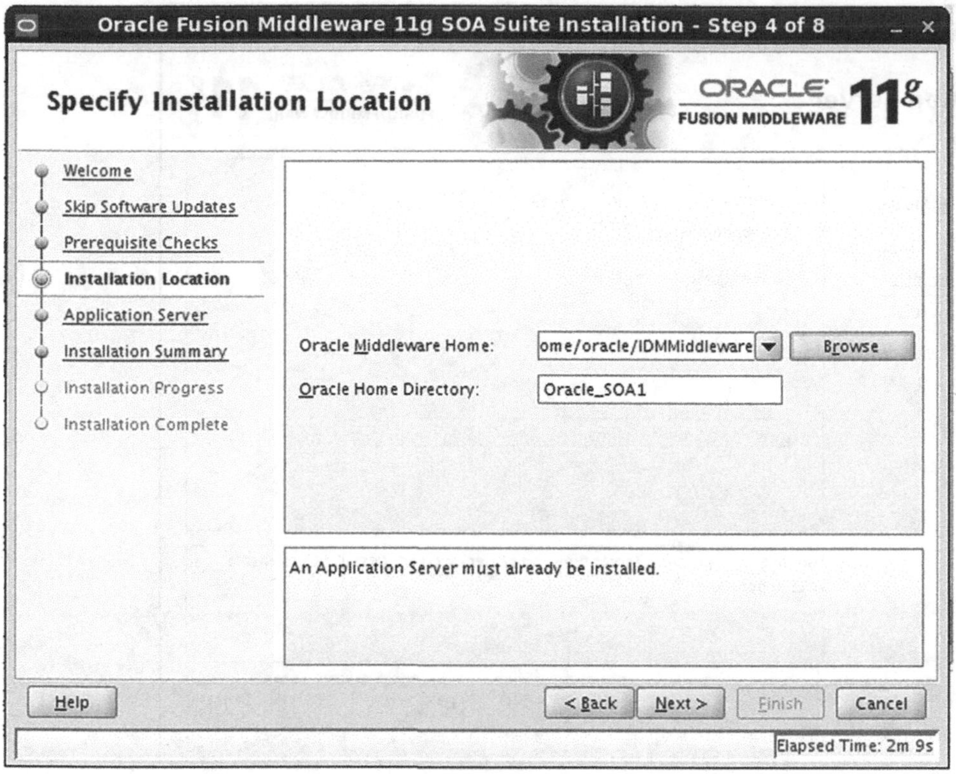

Figure 7-11. *Specify Installation Location screen*

Oracle SOA can be installed on either WLS or WebSphere server. This book focuses on the WLS installation types. Select WebLogic Server, as shown in Figure 7-12, and continue to the next step.

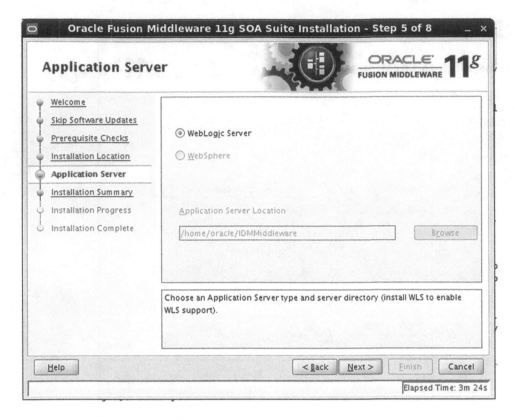

Figure 7-12. *Selecting the application server type*

The Installatio Summary screen, shown in Figure 7-13, displays a summary of the selections made during the installer screens. Confirm the selections and click Install to start the installation.

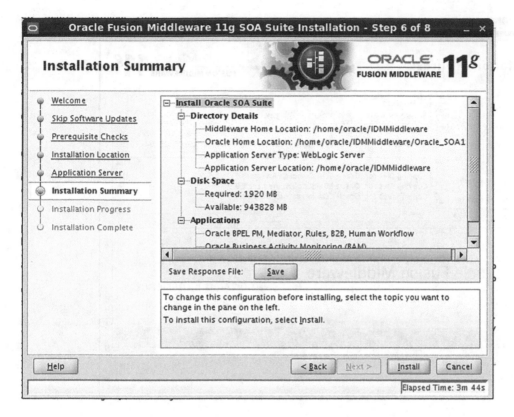

Figure 7-13. Installation Summary screen

The actual installation can take about 10 minutes. The progress screen, shown in Figure 7-14, will keep you apprised of the current status. Do not panic if the progress seems to stall for a while.

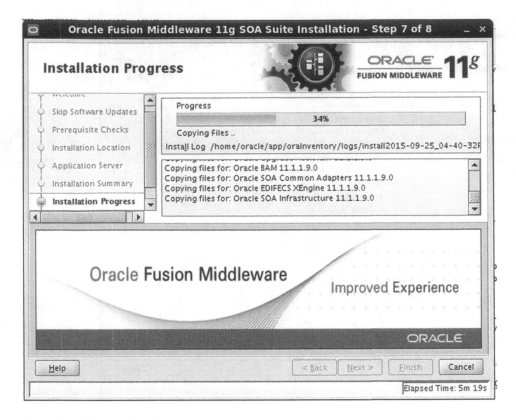

Figure 7-14. *Installation Progress screen*

After the installer has completed copying the necessary files and creating the file system, the Installation Complete screen shown in Figure 7-15, will be displayed. This screen contains details directly related to your new environment. It might be useful to take note of the contents for future reference. At this point, you can click Finish and exit the installer.

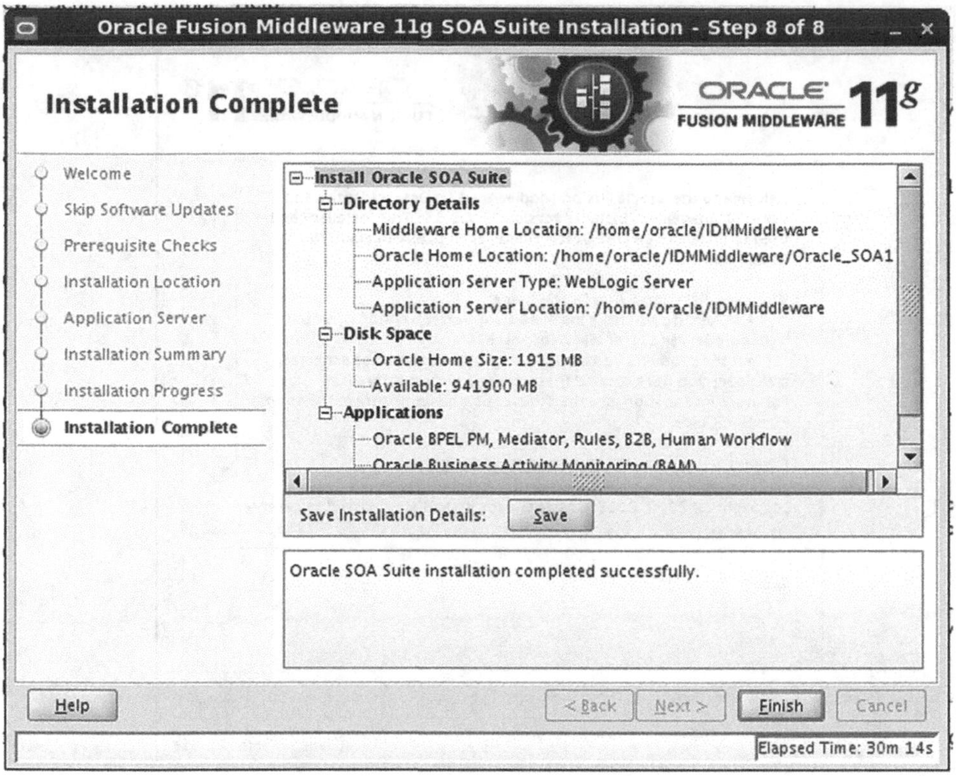

Figure 7-15. Installation Complete screen

Now the required Oracle SOA suite instance has been installed. When configuring the OIM domain, the Configuration Wizard will set up the necessary components of SOA. As you will recall, this SOA instance is installed in the same Middleware Home as the Identity Manager. The next section covers IOM installation.

Identity Manager Installation

The WLS and SOA software has been installed. It is now time to install the Identity Manager software. Again, this process is started using the runInstaller script found on Disk 1 of the installation media. Just like the SOA installation, you must indicate the Java Runtime Environment location for the installer to run properly. Figure 7-16 shows the Universal Installer.

```
./runInstaller.sh -jreLoc /home/oracle/jdk1.6.0_45/jre
```

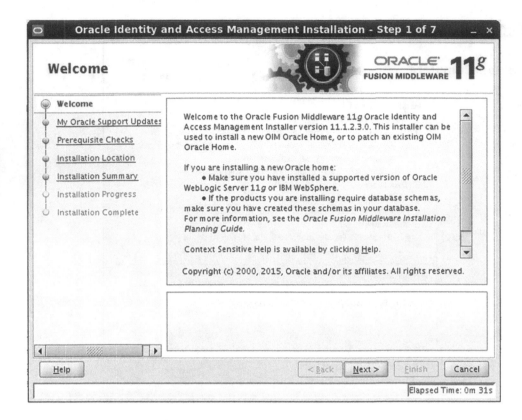

Figure 7-16. *Installation Welcome screen*

The first screen displays important information about the software to be installed. Ensure the version displayed matches your requirements and the version of the RCU previously run.

As with OAM, OIM has its own set of required OS packages, kernel parameters, memory, and storage allowances. These must be met prior to continuing with the installation. As seen in Figure 7-17, the Installer will check these before allowing the process to continue. Although many of these are the same as for the OAM installation, it is important to visit the beginning of this chapter to view them.

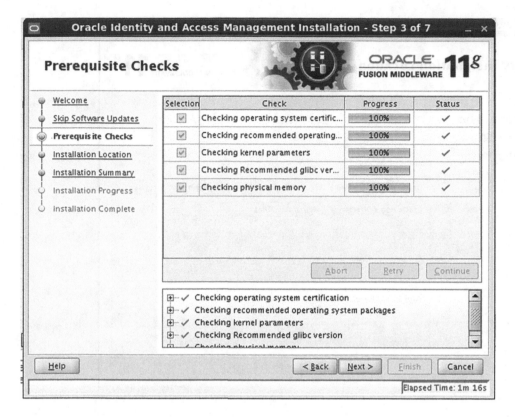

Figure 7-17. *Prerequisite Checks screen*

On the Specify Installation Location screen, you must select a Middleware Home to house the installation. Figure 7-18 provides details on this entry point. This location must be a directory that has WLS installed. Because this physical host houses two instances of WLS, make sure to select the location that is not currently used for OAM. The selected home should be the same as you chose in the previous step for SOA.

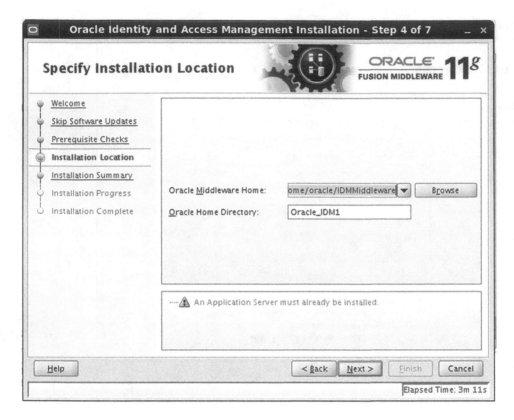

Figure 7-18. *Specify Installation Location screen*

At this point the Universal Installer will begin copying files to their new locations. A progress screen such as the one shown in Figure 7-19 will show the current operation and progress.

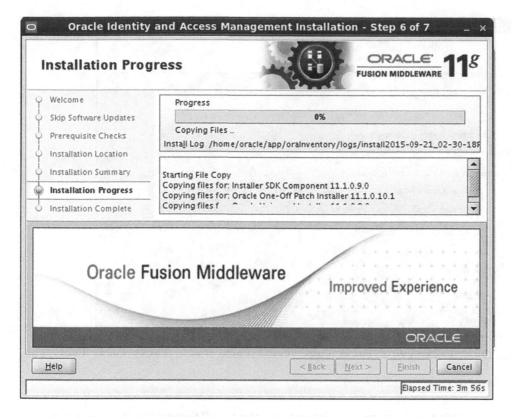

Figure 7-19. *Installation Progress screen*

The actual installation of the software files usually finishes in about 10 minutes. During this time you can see the actual operations on the progress screen, which also shows the location of the installation log file. You can monitor this log for any errors. Once completed, you can close the installer, as all installation operations are complete. In the next sections, you will be configuring the OIM domain.

Configure Identity Manager Domain

After the necessary software components have been installed, you can continue to configure the WebLogic domain to support OIM. This process is started by running the config script located in the IDM_HOME/common/bin directory. It is important to note that you are only configuring the WebLogic domain at this time. OIM will not be ready to run.

To avoid confusion for the rest of this chapter, the following conventions are used. MIDDLEWARE_HOME is the base directory where WLS was installed. IDM_HOME is the directory within the WLS installation where OIM is installed. This is usually a directory called Oracle_IDM1. Figure 7-20 shows the Configuration Wizard.

■ **Note**　There are multiple instances of the config.sh script that can be found within the Middleware Home subdirectories. It is very important to run the correct version found within <MIDDLEWARE_HOME/Oracle_IDM1/common/bin.

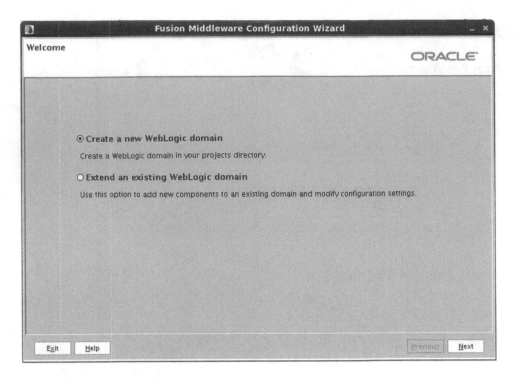

Figure 7-20. Create a new WebLogic domain

Because this is the first time a domain is being created within the WLS environment, choose Create a New WebLogic Domain.

During the next step of the process, select the OIM component. As seen in Figure 7-21, this list is based on the software found within the WebLogic Home directory. You will notice that Oracle SOA Suite is automatically selected. If SOA Suite is not found within the WLS Home, you will be shown an error indicating this. Before continuing, ensure that any missing software is installed.

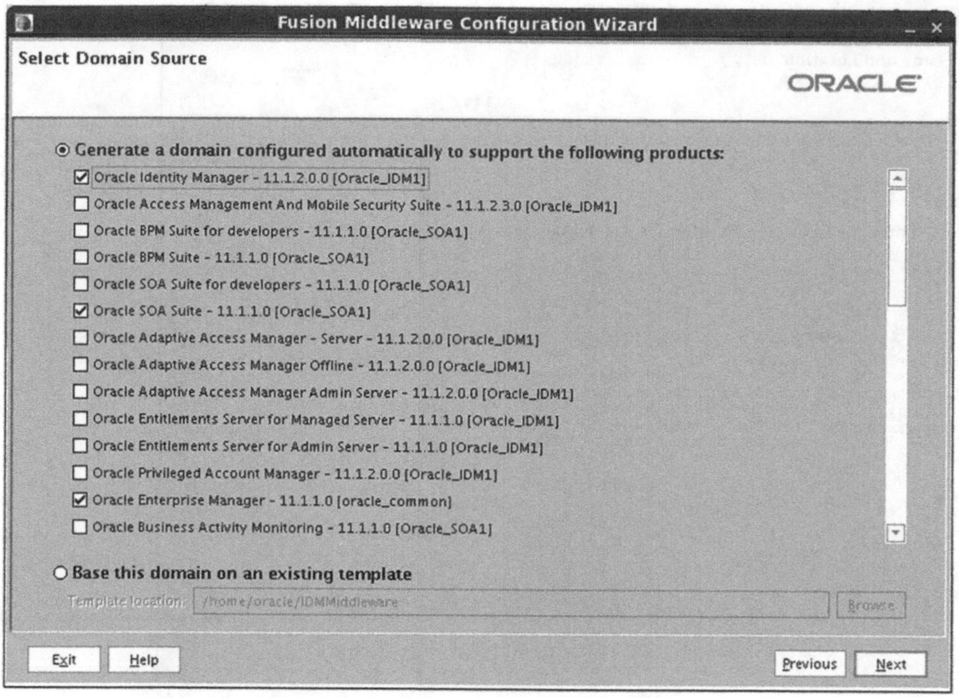

Figure 7-21. *Select domain components*

During the configuration, you are prompted for the name of the domain you wish to create. You can keep the default name of "base_domain" or you can name it something that makes sense in your environment. See Figure 7-22 for an example. In some cases, it might be desirable to locate the associated files separate from the Middleware Home directory. This is often done for clustered environments that require shared storage across the physical hosts.

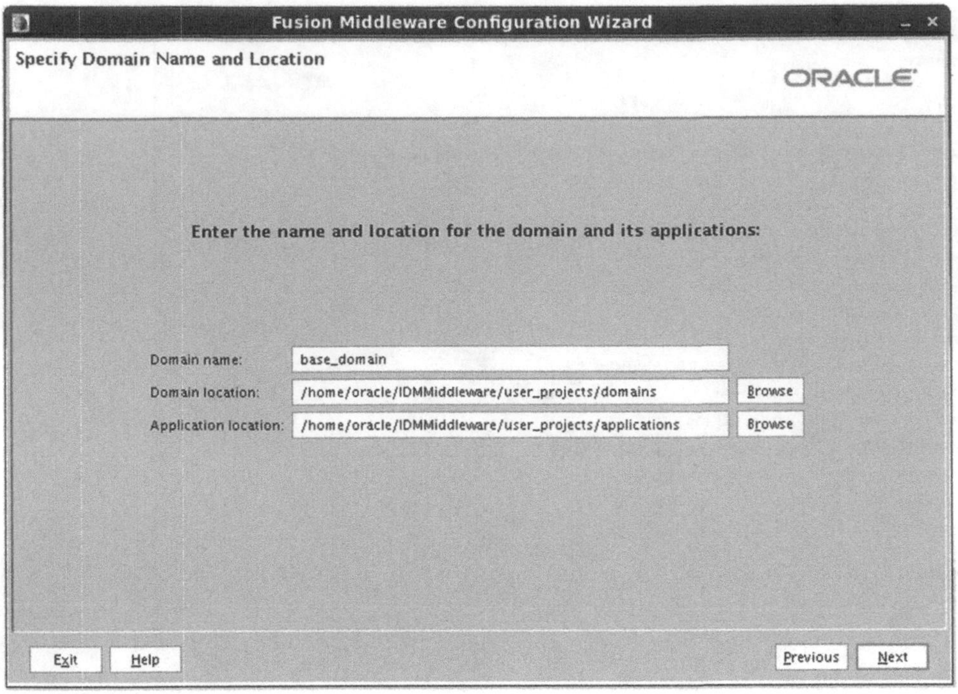

Figure 7-22. *Enter domain name and location*

The user password for weblogic should be set to something standard for your environment. This password will be used for starting and stopping managed servers as well as logging into the WebLogic Admin Console and Fusion Middleware Control. Figure 7-23 shows what the password configuration screen looks like.

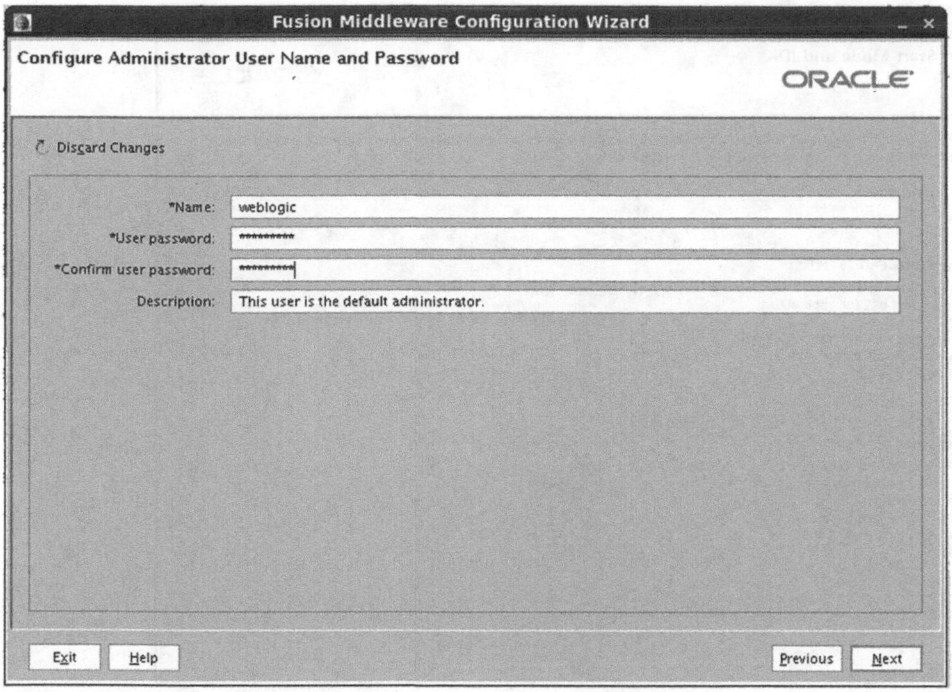

Figure 7-23. *Administrator password*

The Startup Mode determines how the managed servers are started. In Development Mode, the managed servers can be started and stopped from the command line without a password. Also configuration changes can be made and activated within the WebLogic Console without locking the environment. Configuring the Startup Mode to Production Mode locks the environment down to ensure no changes are made without locking the console for edits. Command-line tools will also require a password. These choices are shown in Figure 7-24.

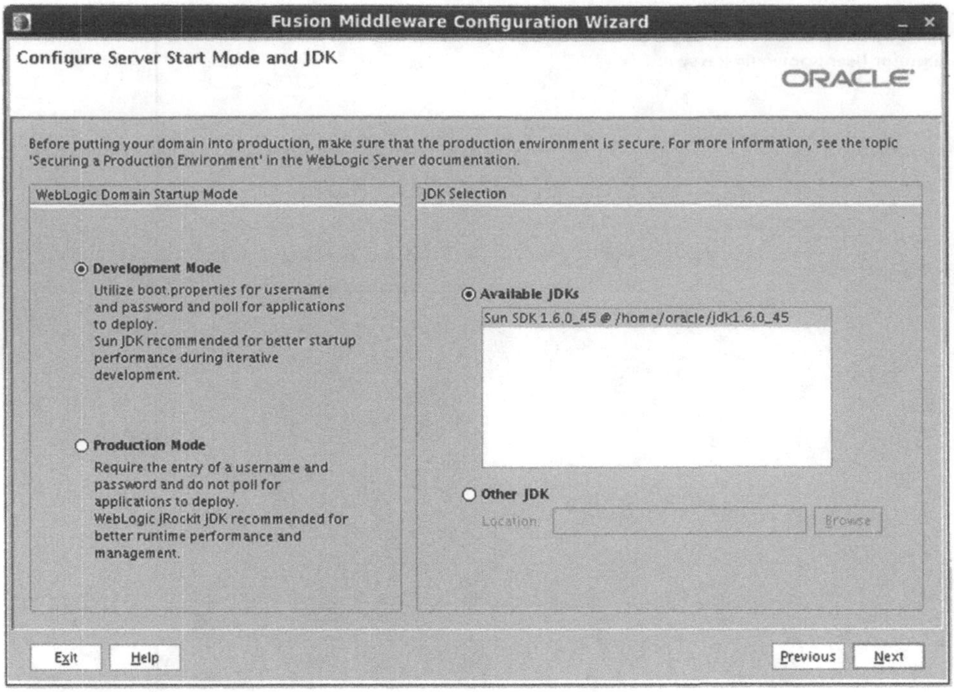

Figure 7-24. *Server Start Mode*

■ **Note**   Locking the Administration Console prevents multiple administrators from making changes and overwriting each other.

After the Java database connectivity (JDBC) connection details are entered, the information is validated by the configuration tool. Any errors will be shown. If a schema was not able to be validated, revisit the previous step to ensure the schema name and details are correct. If the database schema does not exist, rerun the RCU to create it. Figure 7-25 shows a completed database check.

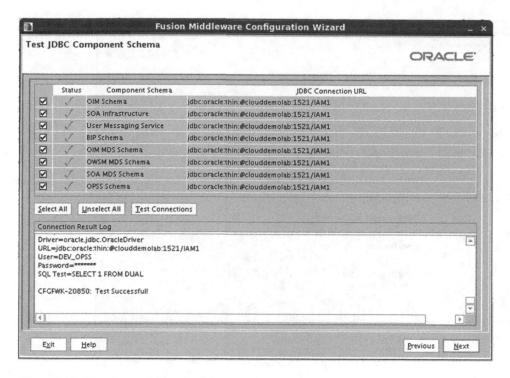

Figure 7-25. *Database schema check*

As discussed in the AOM installation chapter, the example used in this book utilizes a split domain. As such, each component (OID, OAM, and OIM) will have its own Administration server. As shown in Figure 7-26, select Administration Server, Managed Servers, Clusters and Machines.

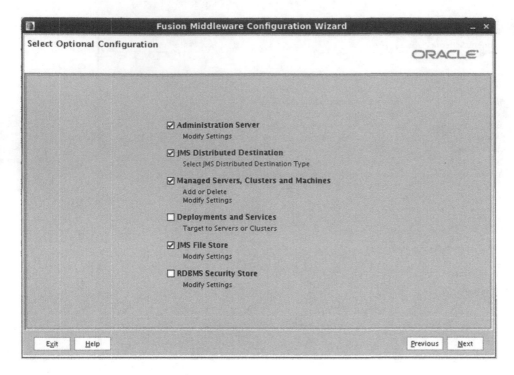

Figure 7-26. *Select Optional Configuration screen*

The default port for the Administration server is 7001, which was used in the previous chapter for the Access Manager Administration listen port. Using a standard port convention will help eliminate confusion or forgotten ports. For this exercise, use Port 7101 as seen in Figure 7-27. Subsequently, if more WLS instances are installed, use Ports 7201, 7301, and so on.

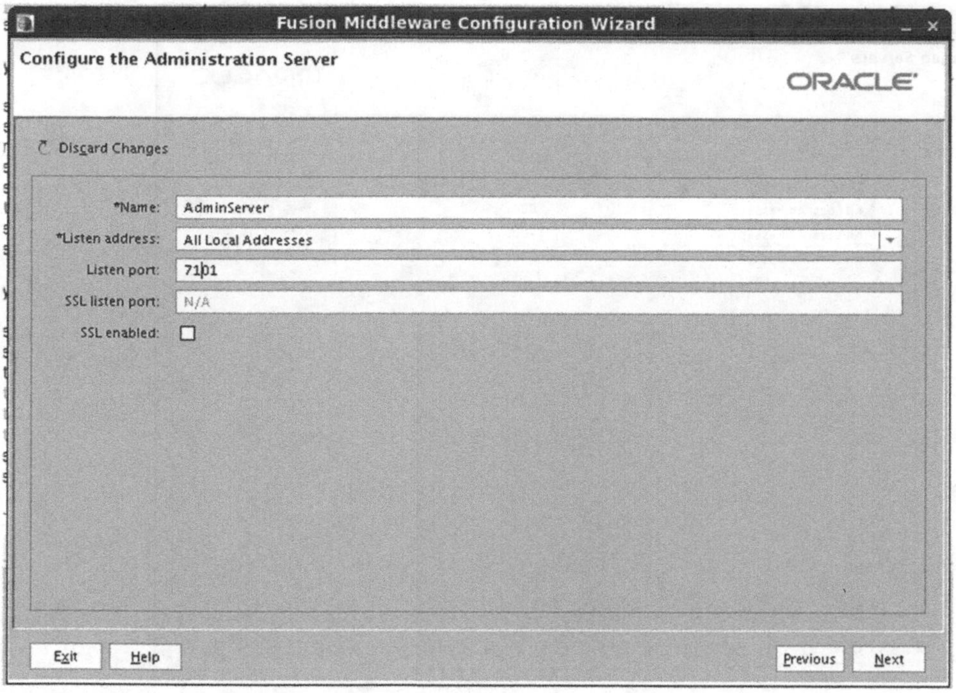

Figure 7-27. *Configure the Administration Server screen*

In this environment, Access Manager and Identity Manager are installed in separate Oracle Middleware Homes. This means that each one consists of WLS, Administration server, and managed servers. As discussed previously, this was done for ease of future maintenance such as patches and upgrades. It also allows the separation of these tiers to different physical hosts at a later time if required. Because these will be running on the same physical host but within separate WLS, each Administration server will require its own listen port.

The managed servers will be prepopulated with the standard ports used by the installation. If desired, you can change the ports or populate a Secure Sockets Layer (SSL) listen port. In many cases, it is sufficient to allow the HTTP server or load balancer to perform the SSL endpoint duties, thus providing some performance gain by offloading the encryption duties to the external device. For ease of troubleshooting and future maintenance, leave the ports as defaults, seen in Figure 7-28.

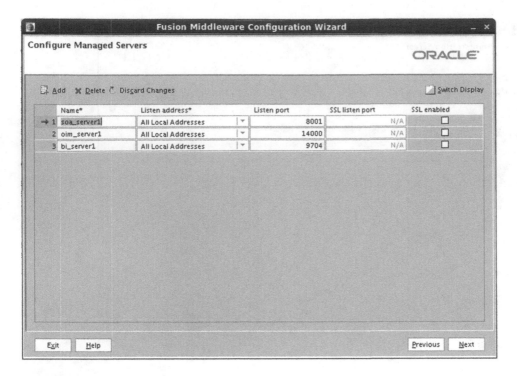

Figure 7-28. *Configure Managed Servers screen*

During the course of this book, clustering is not a concern. However, to facilitate the creation of clusters later, the cluster configuration information is entered here, as shown in Figure 7-29. As such, the WebLogic domain will be preconfigured with the clusters in place. In effect, this step creates a single node cluster that can be later expanded to include multiple machines and instances.

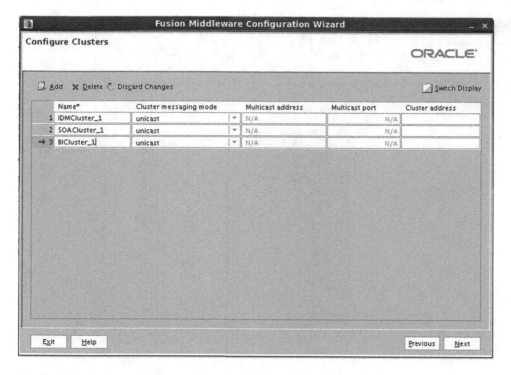

Figure 7-29. *Configure Clusters screen*

Assign the managed servers to the desired cluster, as shown in Figure 7-30. Note that it is possible to create a single cluster and assign all of the managed servers to it. However, for simplification of administrative tasks, each will be assigned to its own cluster within WebLogic.

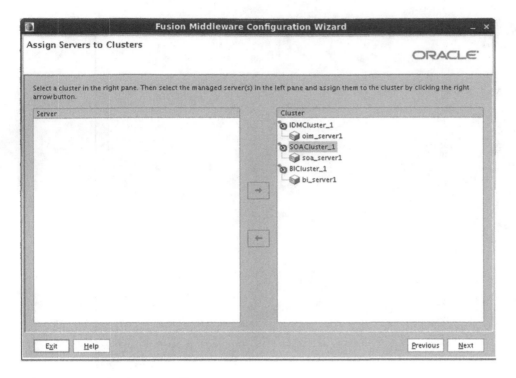

Figure 7-30. *Assign Servers to Clusters screen*

It should be noted at this point that if you only have a single node in your cluster, you might see errors in the managed server logs related to waiting for communication with other members of the cluster. These can be ignored and will go away after adding additional members to the cluster.

As discussed in the previous chapter, machines provide the information necessary for the WebLogic Administration server to communicate with the server processes for status and life cycle events. It is important that any UNIX-based OS use the Unix Machine type. This ensures that any necessary environment settings are properly configured when the Administration server executes its operations. Clusters can contain one or more machines, and machines can include one or more managed servers. Figure 7-31 shows a new Unix Machine.

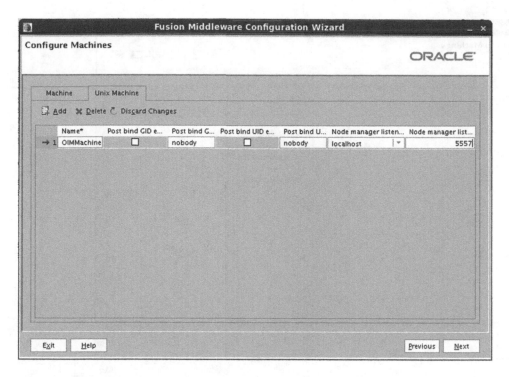

Figure 7-31. *Configure Machines screen*

Assign the managed servers to the machine created in the previous step. In Figure 7-32, you will see that all the new managed servers are assigned to the single Unix_Machine created in the previous step. You can choose to create multiple machines and assign different components to different machines. If you have multiple cluster members, each machine can reside on a separate cluster.

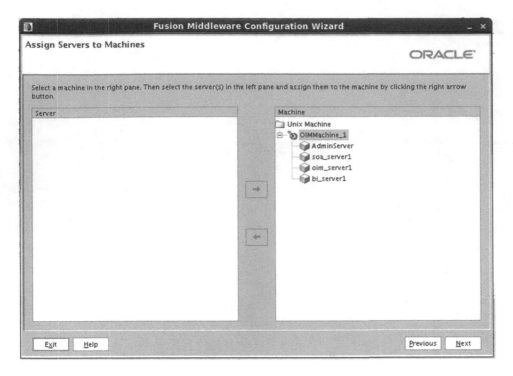

Figure 7-32. Assign Servers to Machines screen

After assigning the managed servers to machines, you will be presented with a summary of all of the inputs you have entered. This Configuration Summary screen, shown in Figure 7-33, provides a last look at the configuration you are about to launch. Review this to ensure that the file locations, names, and configuration parameters look correct. Click Create to start the new WebLogic domain creation.

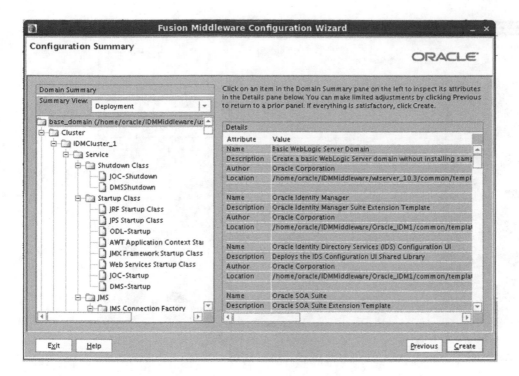

Figure 7-33. *Configuration Summary screen*

During domain creation, a number of files are created and various processes are started. The progress of this can be seen on the Creating Domain screen of the Configuration Wizard, as seen in Figure 7-34. A configuration log will be displayed. Let this run uninterrupted until complete. If there are any errors, check the indicated log.

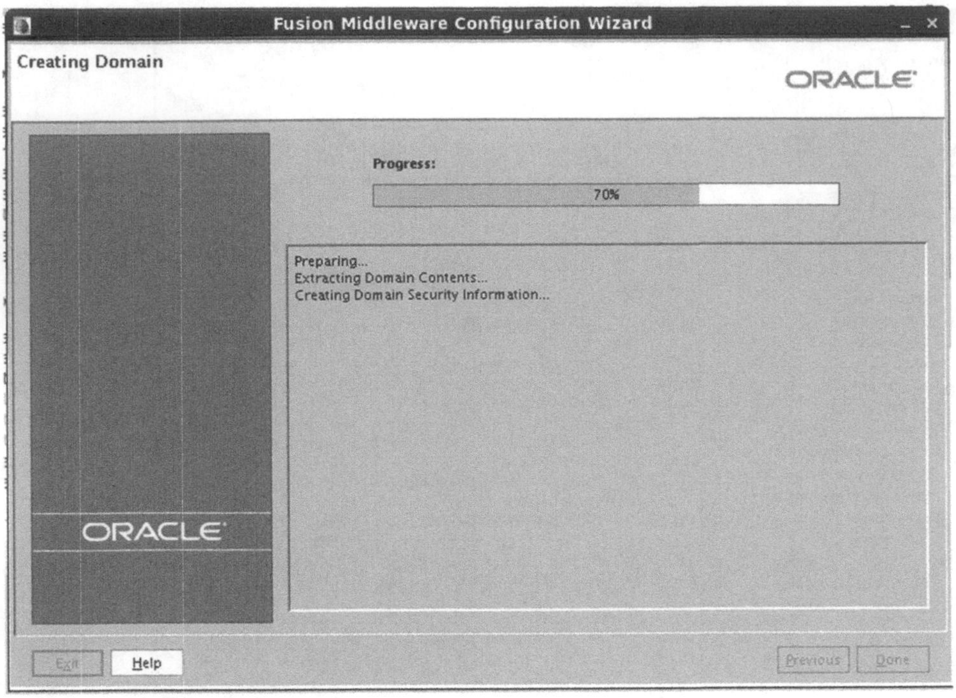

Figure 7-34. *Configuration progress*

Once the domain configuration is complete, click Done to exit the tool. If you have followed the process up to this point, you will have installed OID, OAM, and OIM. Each component resides within its own WebLogic domain and is controlled by its own WebLogic server. This serves to simplify the management processes and facilitate future upgrades and patches. It should also be noted that in some cases, your network infrastructure might require the components to be separated in different network zones. Visit the architecture sections of this book for more information.

Summary

This chapter served to cover the steps required to install OIM in a new WebLogic domain. If followed from the beginning, you were presented with the steps for creating the necessary database objects required for the metadata repository. The chapter also covered the actual software installation and creation of a new WebLogic domain for both OIM and the required Oracle SOA installation. Future chapters cover the configuration of OIM components and the integration with each other.

CHAPTER 8

■ ■ ■

Oracle HTTP Server and WebGate Installation and Configuration

At this point, all of the required components of Oracle Identity and Access Management Suite that will be needed to provide single sign-on (SSO) with Oracle products and applications. The inclusion of Identity Manager provides the ability to manage users within the Oracle Internet Directory (OID) Lightweight Directory Access Protocol (LDAP) user store. Oracle HTTP Server (OHS) and the Oracle Access Manager (OAM) WebGate represent the web server front end for Oracle applications and products. At its core OHS is an Apache web server with Oracle's WebLogic module. Combined with the OAM WebGate software, OHS becomes a central location that handles incoming requests, checks for authentication, and allows authenticated users to access the required resources after OAM performs its operations. This chapter covers the installation and deployment of Oracle HTTP Server and the OAM Webgate.

Preinstallation Tasks

Operating System Users

For most Oracle application installs, operating system (OS) users and groups should be created to perform the installation and configuration tasks. Creating OS groups will allow other OS users to perform certain tasks related to the management of the application environment. The most common OS users and groups related to installing Oracle applications in Linux environments are the oracle user and oinstall or dba groups.

To create the necessary oinstall and dba groups, perform the following commands as the root directory:

```
[root@clouddemolab home]# groupadd oinstall
[root@clouddemolab home]# groupadd osdba
```

After the groups are created, create the oracle user:

```
[root@clouddemolab home]# useradd  -g oinstall -G osdba oracle
```

■ **Note**   -g indicates the primary group to which the user should be added. -G indicates any secondary groups.

© Kenneth Ramey 2016
K. Ramey, *Pro Oracle Identity and Access Management Suite*, DOI 10.1007/978-1-4842-1521-0_8

To set the password for the user, utilize the following command as the root user.

```
[root@clouddemolab home]# passwd oracle
```

Operating System Configuration

Prior to installing the Oracle Fusion Middleware infrastructure and Oracle Identity Management software, it is important to ensure the OS meets the minimum requirements and configuration. The following presents the kernel parameters and packages and the file changes that are required.

The following kernel parameters need to be set:

```
kernel.sem  256  32000  100  143
kernel.shmmax 10737418240
```

To set these parameters, edit the sysctl.conf file located in the /etc directory.

```
[root@clouddemolab home]# vi /etc/sysctl.conf
```

Add or edit the following lines in this section of the file:

```
# Controls the maximum number of shared memory segments, in pages
kernel.shmall = 4294967296
kernel.sem = 256 32000 100 142
kernel.shmmax = 10737418240
```

After setting these values in the sysctl.conf file, you must activate and verify the new values are shown using this command:

```
 [root@clouddemolab home]# /sbin/sysctl -p
net.ipv4.ip_forward = 0
net.ipv4.conf.default.rp_filter = 1
net.ipv4.conf.default.accept_source_route = 0
kernel.sysrq = 0
kernel.core_uses_pid = 1
net.ipv4.tcp_syncookies = 1
net.bridge.bridge-nf-call-ip6tables = 0
net.bridge.bridge-nf-call-iptables = 0
net.bridge.bridge-nf-call-arptables = 0
kernel.msgmnb = 65536
kernel.msgmax = 65536
kernel.shmmax = 68719476736
kernel.shmall = 4294967296
kernel.sem = 256 32000 100 142
kernel.shmmax = 10737418240
```

The open file limits must be set to 4096 to support the instance. To do so, edit the limits.conf file.

```
[root@clouddemolab home]# vi /etc/security/limits.conf
```

If the environment is to be installed on Oracle Linux or RedHat Linux, you must perform the edit in /etc/security/limits.d/90-nproc.conf as well. If this is missed, the values in this file could override the values in the limits.conf file.

In both of these files, ensure the following lines are added or edited:

```
* soft nofile 4096
* hard nofile 65536
* soft nproc 2047
* hard nproc 16384
```

After editing this file, the server must be rebooted to ensure all the changes take effect.

Operating System Packages

Each Oracle application has its own set of required packages. Depending on the version of Linux you are using, the installation procedure might be different. In the following list, you should note that some packages require both 32-bit and 64-bit versions to be installed on a 64-bit OS. If these packages are not installed, the installation will not complete properly. The Oracle Installer will check these and display errors during the installation.

```
binutils-2.20.51.0.2-5.28.el6
compat-libcap1-1.10-1
compat-libstdc++-33-3.2.3-69.el6 for x86_64
compat-libstdc++-33-3.2.3-69.el6 for i686
gcc-4.4.4-13.el6 gcc-c++-4.4.4-13.el6
glibc-2.12-1.7.el6 for x86_64
glibc-2.12-1.7.el6 for i686
glibc-devel-2.12-1.7.el6 for i686
libaio-0.3.107-10.el6
libaio-devel-0.3.107-10.el6
libgcc-4.4.4-13.el6
libstdc++-4.4.4-13.el6 for x86_64
libstdc++-4.4.4-13.el6 for i686
libstdc++-devel-4.4.4-13.el6
libXext for i686
libXtst for i686
libXext for x86_64
libXtst for x86_64
openmotif-2.2.3 for x86_64
openmotif22-2.2.3 for x86_64
redhat-lsb-core-4.0-7.el6 for x86_64
sysstat-9.0.4-11.el6
xorg-x11-utils*
xorg-x11-apps*
xorg-x11-xinit*
xorg-x11-server-Xorg*
xterm
pdksh-5.2.14
```

At this point in the procedure, the OS should be fully prepared for the installation to proceed. Performing these operations prior to installing the software will ensure a problem-free installation. In many cases, the Installer will provide detailed messages if anything was missed. In the event of errors during the installation process, stop the installation and fix any problems before proceeding.

Oracle HTTP Server Software Installation and Configuration

The OHS software installation and configuration is very straightforward. The installer guides you through the installation and configures the server at the end of the process. As such, at the end of the installation, you should be able to test the server by navigating to the hostname and port specified.

Much like the Identity Management installation software, this is started from the software location by running the command. Figure 8-1 shows the Welcome page for the Web Tier Installer.

```
runInstaller -jreLoc /home/oracle/jdk1.6.0_45/jre
```

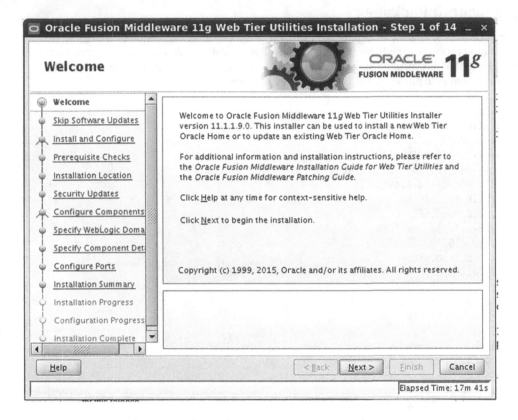

Figure 8-1. *Starting the Universal Installer*

At this stage, ensure that the version of OHS you plan to install is displayed on the Welcome screen. Each version of OHS has its own installer. Prior to installing OHS, you should check the Oracle certification matrices to ensure that the OAM WebGate version is compatible.

OHS is a component that can used the Install and Configure option as seen in Figure 8-2. This is the simplest method of performing this operation as it does not require running additional tools or modifying configuration files at a later time.

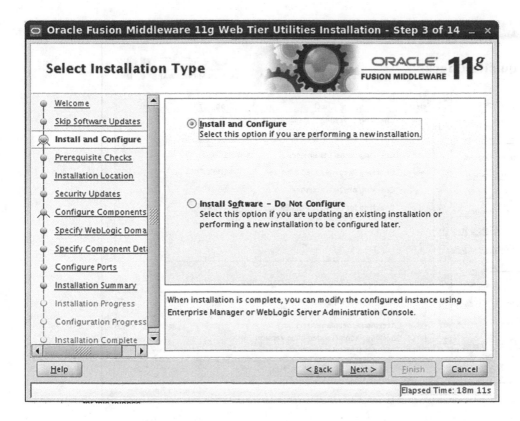

Figure 8-2. *Install and configure setting*

In the beginning of this chapter, the OS prerequisites were listed. If any errors or warnings are displayed, correct them before moving forward. The installer will check the OS and inform you of any missing prerequisites, as displayed in Figure 8-3.

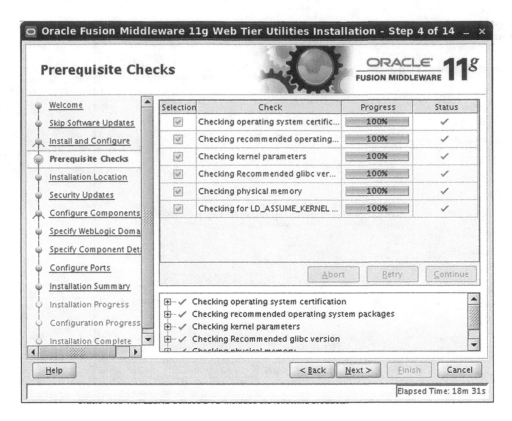

Figure 8-3. *Prerequisite Checks screen*

OHS can be installed within an existing WebLogic home directory, or placed in a new directory. If you plan to register this OHS instance within a domain, you must install the software within the Middleware Home directory of said domain. However, it is completely acceptable to install OHS in its own directory, and not register it with a domain. Although you might lose some monitoring and administrative abilities, most operations can be performed via the command line. As shown in Figure 8-4, enter the location of the new Middleware Home designated for the Web Tier.

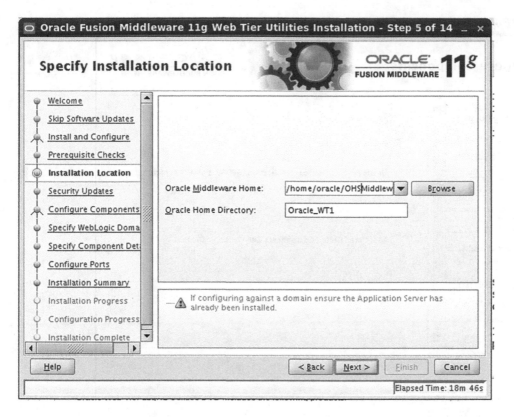

Figure 8-4. *Middleware Home location*

At a minimum, you should install the Oracle HTTP Server component, shown in Figure 8-5. If you require Web Cache in your environment, select it. The Oracle Web Cache check box is selected here solely to display the configuration screens. Web Cache is outside of the scope of this book. Because this OHS instance will be independent of a WebLogic domain, the Associate Selected Components with WebLogic Domain check box has been left unselected.

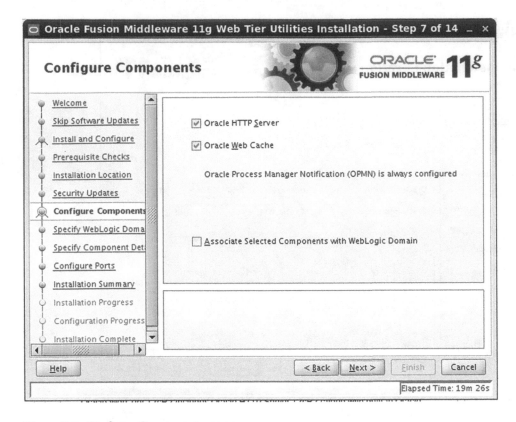

Figure 8-5. *Configure Components screen*

On the Specify Component Details screen, you are afforded the opportunity to specify the instance home directories and names for each component. Ensure these are set to something you can remember. Figure 8-6 shows an example of the Specify Component Details screen.

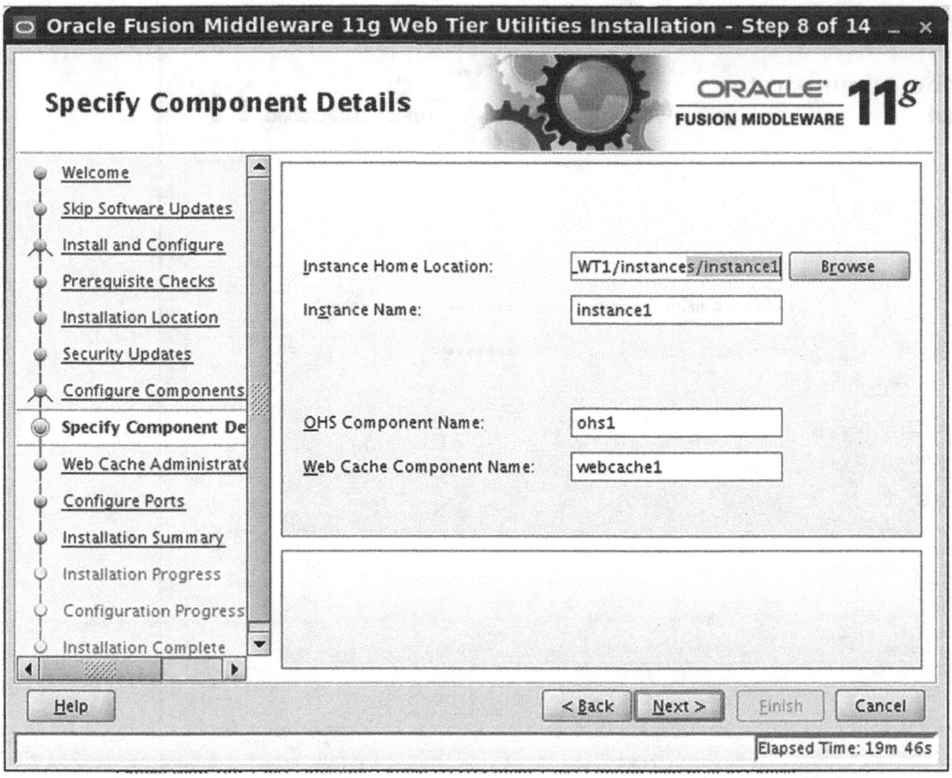

Figure 8-6. *Specify Component Details screen*

If configuring Web Cache, you must provide a password for the administrative user. This user is necessary when making configuration changes to Web Cache. Provide the requested information, as shown in Figure 8-7.

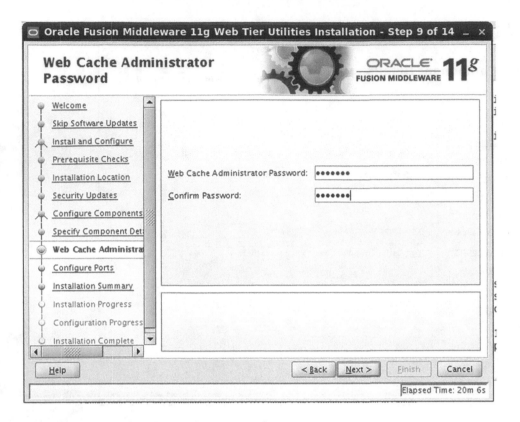

Figure 8-7. *Web Cache Administrator Password screen*

The installation will use Port 7777 by default for the OHS server. If you choose to use different ports such as 80, 443, or both, the configuration can be done by modifying the staticports.ini file. Alternatively, you can later update the httpd.config file located in the instance configuration directory. Figure 8-8 shows an installation using the Auto Port Configuration setting.

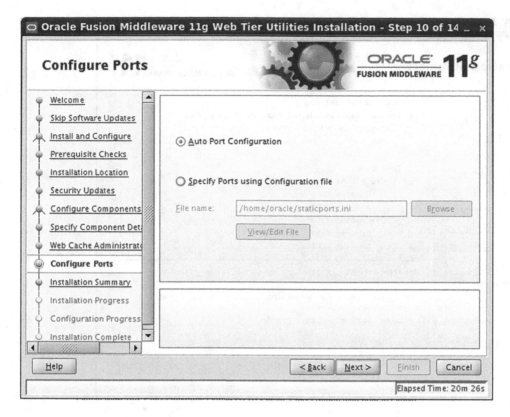

Figure 8-8. *Port configuration*

The Installation Summary screen, shown in Figure 8-9, provides you with an overview of the components to be installed. Click Install to continue.

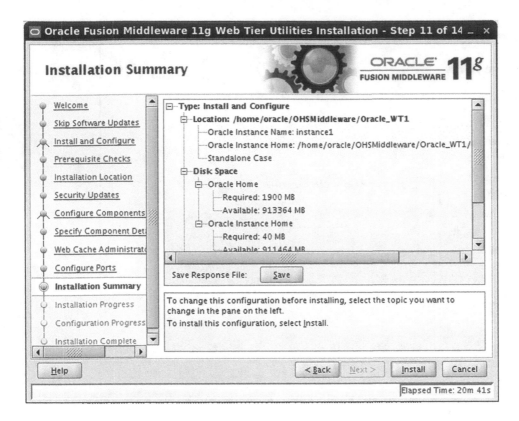

Figure 8-9. *Installation Summary screen*

In general, this process takes between 5 and 10 minutes. The Installation Progress screen, shown in Figure 8-10, will display the progress along with the actual processes that are taking place. If there are any errors, refer to the log file displayed on screen.

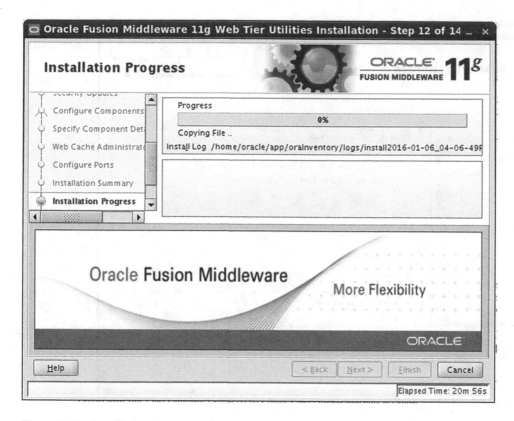

Figure 8-10. *Installation Progress screen*

Immediately after the installer finishes installing, it will move into configuring the new instance created based on the inputs on the previous screens. Each step might take a little time. After the configuration is complete, the installer will start the OHS processes. Monitor the Configuration Progress screen shown in Figure 8-11 and check the indicated log file if there are any errors.

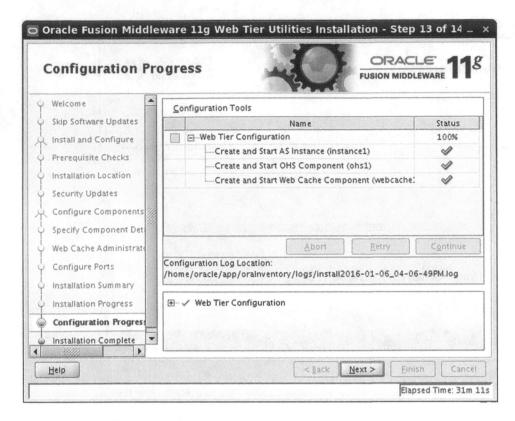

Figure 8-11. *Configuration Progress screen*

The Installation Complete screen in Figure 8-12 indicates all of the installation and configuration details for the new Web Tier.

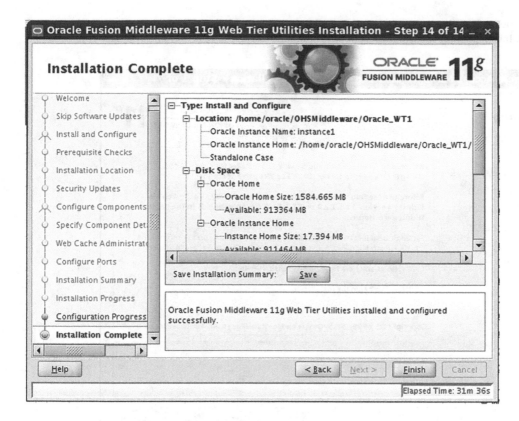

Figure 8-12. Installation Complete screen

You have completed the installation and configuration of OHS and now have a working web server that can be used as a front end for your various applications. With OHS, you receive the Oracle WebLogic Module, which allows you to configure various locations to be handled by underlying WebLogic application servers. Mod_wl_ohs contains the necessary configurations to handle the reverse proxy and cluster failover for WebLogic-based applications. The next section of this chapter presents the steps to install and configure OAM WebGate on the HTTP server.

Oracle Access Manager WebGate Installation and Configuration

The key component that allows OAM to protect resources and handle SSO, is the WebGate. When a request comes in, OAM WebGate evaluates the request and determines if authentication is required. In the case that the requested resource is protected, the WebGate will hand off authentication responsibility to OAM. Once OAM has authenticated the user, it sets up session information within the browser that is utilized by the WebGate to allow the user access to the allowed applications.

The WebGate installation process starts like other installers, with the Welcome screen shown in Figure 8-13. It is important to ensure the version is compatible with the OAM version you have installed.

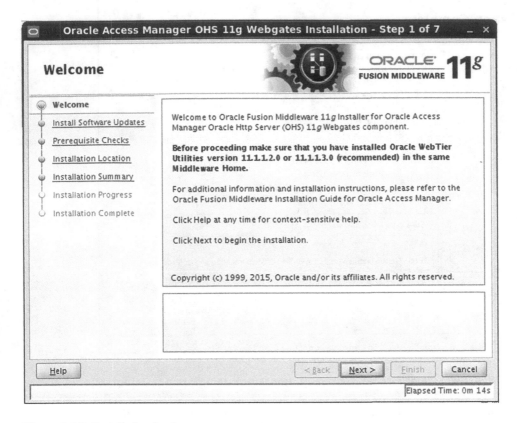

Figure 8-13. Installation begins

The OAM WebGate installation is started much the same way other Oracle applications are installed, using the Universal Installer. From the downloaded installation media, Disk1, execute:

```
./runInstaller.sh -jreLoc /home/oracle/jdk1.6.0_45/jre
```

If you took the time at the beginning to ensure all OS prerequisites were met, this screen should complete with all checks normal. If any check is failed, take this time to correct the issue before proceeding. See Figure 8-14 for an example of a completed prerequisite check.

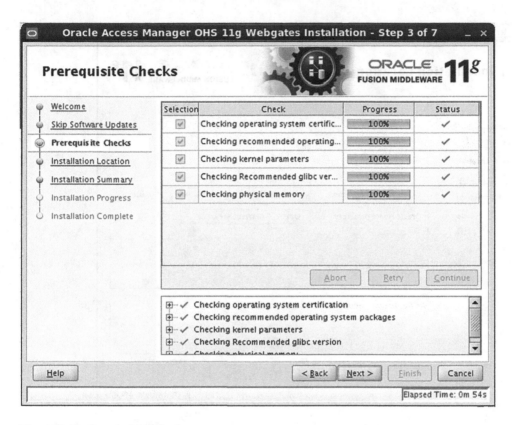

Figure 8-14. *Prerequisite Checks screen*

The Oracle WebGate should be installed within the same Middleware Home location as OHS. If this was done within a WebLogic Middleware Home, ensure the WebGate software shares this home. The Oracle Home Directory listed should be unique within the directory, as shown in Figure 8-15.

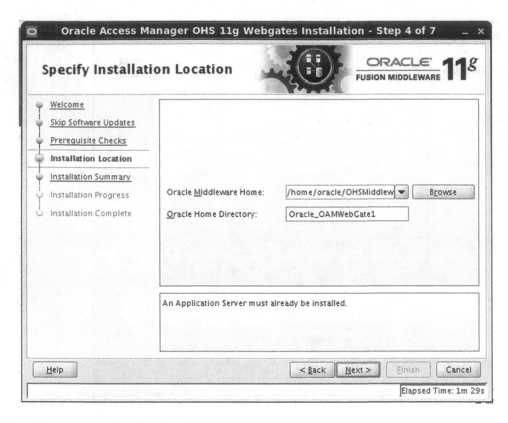

Figure 8-15. Installation location

The Installation Summary screen, shown in Figure 8-16, presents a summary of the components to be installed and their locations. Take time to ensure that everything looks correct.

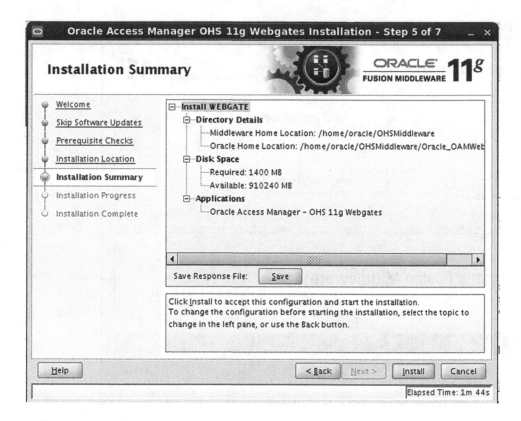

Figure 8 16. Installation details

As with the other products installed within this book, the OHS 11g WebGate installer provides a progress indicator shown in Figure 8-17. You can monitor the installation log indicated if there are any errors.

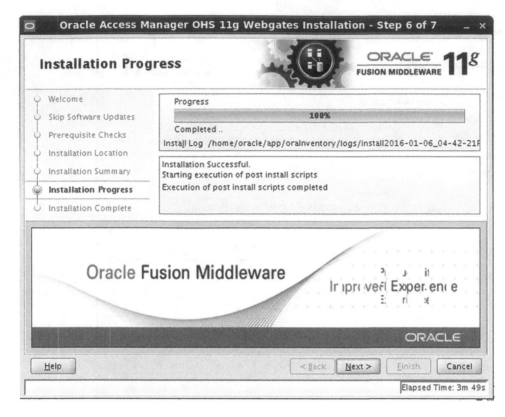

Figure 8-17. *Installation Progress screen*

At the end of the installation phase, make note of the details provided on the completion screen shown in Figure 8-18.

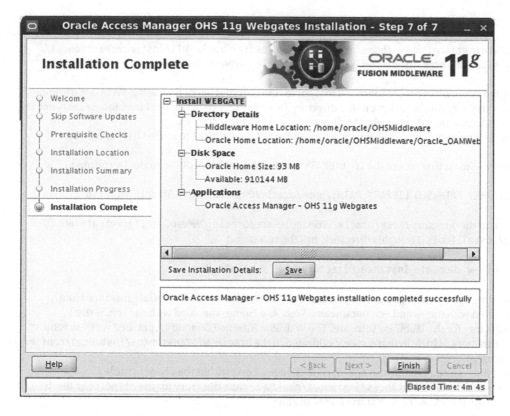

Figure 8-18. *Installation Complete screen*

This completes this installation of OAM WebGate. In the next section, you will progress through the initial configuration and deployment of the WebGate within the OHS environment.

Configure and Deploy Oracle WebGate

Now that the OHS and OAM WebGate software has been installed, it is time to deploy the WebGate into OHS. The tools to do this are located within the Oracle WebGate home directory. This is the directory chosen during the installation.

Using a command prompt, navigate to the directory

```
<WebGate_Home>/webgate/ohs/tools/deployWebGate
```

The tool deployWebGateInstance.sh requires two parameters: WebGate Home and WebGate Instance Home. These are specified with the -w and -oh parameters. WebGate Home, specified with the -oh, is the installation directory for the WebGate software. The WebGate instance directory, specified with -w, is the OHS instance directory, which, in many cases, is located in the Oracle_WT1/instances/instance1/config/OHS/ohs1 directory.

The command should look like this:

```
./deployWebGateInstance.sh -w /home/oracle/OHSMiddleware/Oracle_WT1/instances/instance1/
config/OHS/ohs1 -oh /home/oracle/OHSMiddleware/Oracle_OAMWebGate11g
```

Running the deployWebGateInstance.sh tool copies the required agent files to the WebGate instance directory. You can verify this by looking in the directory /home/oracle/Oracle_WT1/instances/instance1/config/OHS/ohs1. You should see a webgate directory and a webgate.conf file.

The next step in the deployment process is to modify the files required to make OHS aware of the WebGate.

To do this, you must first ensure the LD_LIBRARY_PATH includes the OHS lib folder by running

```
export LD_LIBRARY_PATH=$LD_LIBRARY_PATH:/home/oracle/OHSMiddleware/Oracle_WT1/lib
```

Next move to the directory /home/oracle/OHSMiddleware/Oracle_OAMWebGate11g/webgate/ohs/tools/setup/InstallTools. From this directory, run the command

```
./EditHttpConf -w <WebGate_Instance_Directory> -oh <WebGate_Home>
```

The preceding command requires two parameters: WebGate Home and WebGate Instance Home. These are specified with the -w and -oh parameters. WebGate Home, specified with the -oh, is the installation directory for the WebGate software. The WebGate instance directory, specified with -w, is the OHS instance directory, which, in many cases, is located in the Oracle_WT1/instances/instance1/config/OHS/ohs1 directory.

Verify that the command made the appropriate changes. Look within the /home/oracle/OHSMiddleware/Oracle_WT1/instances/instance1/conf/OHS/ohs1 directory for the httpd.conf file. It should now include the following line at the end of the file:

```
include "/home/oracle/OHSMiddleware/Oracle_WT1/instances/instance1/config/OHS/ohs1/webgate.
conf"
```

Summary

You now have an OHS and OAM 11g WebGate instance. Your OHS can be used as a web server to host applications that must be protected by OAM. The foundation components are now in place to implement the Oracle Identity and Access Management Suite. The next few chapters provide the information necessary to stitch them all together.

CHAPTER 9

■ ■ ■

Configuring Oracle Access Manager

All required components have now been installed. You have created a domain for each of the components in separate Middleware Homes. This simplifies future upgrades and maintenance. After completing this set of operations, the actual components need to be configured and prepared for the actual integrations. The configuration process consists of setting up the components relative to your environment. The following pages discuss how to configure OAM to support single sign-on (SSO) in your environment.

Preparing Access Manager to Use Oracle Internet Directory

OAM, by default, is configured to utilize the WebLogic built-in Lightweight Directory Access Protocol (LDAP) user store for both the system and default store. It is highly recommended that you configure OAM to use an external data store in production environments. Although you might not be setting up a production environment, it is recommended that you configure your development or test environments similar to your production system. As such, this chapter demonstrates how to configure OAM to use Oracle Internet Directory (OID) as its identity store.

To use OID as the identity store, the first step is to configure the WebLogic security realm to recognize OID. Open the OAM WebLogic domain Administration Console by pointing your browser to http:// host:port/console. In this book, the OAM WebLogic Server Administration Console is configured for Host 10.0.70.229 Port 17001. If you recall from previous chapters, OID uses Port 7001 and Oracle Identity Manager (OIM), 27001. Figure 9-1 shows the WebLogic Administration Console Security Realm.

© Kenneth Ramey 2016

K. Ramey, *Pro Oracle Identity and Access Management Suite*, DOI 10.1007/978-1-4842-1521-0_9

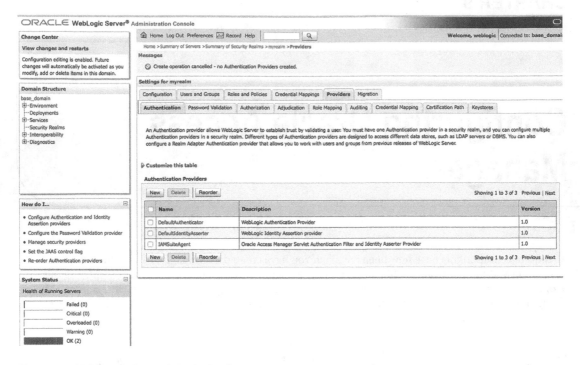

Figure 9-1. *WebLogic Server Security Realm*

Once logged into the Administration Console for the OAM domain, navigate to Security Realms ➤ myrealm. The screen displays the default security realm configured during the domain creation. It consists of the DefaultAuthenticator, IAMSuiteAgent, and the DefaultIdentityAsserter. In this step, you will be adding an authenticator to support OID. Click New to create the new authenticator. This will open the Create a New Authentication Provider screen shown in Figure 9-2.

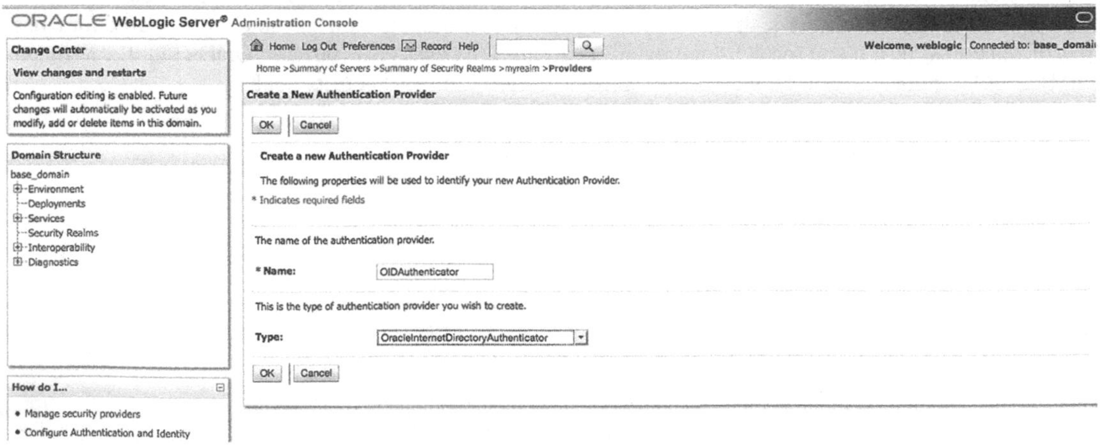

Figure 9-2. *Create OID authenticator*

On this screen, provide a name for the new authenticator. In this case, name it OIDAuthenticator and select OracleInternetDirectoryAuthenticator in the Type field. Click OK.

Figure 9-3 shows the reordering screen for the WebLogic authentication providers.

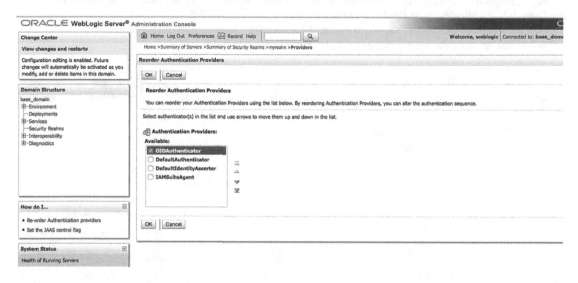

Figure 9-3. *Reorder providers*

After creating the new provider, it should be set to be first in the list of providers. Select the box next to the new OIDAuthenticator and use the arrows to move it up to the appropriate position. Click OK to save this step. You can then move on to setting the Control Flag attribute shown in Figure 9-4.

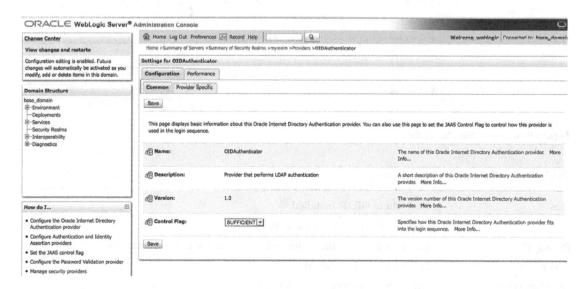

Figure 9-4. *Provider common configuration*

After reordering the providers, you must configure the OIDAuthenticator. First set the control flag to Sufficient. This allows the newly created authenticator to provide authentication services, but not require that a user exist within the OID user store to access resources. This is necessary, as some users, such as weblogic, might not exist in OID. After finishing the configuration of OIDAuthenticator, the control flag on the DefaultAuthenticator must also be set to Sufficient.

On the Provider Details tab, shown in Figure 9-5, enter the configuration details of the new authenticator. In this case, set the values according to the values in Table 9-1.

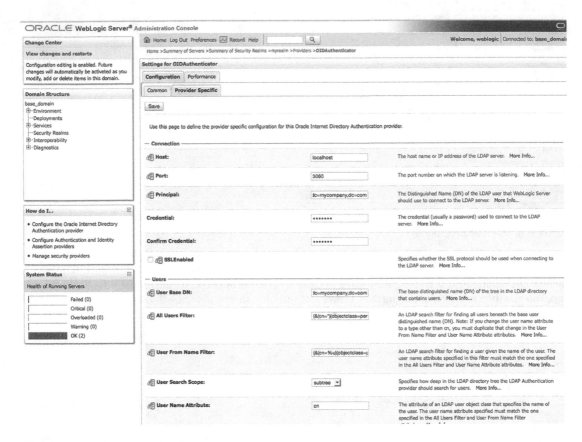

Figure 9-5. *Authenticator details*

Table 9-1. *OID Authenticator Parameters*

Host	Host where OID is installed
Port	OID LDAP port (OID defaults to 3060)
Principal	cn=orcladmin or other principal to be used for the authenticator
Credential	Password used by the principal
User Base DN	cn=users,dc=mycompany,dc=com
Group Base DN	cn=groups,dc=mycompany,dc=com

Customize the other fields as needed. In most cases, the default values will work. Click Save to continue. As mentioned earlier, you will need to configure the DefaultAuthenticator control flag to Sufficient. Use Figure 9-6 as an example of the field to be updated.

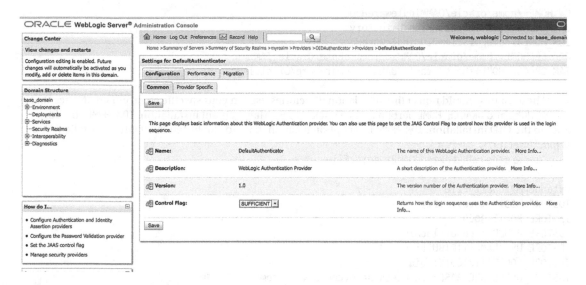

Figure 9-6. *Default authenticator control flag*

After configuring the OIDAuthenticator properties and setting the control flag for both OIDAuthenticator and DefaultAuthenticator, you will need to restart the OAM Managed Server and the WebLogic Administration Server. Follow the steps presented earlier in this book to restart all processes.

Preconfiguring OID for Oracle Access Manager

With the OAM domain configured with the OID Authenticator, it is time to configure the identity store within OAM. This configuration ensures that OAM uses the instance of OID configured previously.

When logging into the OAMConsole for the first time, you will need to use the weblogic user, as OAM is using the default authenticator and oamadmin does not yet have administrator access to the OAMConsole. As such, the first step in the process is to create the necessary users and groups in OID in preparation of the integration.

From a command prompt, set your working directory to <ORACLE_HOME>/idmtools/bin, where <ORACLE_HOME> is the installation directory for OAM. You will run all of the IDM Tool commands for this section from this location.

■ **Note**   The IDM Tool should always be run from the same location to ensure the parameter files are updated properly. However, in a split domain, where OIM is installed in a separate WLS home or on a separate server, you run the -configOIM command in the OIM home.

Prior to running the idmConfigTool.sh command, you must ensure that the environment variables are set properly. Failure to do so will result in a variety of errors, not all of which will point to the cause. Set the environment variables as follows:

```
MW_HOME=/home/oracle/OAMMiddlewareHome
JAVA_HOME=<JDK Installation Directory>
IDM_HOME=/home/oracle/OIDMiddlewareHome
ORACLE_HOME=/home/oracle/OAMMiddlewareHome/Oracle_IAM1
IAM_ORACLE_HOME=/home/oracle/OAMMiddlewareHome/OracleIAM1
```

These values should reflect the installation directories used in your specific environment. Notice that the MW_HOME and ORACLE_HOME pertain to the Oracle Access Management installation. IDM_HOME should refer to the OID installation. IDM_HOME is an optional parameter and can be left out if OID is installed on a separate server.

Create a file called extendOAMPropertyFile:

```
extendOAMPropertyFile
IDSTORE_HOST: 10.0.70.229
IDSTORE_PORT: 3060
IDSTORE_BINDDN: cn=orcladmin
IDSTORE_USERNAMEATTRIBUTE: cn
IDSTORE_LOGINATTRIBUTE: uid
IDSTORE_USERSEARCHBASE: cn=Users,dc=mycompany,dc=com
IDSTORE_GROUPSEARCHBASE: cn=Groups,dc=mycompany,dc=com
IDSTORE_SEARCHBASE: dc=mycompany,dc=com
IDSTORE_SYSTEMIDBASE: cn=systemids,dc=mycompany,dc=com
```

The values in the extendOAMPropertyFile should be set as follows:

- *IDSTORE_HOST*: This should be set to the hostname of the OID instance, or the virtual hostname of a load balanced OID instance.

- *IDSTORE_PORT*: Set this to the LDAP port of the OID instance.

- *IDSTORE_BINDDN*: cn=orcladmin. This value will be used by the tool to log in to OID. This user should have access to create users and groups within the usersearchbase and groupsearchbase.

- *IDSTORE_LOGINATTRIBUTE*: This should be set to the attribute within the LDAP store that contains the login name.

- *IDSTORE_USERSEARCHBASE*: Set this attribute to the location within the ID store where users are stored.

- *IDSTORE_GROUPSEARCHBASE*: Set this attribute to the location within the ID store where groups are stored.

- *IDSTORE_SEARCHBASE*: Parent container that contains the previously mentioned searchbase.

- *IDSTORE_SYSTEMIDBASE*: New container that will store system IDs to be used by the Identity Management suite.

Create a file called preConfigOAMProperties with the following content:

```
vi preconfigOAMPropertyFile
IDSTORE_HOST : 10.0.70.229
IDSTORE_PORT : 3060
IDSTORE_BINDDN : cn=orcladmin
IDSTORE_USERNAMEATTRIBUTE: cn
IDSTORE_LOGINATTRIBUTE: uid
IDSTORE_USERSEARCHBASE: cn=Users,dc=mycompany,dc=com
IDSTORE_GROUPSEARCHBASE: cn=Groups,dc=mycompany,dc=com
IDSTORE_SEARCHBASE: dc=mycompany,dc=com
IDSTORE_SYSTEMIDBASE: cn=systemids,dc=mycompany,dc=com
POLICYSTORE_SHARES_IDSTORE: true
OAM11G_IDSTORE_ROLE_SECURITY_ADMIN:OAMAdministrators
IDSTORE_OAMSOFTWAREUSER:oamLDAP
IDSTORE_OAMADMINUSER:oamadmin
```

The values entered in this file should reflect the values used in your environment.

- *IDSTORE_HOST*: This should be set to the hostname of the OID instance, or the virtual hostname of a load balanced OID instance.

- *IDSTORE_PORT*: Set this to the LDAP port of the OID instance.

- *IDSTORE_BINDDN*: cn=orcladmin. This value will be used by the tool to log in to OID. This user should have access to create users and groups within the usersearchbase and groupsearchbase.

- *IDSTORE_LOGINATTRIBUTE*: This should be set to the attribute within the LDAP store that contains the login name.

- *IDSTORE_USERSEARCHBASE*: Set this attribute to the location within the ID store where users are stored.

- *IDSTORE_GROUPSEARCHBASE*: Set this attribute to the location within the ID store where groups are stored.

- *IDSTORE_SEARCHBASE*: Parent container that contains the previously mentioned searchbase.

- *IDSTORE_SYSTEMIDBASE*: New container that will store system IDs to be used by the Identity Management suite.

- *POLICYSTORE_SHARES_IDSTORE*: Set this to true.

- *OAM11G_IDSTORE_ROLE_SECURITY_ADMIN*: Name of LDAP group that will contain OAM Administrators.

- *IDSTORE_OAMSOFTWAREUSER*: OAM user that will be used by OAM processes.

- *IDSTORE_OAMADMINUSER*: New user that will have administrator rights within the OAM console.

The idmConfigTool.sh command is now ready to be run and create the necessary containers, groups, and users for OAM. Run the command as follows.

First, extend the LDAP identity store for Access Manager integration.

```
./idmConfigTool.sh -preConfigIDStore input_file=extendOAMPropertyFile
```

The output should be similar to the following:

```
[oracle@clouddemolab bin]$ ./idmConfigTool.sh -preConfigIDStore input_
file=extendOAMPropertyFile
Enter ID Store Bind DN Password :
Jan 5, 2016 1:14:42 PM oracle.ldap.util.LDIFLoader loadOneLdifFile
INFO: -> LOADING: /home/oracle/IAMMiddleware/Oracle_IAM1/idmtools/templates/oid/idm_idstore_
                  groups_template.ldif
Jan 5, 2016 1:14:43 PM oracle.ldap.util.LDIFLoader loadOneLdifFile
INFO: -> LOADING: /home/oracle/IAMMiddleware/Oracle_IAM1/idmtools/templates/oid/idm_idstore_
                  groups_acl_template.ldif
Jan 5, 2016 1:14:43 PM oracle.ldap.util.LDIFLoader loadOneLdifFile
INFO: -> LOADING:  /home/oracle/IAMMiddleware/Oracle_IAM1/idmtools/templates/oid/idstore_
                  tuning.ldif
Jan 5, 2016 1:14:43 PM oracle.ldap.util.LDIFLoader loadOneLdifFile
INFO: -> LOADING:  /home/oracle/IAMMiddleware/Oracle_IAM1/idmtools/templates/oid/oid_schema_
                  extn.ldif
Jan 5, 2016 1:14:50 PM oracle.ldap.util.LDIFLoader loadOneLdifFile
INFO: -> LOADING:  /home/oracle/IAMMiddleware/Oracle_IAM1/../oracle_common/modules/oracle.
                  ipf_11.1.1/scripts/ldap/OID_OracleSchema.ldif
Jan 5, 2016 1:15:01 PM oracle.ldap.util.LDIFLoader loadOneLdifFile
INFO: -> LOADING:  /home/oracle/IAMMiddleware/Oracle_IAM1/idmtools/templates/oid/fa_
                  pwdpolicy.ldif
The tool has completed its operation. Details have been logged to automation.log
```

If any errors are reported, check the automation.log file and correct the errors before proceeding.

After the LDAP identity store is preconfigured, you will need to run the second file created to populate the containers, as in the next example.

```
./idmConfigTool.sh -prepareIDStore mode=OAM input_file=preconfigOAMPropertyFile
```

When you run this command, you will be prompted to set passwords for the oblixanonymous, oamLDAP, and oamadmin users. The output will be similar to the following excerpt.

```
[oracle@clouddemolab bin]$ ./idmConfigTool.sh -prepareIDStore mode=OAM input_
file=preconfigOAMPropertyFile
Enter ID Store Bind DN Password :
*** Creation of Oblix Anonymous User ***
Jan 5, 2016 1:17:21 PM oracle.ldap.util.LDIFLoader loadOneLdifFile
INFO: -> LOADING: /home/oracle/IAMMiddleware/Oracle_IAM1/idmtools/templates/oid/oam_10g_
                  anonymous_user_template.ldif
Enter User Password for oblixanonymous:
Confirm User Password for oblixanonymous:
```

```
*** Creation of oamadmin ***
Jan 5, 2016 1:17:33 PM oracle.ldap.util.LDIFLoader loadOneLdifFile
INFO: -> LOADING:  /home/oracle/IAMMiddleware/Oracle_IAM1/idmtools/templates/oid/oam_user_
template.ldif
*** Creation of oamLDAP ***
Jan 5, 2016 1:17:33 PM oracle.ldap.util.LDIFLoader loadOneLdifFile
INFO: -> LOADING:  /home/oracle/IAMMiddleware/Oracle_IAM1/idmtools/templates/oid/oim_user_
template.ldif
Enter User Password for oamLDAP:
Confirm User Password for oamLDAP:
...
*** Creation of ESSO acl ***
Jan 5, 2016 1:17:47 PM oracle.ldap.util.LDIFLoader loadOneLdifFile
INFO: -> LOADING:  /home/oracle/IAMMiddleware/Oracle_IAM1/idmtools/templates/oid/esso_acl.
ldif
The tool has completed its operation. Details have been logged to automation.log
```

After this has completed, the necessary users and groups have been created within OID. Check within OID, using the Oracle Directory Service Manager (ODSM) tool to ensure the oamAdministrators and oamAdmin user have been created.

Configuring Oracle Access Manager Identity Store

With OID extended to support OAM, it is now time to configure OAM to use OID as the System and Default user stores. Log in to the AOM Administration Console by navigating to the URL http://host:wls_console_port/oamconsole. An example of the OAM Administration Console is shown in Figure 9-7. Log in using the weblogic user and password. Until the OAM system and default identity stores are configured, the newly created admin user will be unusable.

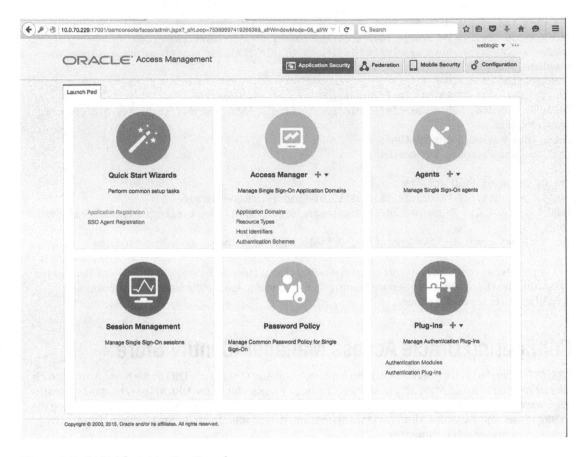

Figure 9-7. *OAM Administration Console*

The Administration Console landing page is split into sections that make it easier to find configuration settings. Along the top are the main configuration categories: Application Security, Federation, Mobile Security, and Configuration. Each has several options that allow you to configure the various components. To begin, select the Configuration option at the top right corner of the screen. The Configuration menu is shown in Figure 9-8.

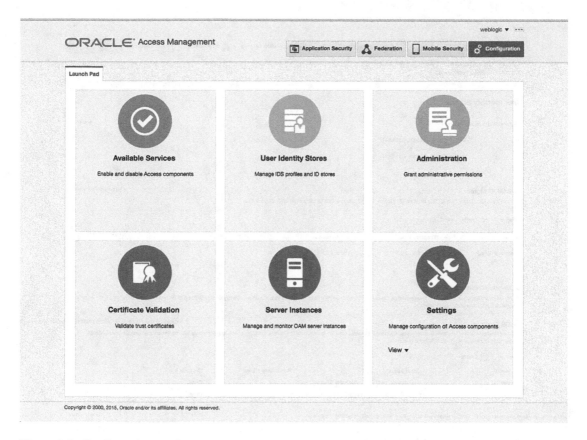

Figure 9-8. *Configuration menu*

Complete configuration and administration is outside the scope of this book. However, this guide covers the parts necessary to complete the overall integration. On the Configuration menu, click the User Identity Stores icon to view the current configuration. Figure 9-9 displays the User Identity Stores screen as you will see it before creating a new store.

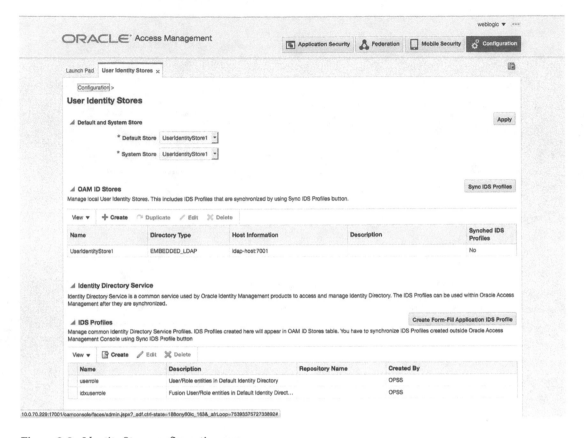

Figure 9-9. *Identity Store configuration screen*

The first time you visit the User Identity Stores screen, you will see that Access Manager is using the Embedded LDAP as the UserIdentityStore, and that it is set as the Default and System Stores. The Embedded LDAP is referring to the WLS built in. In this section, you are creating a new identity store called OID and changing the System and Default stores to use it.

On the Create: User Identity Store screen, shown in Figure 9-10, enter the necessary connection details for OID. The list that follows in Table 9-2 displays the values expected during this stage.

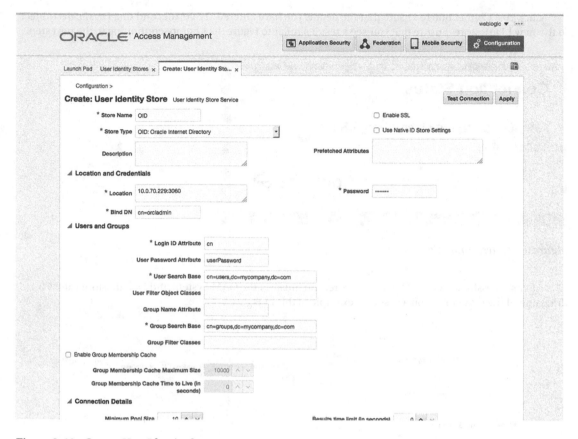

Figure 9-10. *Create: User Identity Store screen*

Table 9-2. *OID Identity Store Connection Details*

Store Name	Give the new identity store a name that will be used
Store Type	OID Oracle Internet Directory
Bind DN	Cn=orcladmin, or other user that has read access to the user and group searchbases
Password	Password set for the user listed in Bind DN
Description	(Optional)
Location	Hostname and LDAP port number for OID
Login ID Attribute	CN is the default value; if you are using a different attribute, enter it here
User Password Attribute	userPassword
User Search Base	Cn=Users,dc=mycompany,dc=com; this value should match the user searchbase that was used in the extendOAMPropertyFile
Group Search Base	Cn=Groups,dc=mycompany,dc=com; this value should match the group searchbase that was used in the extendOAMPropertyFile

Click Test Connection to ensure that the details you have entered are correct and that OAM can connect to the new LDAP store. Ensure that you see a result similar to Figure 9-11 before continuing to the next step.

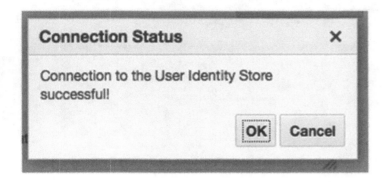

Figure 9-11. *Test connection*

After successful creation of the LDAP store, you must set the OAM System and Default store values to the name of the new store. You will see an example of this in Figure 9-12.

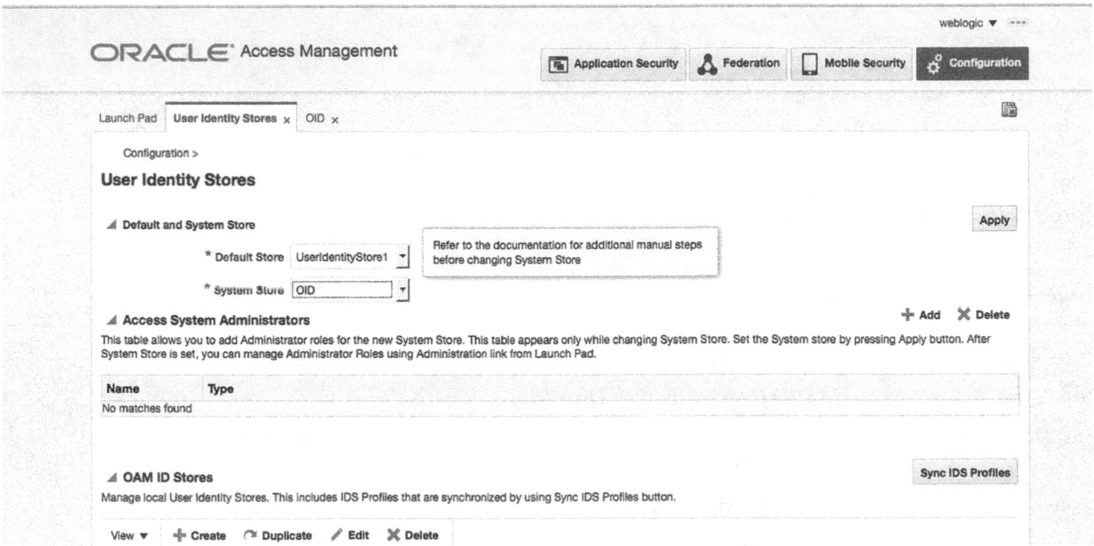

Figure 9-12. *Set Default and System stores*

When you update the store values, you will see a pop-up message informing you that there is a step that must be completed before you apply the changes. A new section called Access System Administrators will show up on the page. In this section, you will add the oamadmin user and oamadministrators group created in the preconfigOAMProperties file. Click Add Button and use the search screen to find the user and group. Add any additional users that might be required in your environment. After you have added the users, click Apply. You will be asked for the oamadmin username and password to validate that the new user store works properly.

After validation of the administration user, and after the new configuration is saved, you must configure the LDAP Authentication Module to use the new Identity Store. Failure to complete this step before exiting the Administration Console can prevent you from logging into the OAM console again. To continue, select the Application Security option at the top center of the screen as seen in Figure 9-13.

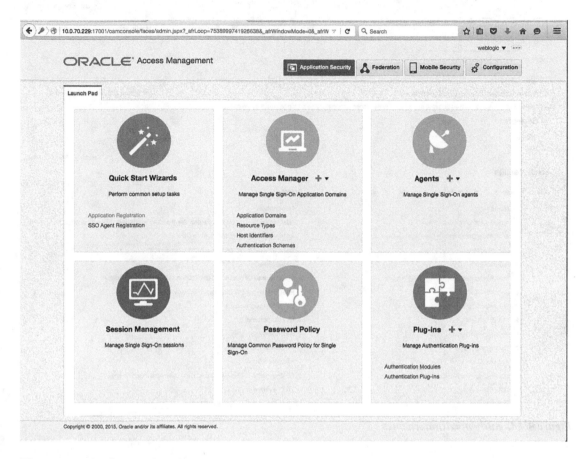

Figure 9-13. *Application Security menu*

On the Application Security menu, under Access Manager, click the Authentication Schemes link. Figure 9-14 shows a list of the authentication schemes that come preconfigured with OAM.

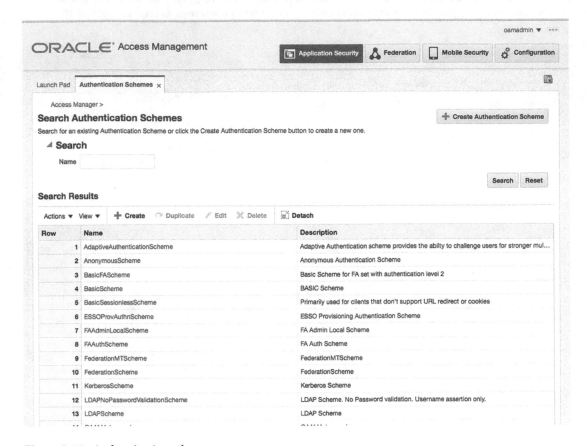

Figure 9-14. *Authentication schemes*

On the Search Authentication Schemes screen, click Search to display a list of the currently available schemes. Click the LDAPScheme listed to bring up the configuration. This will show the name of the Authentication Module used. Figure 9-15 shows the configuration screen that will be used.

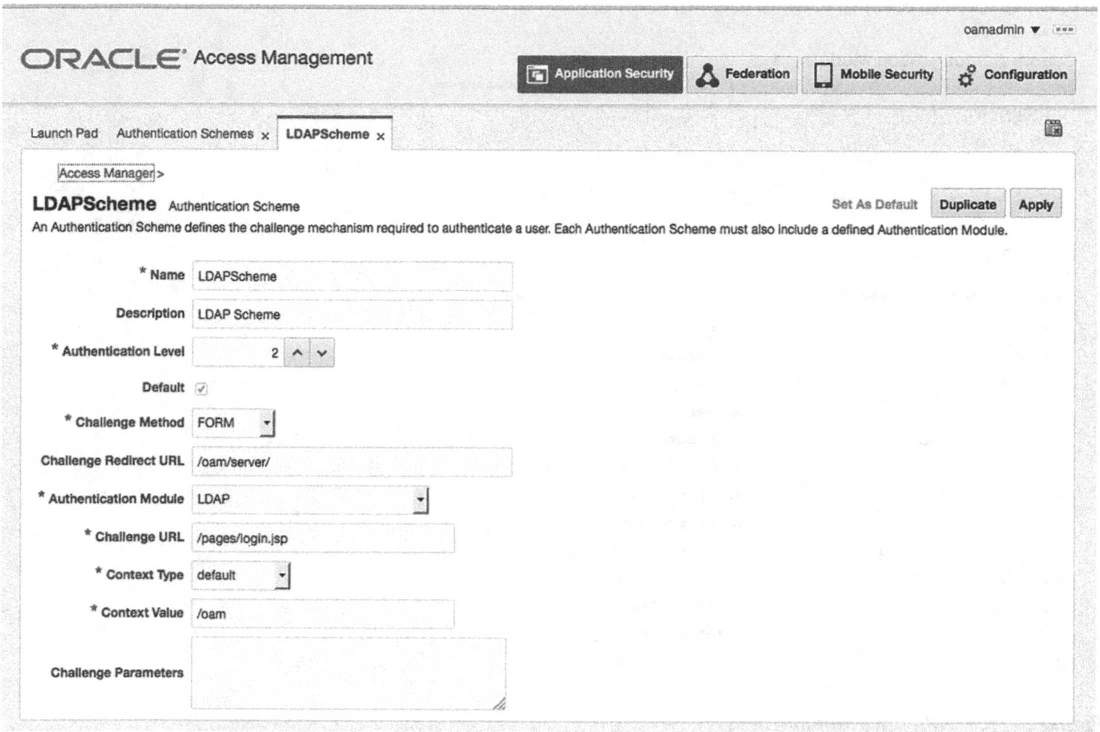

Figure 9-15. *LDAPScheme configuration screen*

In this case, the LDAPScheme is configured to use the LDAP Authentication Module. This is the module you will need to change to ensure proper login and access within Access Manager configured with an external LDAP store such as OID. Figure 9-16 shows the result set on the Authentication Modules tab.

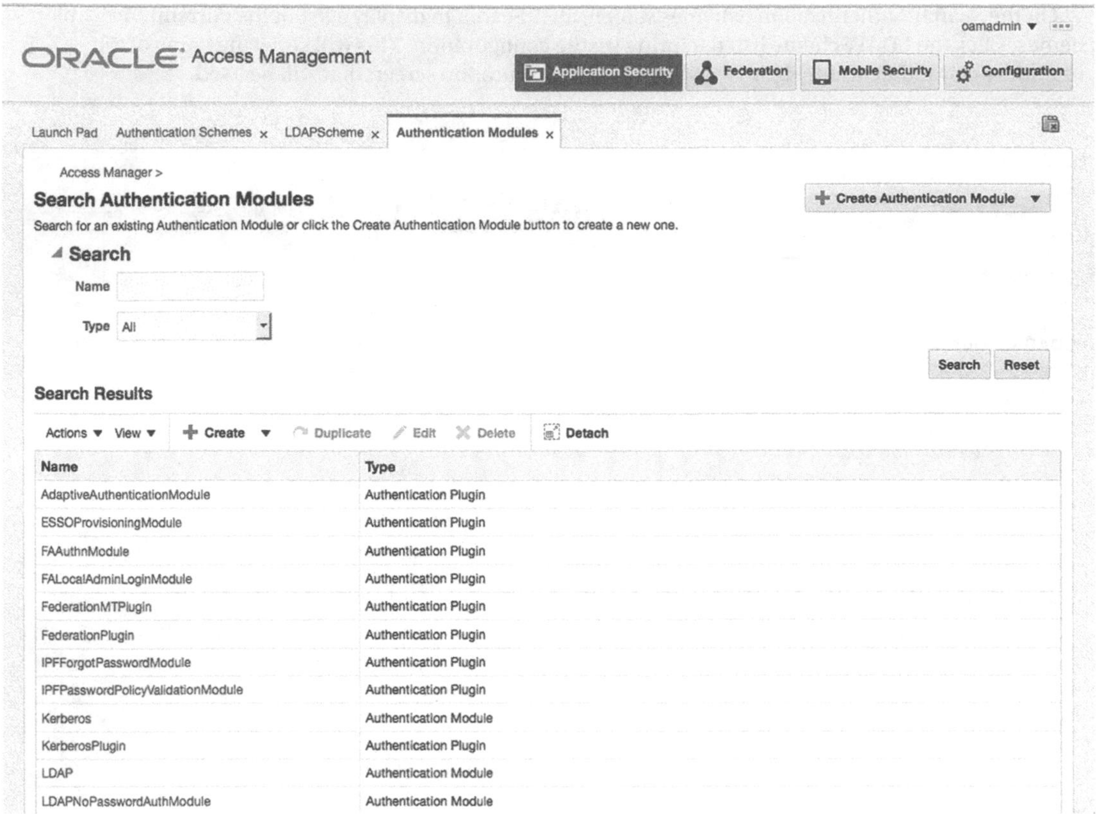

Figure 9-16. *Authentication modules*

Now that you have the name of the authentication module used by the LDAP Authentication Scheme, return to the launch page and click the Authentication Modules link under Plugins on the Application Security screen. Click Search to display the available modules and click the LDAP link. This will bring up the configuration parameters for the selected module as seen in Figure 9-17.

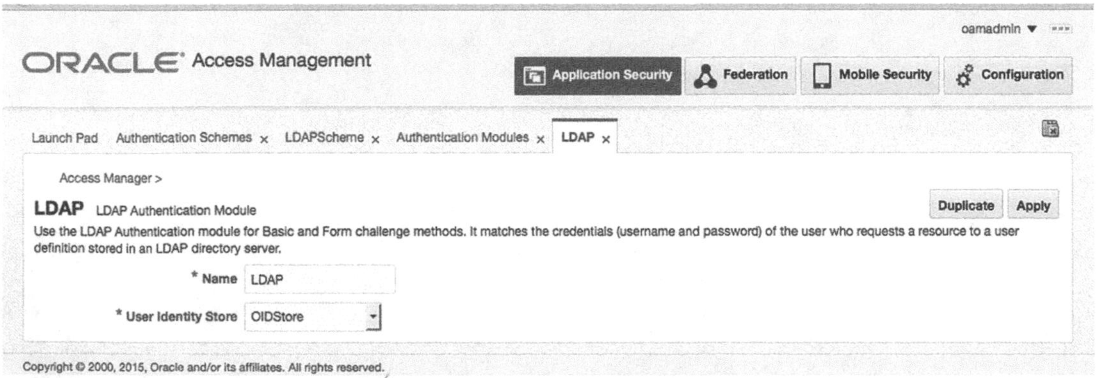

Figure 9-17. *LDAP Authentication module configuration*

On the configuration screen, for the User Identity Store, select OIDStore, the name of the Identity Store created previously. Click Apply to save the changes. You have now finished configuring AOM to use OID and are ready to proceed to the next step of configuring OIM in the next chapter. For now close the browsers and restart OAM. Once restarted, test to ensure you can log into the OAMConsole as the oamadmin user you created.

Summary

This chapter demonstrated the steps required to configure OAM. It included preconfiguring the OID schema to include the necessary containers, users, and groups necessary to integrate OAM with an external LDAP provider. Although these instructions were specific to OID, similar instructions can be used with most other supported LDAP directories with some modification. This step is required whether configuring OAM for integration with OIM or not. It will ensure that the user and permissions will be contained in the centralized LDAP store and not depend on the embedded WebLogic store.

CHAPTER 10

■ ■ ■

Oracle Identity Management Configuration

Oracle Identity Manager (OIM) provides a user interface that can be used by administrators to create and manage user accounts, set up roles, configure workflows, and more. It can also be integrated with Oracle Access Manager (OAM) to provide user self-service screens that will allow end users to reset forgotten passwords, manage their profile information, and set up challenge questions. This all results in a complete identity life cycle management environment for the organization.

Chapter 7 presented the steps to configure a new domain for OIM. That only set up the structures necessary to run OIM within a WebLogic Server, and deployed the necessary components. This chapter guides you through the actual configuration required to run the Identity Manager tools.

Preconfiguration Steps

After creating the new OIM domain, there are a few steps that must be completed prior to actually configuring the Identity Manager server. Begin the preconfiguration by upgrading the Oracle Platform Security Services (OPSS) Schema.

The Oracle Fusion Middleware Patch Set Assistant will be used to upgrade the OPSS. You can find the Patch Set Assistant executable in the directory /home/oracle/IDMMiddleware/oracle_common/bin/psa. This will launch a graphical user interface (GUI) to walk you through the process. Figure 10-1 shows the Patch Set Assistant.

© Kenneth Ramey 2016

K. Ramey, *Pro Oracle Identity and Access Management Suite*, DOI 10.1007/978-1-4842-1521-0_10

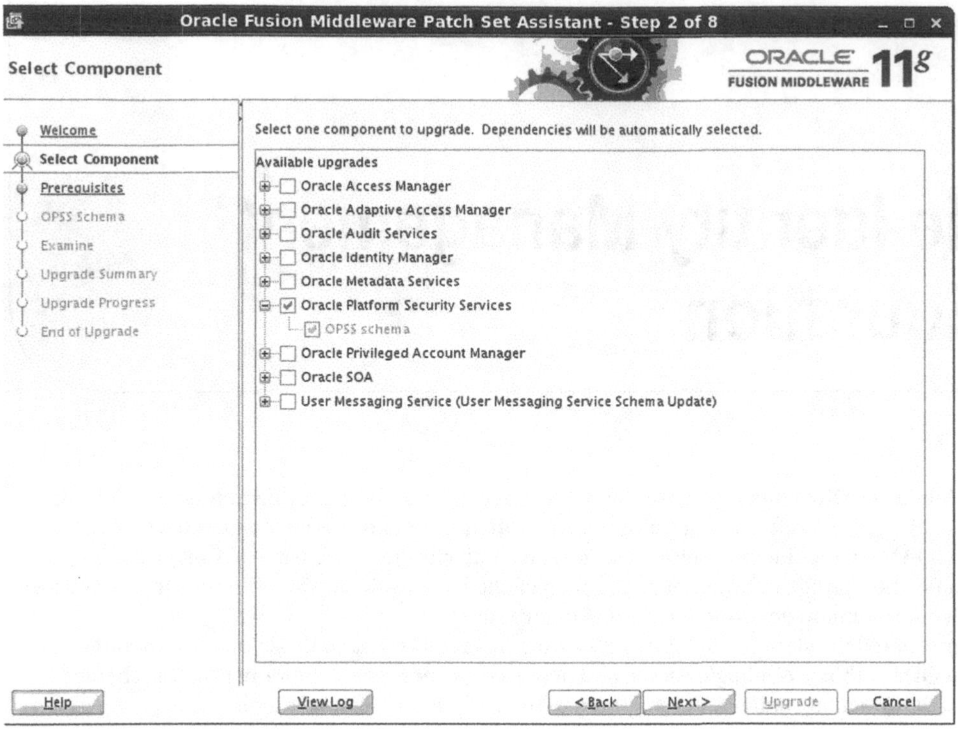

Figure 10-1. *Starting the Patch Set Assistant*

On the Select Component screen, select the Oracle Platform Security Services check box.

The Patch Set Assistant will ask you to verify that you have completed a database backup and that the database version being used is certified with Fusion Middleware. This is shown in Figure 10-2. If you have not already checked Oracle's certification matrix, do so now. Once completed, select the check boxes, and click Next.

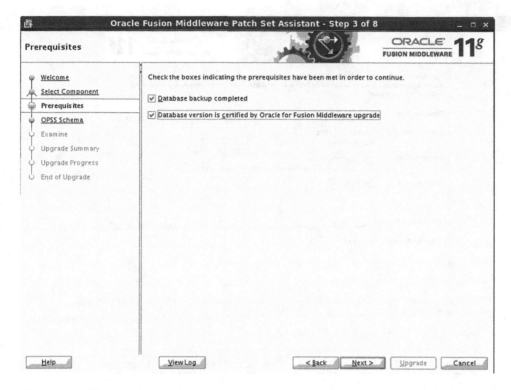

Figure 10-2. *Check prerequisites*

On the OPSS Schema screen, you will need to enter the connection details for the database in your environment. The fields and values entered are shown in Figure 10-3.

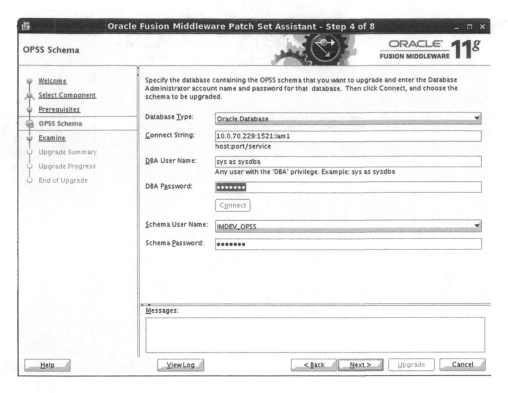

Figure 10-3. *Connection details*

For a description of the fields and the data that should be entered in each, see Table 10-1.

Table 10-1. *OPSS Schema Upgrade Connection Details*

Database Type	Oracle Database
Connect String	The connect string should be entered in the following format: hostname:port:servicename
DBA User Name	The user entered in this field must have sysdba privileges. Enter it in the format "sys as sysdba"
DBA Password	Password for the user entered above
Schema User Name	This should be the OPSS schema name created with the Repository Creation Utility (RCU)
Schema Password	Enter the password set during the RCU creation

Prior to actually upgrading the OPSS Schema, the Patch Set Assistant will validate the database and schema objects to ensure that they meet the requirements. Figure 10-4 shows the validation. It should be noted that if the OPSS is already at the proper version or if it does not meet the minimum, this screen will inform you of that condition.

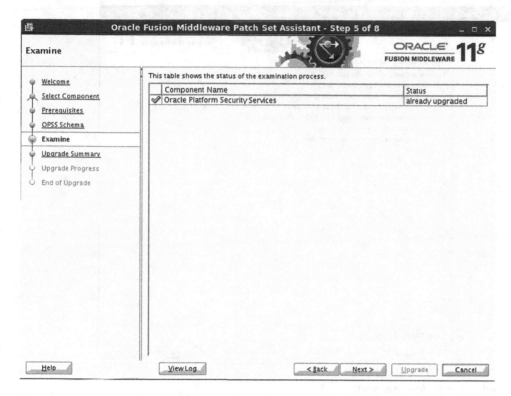

Figure 10-4. *Checking the schema to be upgraded*

The Patch Set Assistant will check the schema and validate its upgrade status, then provide you with a summary of the environment it will upgrade. Take this time to review the Upgrade Summary screen shown in Figure 10-5 before continuing.

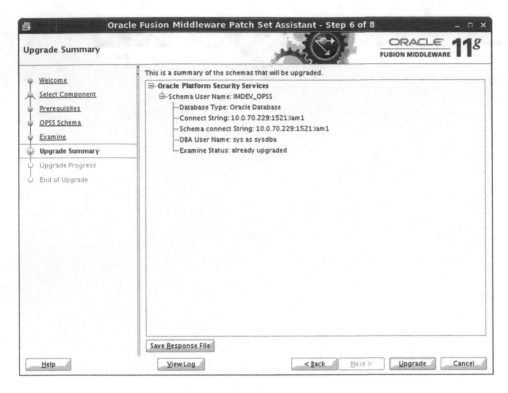

Figure 10-5. *Confirm upgrade components*

Figure 10-6 shows the Patch Set Assistant progress indicator. Once this shows 100 percent, you can click Next to continue.

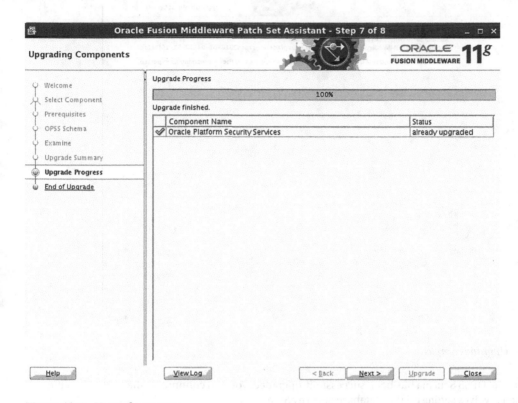

Figure 10-6. Upgrade progress

At the end of the process, you will be presented with the Upgrade Success screen, shown in Figure 10-7. If any errors were encountered, address them now before proceeding.

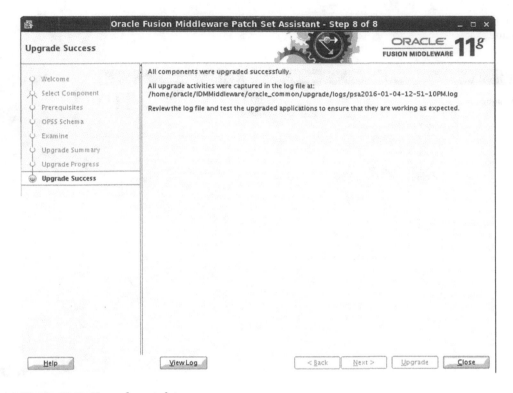

Figure 10-7. *Upgrade complete*

Now that the OPSS Schema has been successfully upgraded, you can continue to the next step in the process, which involves setting up the Database Security Store.

Configure the Database Security Store

After upgrading the OPSS database schema, you must also configure the Database Security Store for the new OIM instance. Oracle Identity and Access Management only supports a Database Security Store. As such, the following steps help you configure this store.

You performed this same activity while configuring OAM. If configuring OAM and OIM in a single domain sharing the same database, you would need to follow steps that would have OIM join the Access Manager Database Security Store. However, if you have followed the steps presented in this book, you installed OAM and OIM in a split domain. The repository objects were installed in separate databases as well. This requires you to create a separate security store for each product.

The configureSecurityStore.py script is located in the OIM home directory under common/tools. To run the script you will use wlst.sh found under the Middleware Home directory under oracle_common/ common/tools.

As mentioned earlier, if you have both OIM and OAM installed in a single domain, and you have already run this for Access Manager, you will need to use the -m join option. However in this case, you will be using the -m create option to create the new security store in the OIM database repository.

To configure the new security store, run the following command from /home/oracle/IDMMiddleware/ oracle_common/common/tools.

```
./ wlst.sh /home/oracle/IDMMiddleware/Oracle_IDM1/common/tools/configureSecurityStore.py -d /home/oracle/IDMMiddleware/user_projects/idm_domain -c IAM -p Password123 -m create
```

In this command, you need to specify the location of the configureSecurityStore.py file and the location of the OIM domain. Specify IAM as the component and the OPSS schema password.

Preconfigure OID Identity Store for OIM

Because the plan consists of integrating OIM and OAM, you must enable Lightweight Directory Access Protocol (LDAP) sync within the OIM server. There will be a step during the configuration to enable the LDAP sync. However, to prepare for that step, you must complete the prerequisite steps prior to continuing. This ensures your LDAP Store, OID, will be ready to be used as the OIM identity store. These instructions apply to using OID. Oracle supports other LDAP stores such as Oracle Unified Directory, Oracle Virtual Directory, Active Directory and iPlanet/ODSEE, but those are outside the scope of this book.

Before continuing, set the environment variables as follows:

```
MW_HOME=/home/oracle/OIDMiddleware
ORACLE_INSTANCE=/home/oracle/OIDMiddleware/asinst_1
ORACLE_HOME=/home/oracle/OIDMiddleware/Oracle_IDM1
```

To preconfigure OID as the LDAP identity store for OIM, begin by creating a file called oidContainers. ldif with the following content:

```
dn: cn=oracleAccounts,dc=mycompany,dc=com
cn: oracleAccounts
objectClass: top
objectClass: orclContainer

dn: cn=Users,cn=oracleAccounts,dc=mycompany,dc=com
cn: Users
objectClass: top
objectClass: orclContainer

dn: cn=Groups,cn=oracleAccounts,dc=mycompany,dc=com
cn: Groups
objectClass: top
objectClass: orclContainer

dn: cn=Reserve,cn=orcleAccounts,dc=mycompany,dc=com
cn: Reserve
objectClass: top
objectClass: orclContainer
```

This file contains the information needed to create new containers for OIM to use for synchronization. Create the containers in OID using the ldapadd command. For example:

```
ldapadd -h 10.0.70.229 -p  3060 -D cn=orcladmin -w ****** -c -f oidContainers.ldif
```

In this example, -h is the hostname of the OID server, -p is the LDAP port of the OID server, -D is cn=orcladmin, -w is the oracladmin password, and -f is the full path to the oidContainers.ldif file.

The ldapadd command is found within the ORACLE_HOME/bin directory for OID.

After creating the containers for enabling LDAP synchronization, you must create the users, groups, and ACIs required by Oracle Identity Manager's LDAP synchronization process. Begin by creating another file called oimAdmin.ldif with the following content.

```
dn: cn=systemids,dc=mycompany,dc=com
changetype: add
objectclass: orclContainer
objectclass: top
cn: systemids

dn: cn=oimAdminUser,cn=systemids,dc=mycompany,dc=com
changetype: add
objectclass: top
objectclass: person
objectclass: organizationalPerson
objectclass: inetorgperson
objectclass: orclusers
objectclass: orcluserV2
mail: oimAdminUser
givenname: oimAdminUser
sn: oimAdminUser
cn: oimAdminUser
uid: oimAdminUser
userPassword: gundam1

dn: cn=oimAdminGroup,cn=systemids,dc=mycompany,dc=com
changetype: add
objectclass: groupOfUniqueNames
objectclass: orclPrivilegeGroup
objectclass: top
cn: oimAdminGroup
description: OIM administrator role
uniquemember: cn=oimAdminUser,cn=systemids,dc=mycompany,dc=com

dn: cn=oracleAccounts,dc=mycompany,dc=com
changetype: modify
orclaci: access to entry by group="cn=oimAdminGroup,cn=systemids,dc=mycompany,dc=com"
(add,browse,delete) by * (none)
orclaci: access to attr=(*) by group="cn=oimAdminGroup,cn=systemids,dc=mycompany,dc=com"
(read,search,write,compare) by * (none)

dn: cn=changelog
changetype: modify
add: orclaci
orclaci: access to entry by group="cn=oimAdminGroup,cn=systemids,dc=mycompany,dc=com"
(browse) by * (none)
orclaci: access to attr=(*) by group="cn=o1mAdminGroup,cn=systemids,dc=mycompany,dc=com"
(read,search,compare) by * (none)
```

With this file created, you will import the new objects into OID using the ldapmodify command also located in the ORACLE_HOME/bin directory.

```
ldapmodify -h 10.0.70.229 -p 3060 -d cn=orcladmin -w gundam1 -c -v -f oidAdmin.ldif
```

Validate that this ldapmodify command worked properly by performing the following commands. They should both return no errors.

```
ldapsearch -h <OID Server> -p <OID Port> -D "cn=orcladmin"  -w gundam1-b
"dc=mycompany,dc=com" -sone "objectclass=*" orclaci
```

```
ldapsearch -h <OID Server> -p <OID Port> -D  "cn=oimAdminUser,cn=systemids,dc=mycompany,dc=c
om" -w * -b  "cn=changelog" -s sub "changenumber>=0"
```

In environments such as this, where OAM and OIM are to be integrated, you must extend OID for OAM and OIM integration by extending the OAM schema. You will need to use the ldapmodify script to import four files located in the OAM home directory.

Move your working directory to /home/oracle/IAMMiddleware/Oracle_IAM1/oam/server/oim-intg/ldif/oid/schema/oim-intg/ldif/oid/schema. There are four files: OID_oblix_pwd_schema_add.ldif, OID_oblix_schema_add.ldif, OID_oim_pwd_schema_add.ldif, and OID_oblix_schema_index_add.ldif. Use the following examples to import the new schema information.

```
ldapmodify -h 10.0.70.229 -p 3060 -D cn=orcladmin -w gundam1 -f OID_oblix_pwd_schema_add.ldif
```

```
ldapmodify -h 10.0.70.229 -p 3060 -D cn=orcladmin -w gundam1 -f OID_oblix_schema_add.ldif
```

```
ldapmodify -h 10.0.70.229 -p 3060 -D cn=orcladmin -w gundam1 -f OID_oim_pwd_schema_add.ldif
```

```
ldapmodify -h 10.0.70.229 -p 3060 -D cn=orcladmin -w gundam1 -f OID_oblix_schema_index_add.
ldif
```

Configure Oracle Identity Manager Server

At this point OID has been set up to be used as the Identity Store for OIM, and you can move on to configuring the Identity Manager Server. In a previous chapter, you created the new OIM domain in its own WebLogic Middleware Home. That step configured an Administration Server, Service-Oriented Architecture (SOA) Server, and Identity Management Server. This continues where that left off and prepares OIM to be started.

It is time to start the WebLogic Administration Server and SOA Server. These must be running before configuring Identity Manager. Move to the Identity Management domain directory /home/oracle/IDMMiddleware/user_projects/oim_domain. Execute the command startWeblogic.sh. If you wish to have this start in the background, you can execute the command using nohup, such as nohup ./startWeblogic.sh > weblogic.out &. This will direct the output of the command to the file weblogic.out. To do this, WLS must be configured to start in Development mode. If the server is configured to start in Production mode, then you will need to ensure there is a boot.properties file in place. Next start SOA. This can be accomplished by executing ./startManagedWebLogic.sh soa_server1 in the bin directory.

■ **Note**   To start servers in the background, either the file boot.properties must be present in the security directory, or the server must be in Development mode.

Create a file called boot.properties formatted as follows in the <Domain Home/servers/<ServerName>/ security directory.

```
username=weblogic
password=<weblogic password>
```

Now that the WebLogic Administration Server and SOA Servers are started, you can continue configuring the Identity Manager Server.

Navigate to <Middleware_Home>/Oracle_IDM1/bin, where Middleware_Home is the directory in which you installed OIM. In the case of this example, it is /home/oracle/IDMMiddleware. In the bin directory, execute config.sh:

```
<MW_HOME>/<IDM_HOME>/bin/config.sh
```

■ **Note**   Only run the config.sh file located in this directory for this step. There are other locations where config.sh might be found. Only this one will launch the correct GUI.

The first step is to select the components to be configured during this step. The required component is OIM Server. OIM Design Console and OIM Remote Manager can only be installed on Microsoft Windows and as such, you will not be installing them here. If you decide at a later time to install these on a separate server, you may do so. Make your selection as shown in Figure 10-8.

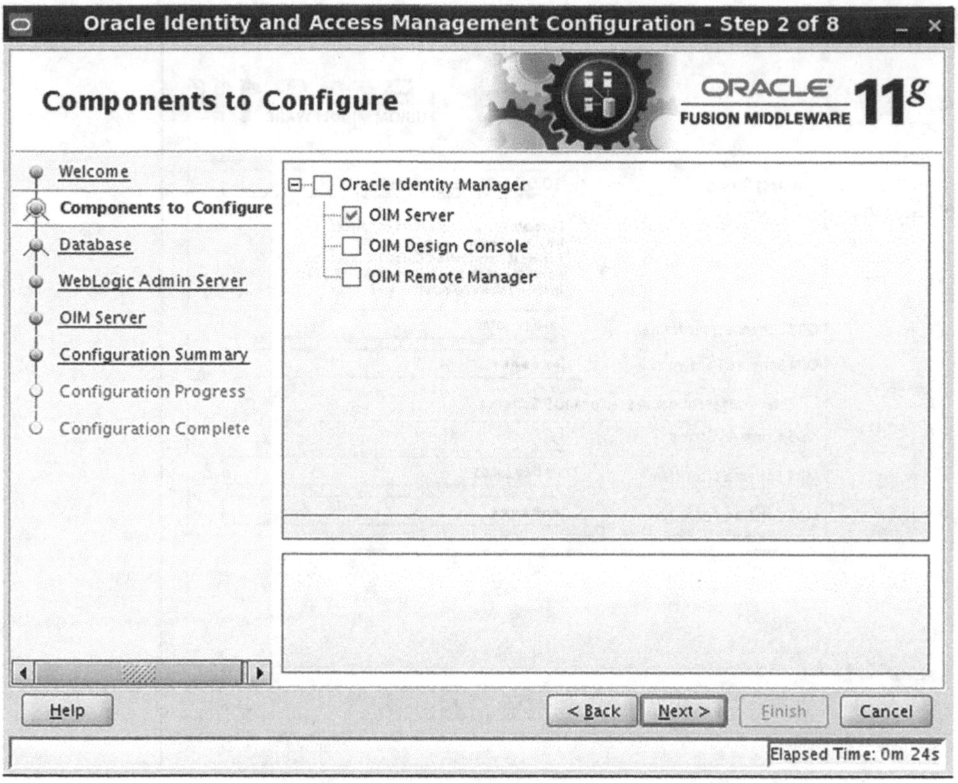

Figure 10-8. Select components to configure

After selecting the component to configure, the tool will ask for database information regarding the OIM Installation. You created the necessary repository database objects when installing the software. Here you will specify the details. Figure 10-9 shows the database connection screen.

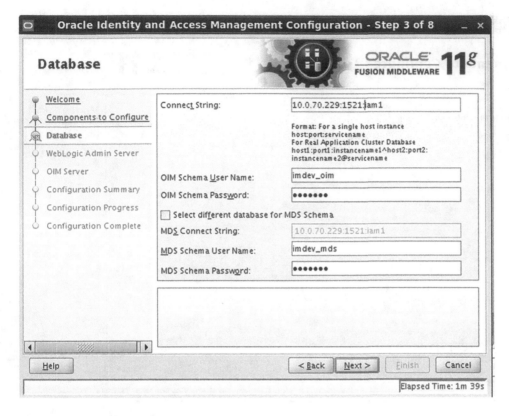

Figure 10-9. *Database information*

Connect String should be entered in the format hostname:port:sid. In the case of this example, you have a single database instamce. If you are using a RAC database, you can enter both nodes as follows: `host1:por`
`t1:instancename1^host2:port2:instancename2@<ServiceName.`

OIM Schema User Name is the schema name entered during the RCU operation earlier in the book. In this case, use `imdev_oim`.

OIM Schema Password is entered in the next line. You provided this password during the RCU operation.

MDS Connect String will default to the same as the Connect String value already entered. If you installed the MDS schema in a different database, select the Select different database for MDS Schema check box and you will be able to edit this field.

MDS Schema User Name should contain the username configured during the RCU operation, `imdev_mds` in this case.

MDS Schema Password should contain the password for `imdev_mds`.

During the initial domain creation step, you configured a WebLogic domain to house OIM. You configured the Administration Server on Port 27001. Enter the URL for the Administration Server, including port as seen in Figure 10-10. Note that in this case you must enter the URL using the T3 protocol in the format t3://hostname:port. Enter the WebLogic username and password and click Next to continue.

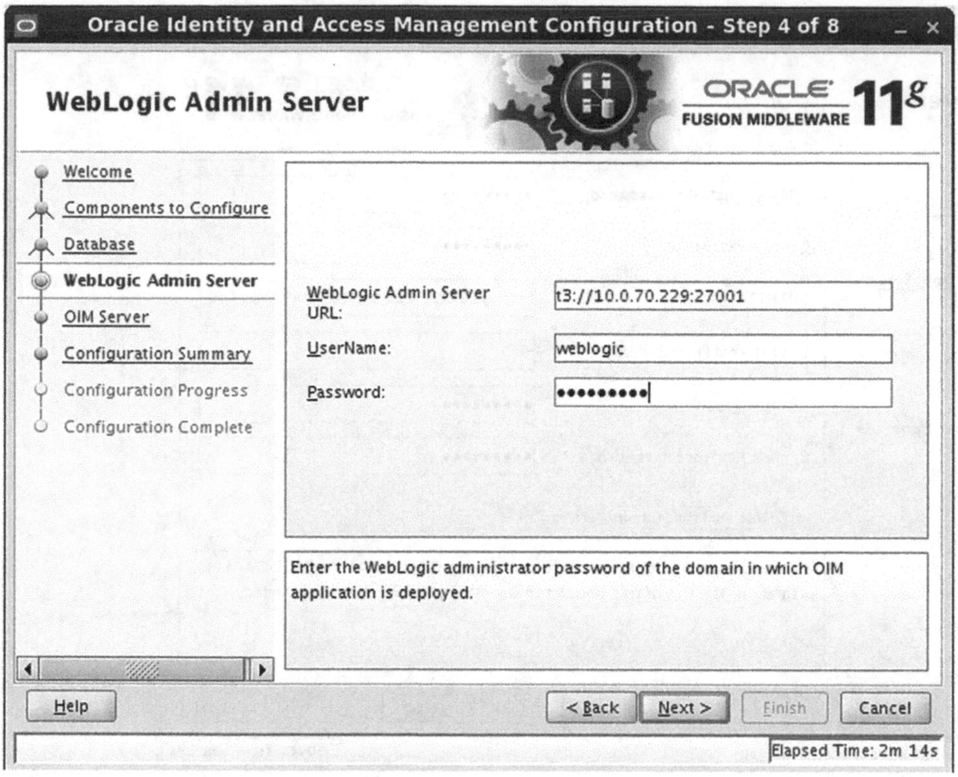

Figure 10-10. *WLS information*

The next step allows you to configure the details around the new OIM server. Figure 10-11 shows the screen that collects the new OIM administrator password and keystore passwords. Make note of these values, as they will be necessary later in the process.

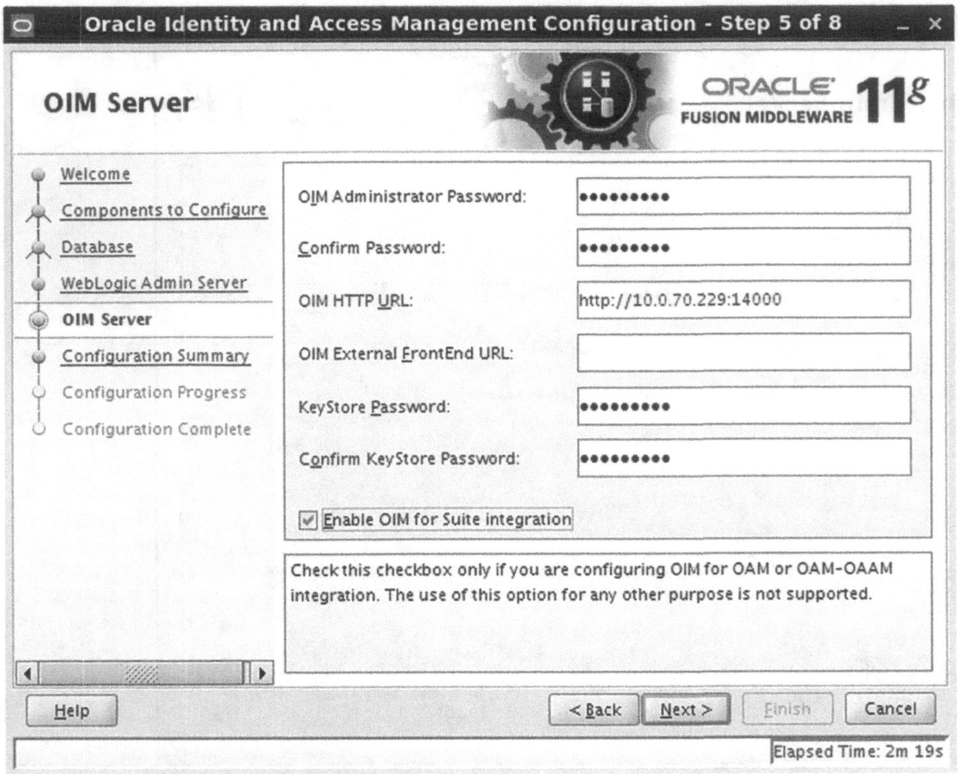

Figure 10-11. *OIM Server configuration*

OIM Adminstrator Password should be set to something you will remember. The OIM HTTP URL is the URL that will be used for Identity Manager. If you have an Oracle HTTP Server (OHS) server in front of the OIM server, enter the URL for it here. You can update this later if you have not yet installed an OHS server. Enter and confirm a Keystore Password.

Select the Enable OIM for Suite Integration check box. This environment will include OAM and OIM integration. Synchronization is required. Earlier in the chapter, the prerequisite steps for this were presented. If you have not yet completed those steps, go do them now before proceeding.

On Step 6 of 10, you will be prompted for the LDAP identity store to be used by OIM. Figure 10-12 shows the LDAP Server screen.

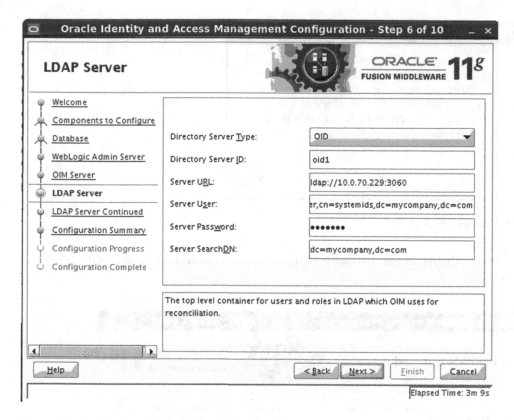

Figure 10-12. *Directory Server configuration*

In an earlier step, you preconfigured this identity store. In this example, you are using OID.

- Choose OID as the Directory Server Type.

- Enter a Directory Server ID. This should be unique.

- Enter the LDAP Server connection information in the format `ldap://hostname:ldapport`.

- Enter the Server User to be used by OIM to connect and perform operations. This should not be the `cn=orcladmin` user. Instead, in the preconfiguration steps, you created a user called `oimadminuser`. Enter it using the full distinguished name: `cn=oimadminuser,cn=systemids,dc=mycompany,dc=com`.

- Server Password is expecting the password you set during the preconfiguration step.

- Enter the Server SearchDN as the overall container name that contains the user and group containers.

Because you have selected to enable LDAP synchronization, the configuration tool will remind you to complete the preconfiguration steps as seen in Figure 10-13. If you have not done this, return to that section of this chapter and complete the steps now.

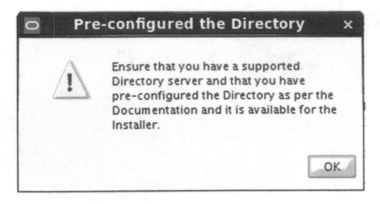

Figure 10-13. *Prerequisite check*

The LDAP Server Continued screen shown in Figure 10-14 continues the configuration of the LDAP identity directory.

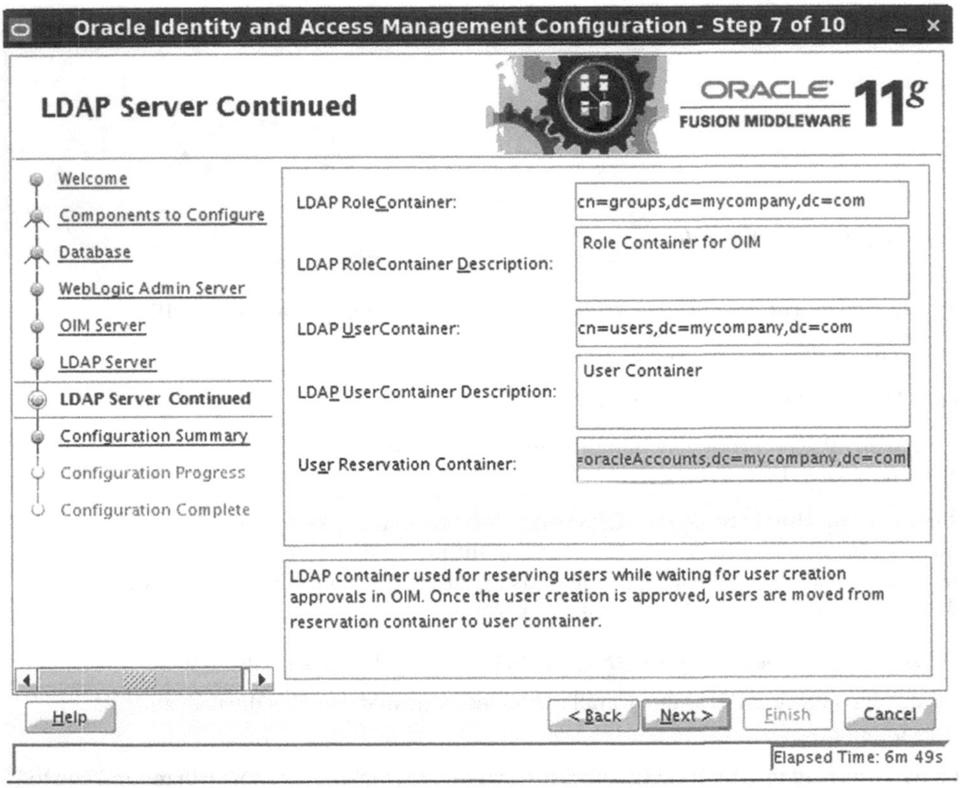

Figure 10-14. *LDAP Server information*

On this screen, you will enter the information pertaining to the user and group containers OIM will use to create users.

- LDAP RoleContainer is the group container.

- Enter a description.

- LDAP UserContainer is the location for all users OIM will manage.

- Enter a description.

- User Reservation Container is the holding place for newly created users waiting for approval.

The Configuration Summary screen shown in Figure 10-15 displays a consolidation of the configuration parameters that have been entered.

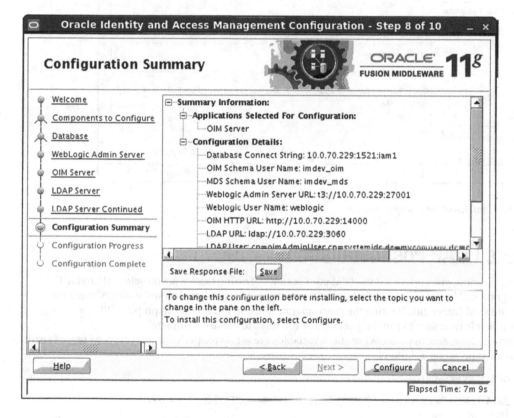

Figure 10-15. *Configuration Summary screen*

Ensure that the components you have chosen to configure are listed. This is also a chance to double-check the values you have used for the configuration. Click Configure to continue.

You have now completed the OIM configuration. The server should now be configured with an OID identity store and LDAP synchronization enabled. Figure 10-16 shows the completed configuration.

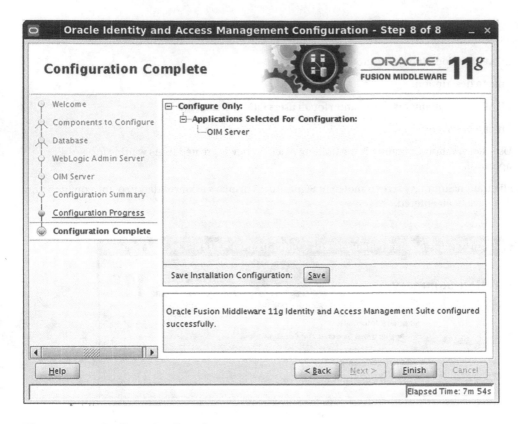

Figure 10-16. Configuration Complete screen

Complete LDAP Postinstallation

In the previous section, you completed the OIM configuration. During that step, you selected Enable OIM for Suite Integration. This informs OIM that you will be using LDAP synchronization, which is required for an OAM and OIM integration. During the preconfiguration, you ran utilities to prepare OID for synchronization. It is now time to run the postinstallation tasks to make it complete.

Before proceeding, ensure your environment variables are set up properly for the ldapconfigpostsetup utility. These must be set up as follows.

- APP_SERVER=weblogic

- JAVA_HOME=/home/oracle/java/jdk1.6.0_45 MW_HOME=/home/oracle/IDMMiddleware

- OIM_ORACLE_HOME=/home/oracle/IDMMiddleware/Oracle_IDM1

- WL_HOME=/home/oracle/IDMMiddleware/wlserver_10.3

- DOMAIN_HOME=/home/oracle/IDMMiddleware/user_projects/domains/idm_domain

In the directory /home/oracle/IDMMiddleware/Oracle_IDM1/server/ldap_config_util, you will find a file called ldapconfig.props. Make a backup copy of this file and edit it as follows.

```
# OIMServer Type, Valid values can be WLS, JBOSS, WAS
# e.g.: OIMServerType=WLS
OIMServerType=WLS

# OIM Provider URL
# if OIMServerType is WAS then
#    OIMProviderURL=corbaloc:iiop:OIMServerBootStrapHost:OIMServerBootStrapPort
#    hint:look for the OIM server bootStrapPort number in WAS admin console
#    e.g.: corbaloc:iiop:hostName:2809
# else OIMServerType is WLS then
#      OIMProviderURL=t3://localhost:ManagedServerPort
#      e.g.: OIMProviderURL=t3://localhost:14000
OIMProviderURL=t3://10.0.70.229:14000

# LDAP/OVD Server URL
# If OVD server is selected during OIM installation, then provide
# value for LDAPURL.
# LDAPURL=ldap://<OVD server>:<OVD Port>
# e.g.: LDAPURL=ldap://OVDserver.us.oracle.com:6501
#
# If not, leave LDAPURL empty
# e.g.: LDAPURL=
LDAPURL=

# If OVD server is selected during OIM installation, then provide
# Admin user name to connect to LDAP/OVD Server
# e.g.: LDAPAdminUsername=cn=oimAdminUser,cn=systemids,dc=us,dc=oracle,dc=com
#
# If not, leave LDAPAdminUsername empty
# e.g.: LDAPAdminUsername=
LDAPAdminUsername=

# If OVD server is NOT selected during OIM installation, then provide
# LIBOVD_PATH_PARAM=
# e.g.: #LIBOVD_PATH_PARAM=/scratch/suramesh/Oracle/Middleware/user_projects/domains/base_
domain/config/fmwconfig/ovd/oim
LIBOVD_PATH_PARAM=

# This is for FA C9, MT scenario where last changenumber from the standby
# server is to be updated to the incremental recon. jobs, to be picked up,
# once the primary/secondary replicated server comes up.
# If the change number is not passed through this parameter, then logic is to
# query the OVD and retrieve the same.
ChangeLogNumber=
```

Make these changes to the file and save the changes:

- OIMServerType=WLS

- Leave the LDAP URL empty as you are not using Oracle Virtual Directory (OVD).

- Leave the LDAPUsername empty as you are not using OVD.

- Leave the LIBOVD_PATH_PARAM empty as you are not using OVD.

You will next run the command LDAPConfigPostSetup.sh, providing it with the directory of the ldap_config_util.

```
[oracle@clouddemolab ldap_config_util]$ ./LDAPConfigPostSetup.sh /home/oracle/IDMMiddleware/
Oracle_IDM1/server/ldap_config_util
```

The output of this command should be similar to the following.

```
For running the Utilities the following environment variables need to be set
APP_SERVER is weblogic
OIM_ORACLE_HOME is /home/oracle/IDMMiddleware/Oracle_IDM1
JAVA_HOME is /home/oracle/java/jdk1.6.0_45
MW_HOME is /home/oracle/IDMMiddleware
WL_HOME is /home/oracle/IDMMiddleware/wlserver_10.3
DOMAIN_HOME is /home/oracle/IDMMiddleware/user_projects/domains/idm_domain
Executing oracle.iam.platformservice.utils.LDAPConfigPostSetup in IPv4 mode
[Enter LDAP admin password:]
[Enter OIM admin password:]
LDAP server is OID 11.1.1.5.0
Obtained LDAP Connection.....
UsernamePasswordLoginModule.initialize(), debug enabled
UsernamePasswordLoginModule.login(), username xelsysadm
UsernamePasswordLoginModule.login(), URL t3://10.0.70.229:14000
log4j:WARN No appenders could be found for logger (org.springframework.jndi.JndiTemplate).
log4j:WARN Please initialize the log4j system properly.
Authenticated with OIM Admin.....
Obtained Scheduler Service.....
------------------------------------
Following attributes were returned by changelog search:
lastchangenumber
------------------------------------
Successfully Enabled Changelog based Reconciliation schedule jobs.
Successfully Updated Changelog based Reconciliation schedule jobs with last change number :
167990
```

You can now take steps to verify that the LDAP synchronization is running as expected.

Summary

In this chapter, you were presented with the necessary steps to configure an OIM server. In a previous chapter, you installed the necessary software and created a WebLogic domain. Here, you built on that effort and now should have an OIM instance that can be used to create and manage users within the OID Identity Store. You also preconfigured this installation in preparation for integrating OIM with OAM. The next step in this process will be to begin the actual integration of these two products.

CHAPTER 11

■ ■ ■

Oracle Identity and Access Manager Integration

In the previous chapters, you installed Oracle Internet Directory (OID), Oracle Access Manager (OAM), and Oracle Identity Manager (OIM) in preparation for integration. This integration provides several benefits, including increased user productivity, increased identity security, and fewer help calls for forgotten passwords or locked accounts.

Organizations using an integrated environment are able to not only leverage OIM's user provisioning and auditing, but also to combine user self-service functionality with OAM's single sign-on (SSO) enablement. The combination of these two major components creates a seamless interface for users who might need to manage their account access, passwords, or profile information. Just as the SSO environment allows users to log in to an application one time, then be automatically logged in to the other applications they might need, this integration adds Identity Manager as a protected resource. This facilitates user self-service by automatically logging in users after certain events, such as a password change, a forgotten password, and so on. Another feature is the ability for OIM and OAM to communicate to determine user status such as first-time logins and expired accounts.

At the end of this chapter, you will have an integrated environment with one protected resource or URL. From the login screen, your users will be able to use the First Time Login, Forgot Password, and other Identity Manager functionalities in an SSO environment.

IdmConfigTool

Oracle has provided a tool that can be used to ensure that all of the necessary configurations are performed for a successful integration. There are a great number of configuration parameters that must be set or updated. Running this tool correctly ensures a seamless integration with fewer hassles during setup.

Adding new applications and resources into the OAM SSO environment can be relatively simple. In the case of most Oracle products and applications, this involves creating a new Oracle Access Manager Identity Asserter in the WebLogic domain and configuring the WebGate. In the case of OIM, however, there are a number of components that must be configured to ensure the communication between the two components is performing properly. Luckily Oracle has provided a tool called IDMConfigTool. In the previous chapters, you used this tool to preconfigure the Identity Store. In this chapter, it is used to configure the integration of OAM, OIM, and WLS.

The IdmConfigTool can assist with the tasks of integrating Identity Manager components. It can also be used to validate the configuration parameters and extract configuration parameters of an integrated environment to assist with troubleshooting or replication in another environment. It supports integration of the Identity Manager components in single and split domain environments, 11g and 10g WebGates, and multiple identity store types such as OID and Oracle Unified Directory (OUD).

© Kenneth Ramey 2016
K. Ramey, *Pro Oracle Identity and Access Management Suite*, DOI 10.1007/978-1-4842-1521-0_11

Although idmConfigTool provides a number of tools for integration, the proper functioning of the tool depends on correct environment management. It is important to note where you run the idmConfigTool. In this book, you have set up OAM and OIM in a split domain. The Oracle documentation mentions that you should always run the idmConfigTool from the same location. However, if running in a split domain, you must run the OAM-specific commands in the OAM home location, whereas OIM-specific commands are run from the OIM home.

Because this chapter covers both OAM and OIM tasks, the proper setup for idmConfigTool is covered in each section.

Configure Oracle Access Manager

In Chapter 9, you configured OAMand preconfigured it for integration with OIM. You also created the necessary objects in the OID Lightweight Directory Access Protocol (LDAP) store. This was all to get OAM up and running and ensure the proper administrative users were created. You also integrated OID as an authenticator at the WebLogic layer.

As stated earlier, this environment is a split domain where OAM and OIM are installed in separate Middleware Homes and in separate WebLogic domains. As such, the configuration of OAM will use the idmConfigTool located in the OAM home directory. See Table 11-1 for details on how to prepare your environment variables to use this tool.

Table 11-1. *Environment Variables for the idmConfigTool*

MW_HOME	Set this to the installation directory of the OAM middleware software; for example, /home/ oracle/IAMMiddleware/
JAVA_HOME	Set this to the Java installation directory; for example, /home/oracle/java
IDM_HOME	If you have installed OID on the same physical server, set this to the OID installation directory; for example, /home/oracle/OIDMiddleware; if OID is installed on a separate server, leave this null
ORACLE_HOME	Set this to the OAM installation directory; for example, /home/oracle/IAMMiddleware/ Oracle_IAM

The idmConfigTool.sh file is located in the $ORACLE_HOME/idmtools/bin directory. When performing these steps, the various steps should be run from this directory. During the process, a file called automation. log will be created and appended.

To start the process, create a file called OAMConfigPropertyFile. This will contain the pertinent information to configure OAM for the OAM and OIM integration. The file should contain the following information about your configuration. Update the values accordingly:

```
vi OAMConfigPropertyFile

WLSHOST: 10.0.70.229
WLSPORT: 17001
WLSADMIN: weblogic
WLSPASSWD: weblogic11
ADMIN_SERVER_USER_PASSWORD: weblogic1
```

```
IDSTORE_HOST: 10.0.70.229
IDSTORE_PORT: 3060
IDSTORE_BINDDN: cn=orcladmin
IDSTORE_USERNAMEATTRIBUTE: cn
IDSTORE_LOGINATTRIBUTE: uid
IDSTORE_USERSEARCHBASE: cn=Users,dc=mycompany,dc=com
IDSTORE_SEARCHBASE: dc=mycompany,dc=com
IDSTORE_SYSTEMIDBASE: cn=systemids,dc=mycompany,dc=com
IDSTORE_GROUPSEARCHBASE: cn=Groups,dc=mycompany,dc=com
IDSTORE_OAMSOFTWAREUSER: oamLDAP
IDSTORE_OAMADMINUSER: oamadmin
IDSTORE_DIRECTORYTYPE: OID
POLICYSTORE_SHARES_IDSTORE: true
PRIMARY_OAM_SERVERS: 10.0.70.229:5575
WEBGATE_TYPE: ohsWebgate11g
ACCESS_GATE_ID: Webgate_IDM
OAM11G_IDM_DOMAIN_OHS_HOST:10.0.70.229
OAM11G_IDM_DOMAIN_OHS_PORT:7777
OAM11G_IDM_DOMAIN_OHS_PROTOCOL:http
OAM11G_WG_DENY_ON_NOT_PROTECTED: false
OAM11G_IMPERSONATION_FLAG: false
OAM_TRANSFER_MODE: open
OAM11G_OAM_SERVER_TRANSFER_MODE:open
OAM11G_IDM_DOMAIN_LOGOUT_URLS: /console/jsp/common/logout.jsp,/em/targetauth/emaslogout.
jsp,/oamsso/logout.html,/cgi-bin/logout.pl
OAM11G_OIM_WEBGATE_PASSWD: gundam1
OAM11G_SERVER_LOGIN_ATTRIBUTE: uid
COOKIE_DOMAIN: .centroid.com
OAM11G_IDSTORE_NAME: OIDIdentityStore
OAM11G_IDSTORE_ROLE_SECURITY_ADMIN: OAMAdministrators
OAM11G_SSO_ONLY_FLAG: false
OAM11G_OIM_INTEGRATION_REQ: true
OAM11G_SERVER_LBR_HOST:10.0.70.229
OAM11G_SERVER_LBR_PORT:7777
OAM11G_SERVER_LBR_PROTOCOL:http
COOKIE_EXPIRY_INTERVAL: 120
OAM11G_OIM_OHS_URL:http://10.0.70.229:7777/
SPLIT_DOMAIN: false
```

In this file, the values should be set as seen in Table 11-2.

Table 11-2. *OAMConfigPropertyFile Parameter Values*

WLSHost	Hostname of the server where OAM is installed
WLSPort	OAM WebLogic Administration Server listen port
WLSADMIN	OAM WebLogic administrator username <weblogic>
WLSPASSWD	OAM WebLogic administrator password
ADMIN_SERVER_USER_PASSWORD	OAM administrator password
IDSTORE_HOST	Hostname of the server with OID installed
IDSTORE_PORT	LDAP port of the OID
IDSTORE_BINDDN	Fully qualified username of the Identity Store administrator user
IDSTORE_USERNAMEATTRIBUTE	Indicates the Identity Store attribute that contains a user's username; for example, cn
IDSTORE_LOGINATTRIBUTE	Enter the attribute that contains user's login name
IDSTORE_USERSEARCHBASE	This value indicates where within the Identity Store OAM should start its search for users; for example, cn=users,dc=mycompany,dc=com
IDSTORE_SEARCHBASE	Use the top level of the Identity Store; for example, dc=mycompany, dc=com
IDSTORE_SYSTEMIDBASE	Enter the location of adminsitrative or system accounts within the Identity Store
IDSTORE_GROUPSEARCHBASE	Location of groups within the Identity Store
IDSTORE_OAMSOFTWAREUSER	This should be the name of the user OAM will use to connect to the Identity Store; for example, oamLDAP
IDSTORE_OAMADMINUSER	The username of the user OAM will modify Identity Store entries with
IDSTORE_DIRECTORYTYPE	Indicate the type of server used as the identity store; for example, OID, AD, OpenLDAP
POLICYSTORE_SHARES_IDSTORE	Set this value to true if OAM policies are stored in the same store as the Identity Store
PRIMARY_OAM_SERVERS	List the OAM hostnames
WEBGATE_TYPE	Enter the type of WebGate: ohsWebgate11g or ohsWebGate10g
ACCESS_GATE_ID	Enter the name to use as the WebGate in the OAM configuration
OAM11G_IDM_DOMAIN_OHS_HOST	Hostname where Oracle HTTP Server (OHS) is installed
OAM11G_IDM_DOMAIN_OHS_PORT	Port OHS is listening on
OAM11G_IDM_DOMAIN_OHS_PROTOCOL	Indicate whether this OHS is Secure Sockets Layer (SSL) or not; for example, http or https
OAM11G_WG_DENY_ON_NOT_PROTECTED	Set this to true to make all URL patterns deny access if they are not otherwise configured in OAM
OAM11G_IMPERSONATION_FLAG	Indicate whether OAM should allow impersonation; this is useful in fusion application environments

(continued)

Table 11-2. (*continued*)

OAM_TRANSFER_MODE	Configure the communication mode of OAM; valid values are Open and Simple
OAM11G_OAM_SERVER_TRANSFER_MODE	Indicate what type of communication OAM will support; note that this should match the OAM_Transfer_Mode
OAM11G_IDM_DOMAIN_LOGOUT_URLS	Configure the URL that will be used for Logout operations
OAM11G_OIM_WEBGATE_PASSWD	Enter the password for the WebGate
OAM11G_SERVER_LOGIN_ATTRIBUTE	Configure the name of the attribute to be used for user login
COOKIE_DOMAIN	Indicate the name of the domain where the cookie will be valid
OAM11G_IDSTORE_NAME	Enter the name of the system Identity Store
OAM11G_IDSTORE_ROLE_SECURITY_ADMIN	Enter the name of the group or role within the Identity Store that contains the adminsitration users
OAM11G_SSO_ONLY_FLAG	Set this to true to provide Authentication functions only; setting this to false will configure OAM to perform Authorization checks as well
OAM11G_OIM_INTEGRATION_REQ	Enter true to indicate that OIM and OAM will be integrated
OAM11G_SERVER_LBR_HOST	Provide the load balancer URL for the OAM location
OAM11G_SERVER_LBR_PORT	Provide the load balancer port
OAM11G_SERVER_LBR_PROTOCOL	Indicate whether the URL is SSL or not
COOKIE_EXPIRY_INTERVAL	Set this
OAM11G_OIM_OHS_URL	If OAM and OIM are fronted by an OHS, provide the URL
SPLIT_DOMAIN	Set this to true if OAM and OIM are installed in separate WebLogic servers

With the file created, you can now run the idmConfigTool with the –configOAM option to set OAM up for integration. When run, this step will configure the OAM Identity Store and register necessary authentication policies. You will be prompted to configure passwords for the OAM software user, OAM admin user, and OAM WebLogic user. If no errors are reported, restart the OAM environment including the OAM managed server and Administration Server. The output should be similar to the following. You should also check the Automation.log file for any errors.

```
[oracle@clouddemolab bin]$ ./idmConfigTool.sh  -configOAM input_file=OAMConfigPropertyFile
Enter ID Store Bind DN Password :
Enter User Password for IDSTORE_PWD_OAMSOFTWAREUSER:
Confirm User Password for IDSTORE_PWD_OAMSOFTWAREUSER:
Enter User Password for IDSTORE_PWD_OAMADMINUSER:
Confirm User Password for IDSTORE_PWD_OAMADMINUSER:
^[[BConnecting to t3://10.0.70.229:17001
Connection to domain runtime mbean server established
Starting edit session
Edit session started
Connected to security realm.
Validating provider configuration
Validated desired authentication providers
Created OAMIDAsserter successfuly
```

```
A type of LDAP Authenticator already exists in the security realm. Please create
authenticator manually if different LDAP provider is required.
Control flags for authenticators set sucessfully
Reordering of authenticators done sucessfully
Saving the transaction
Transaction saved
Activating the changes
Changes Activated. Edit session ended.
Connection closed sucessfully
The tool has completed its operation. Details have been logged to automation.log
```

You have now configured OAM in preparation for integration with OIM. To continue the process, you will be using the idmConfigTool.sh command. If you are working in a split domain or if your OIM instance is on a separate server, move to that server or to the OIM software home directory

Configure Oracle Identity Manager

OIM requires a system user to connect to the Identity Store and browse, create, and edit users. Just like you did for the OAM configuration, you will use the idmConfigTool command to accomplish this. The following instructions will guide you through the creation of the system account.

Prior to running the idmConfigTool.sh command, you must ensure that the environment variables are set properly. Failure to do so will result in a variety of errors, not all of which will point to the cause. Set the environment variables as follows:

```
MW_HOME=/home/oracle/OAMMiddlewareHome
JAVA_HOME=<JDK Installation Directory>
IDM_HOME=/home/oracle/OIDMiddlewareHome
ORACLE_HOME=/home/oracle/OAMMiddlewareHome/Oracle_IAM1
IAM_ORACLE_HOME=/home/oracle/OAMMiddlewareHome/OracleIAM1
```

To create the system account, start by creating a properties file called preconfigOIMProperties as shown here.

```
IDSTORE_HOST: 10.0.70.229
IDSTORE_PORT: 3060
IDSTORE_BINDDN: cn=orcladmin
IDSTORE_USERNAMEATTRIBUTE: cn
IDSTORE_LOGINATTRIBUTE: uid
IDSTORE_USERSEARCHBASE: cn=Users,dc=mycompany,dc=com
IDSTORE_GROUPSEARCHBASE: cn=Groups,dc=mycompany,dc=com
IDSTORE_SEARCHBASE: dc=mycompany,dc=com
POLICYSTORE_SHARES_IDSTORE: true
IDSTORE_SYSTEMIDBASE: cn=systemids,dc=mycompany,dc=com
IDSTORE_OIMADMINUSER: oimLDAP
IDSTORE_OIMADMINGROUP: OIMAdministrators
```

In the preconfigOIMProperties file, the values should be set according to the list in Table 11-3.

Table 11-3. *Parameter Definitions for* `preconfigOIMProperties` *File*

`IDSTORE_HOST`	Set this to the hostname of the server running OID
`IDSTORE_PORT`	This should be set to the LDAP port of the OID server
`IDSTORE_BINDDN`	`cn=orcladmin`
`IDSTORE_USERNAMEATTRIBUTE`	Set this to the LDAP attribute that stores the username; this value is what will be used to search for users
`IDSTORE_LOGINATTRIBUTE`	Set this value to the attribute that stores the user's login name
`IDSTORE_USERSEARCHBASE`	This should be set to the container that contains the users in your environment
`IDSTORE_GROUPSEARCHBASE`	Enter the name of the container that stores the groups in your environment
`IDSTORE_SEARCHBASE`	The overall container in which the preceding searchbase values are stored
`POLICYSTORE_SHARES_IDSTORE`	Set to true if your Identity Store also stores policy information
`IDSTORE_SYSTEMIDBASE`	This location will be used to store user reconciliation data from Oracle Identity Management
`IDSTORE_OIMUSER`	The account that will be created in the LDAP store for use by OIM
`IDSTORE_OIMADMINGROUP`	Enter the group that will store OIM Administrative users

Once the `preconfigOIMProperties` file has been created, you are ready to run the `idmConfigTools.sh` command to prepare the OID Identity Store.

At the beginning of this step, you set the environment variables to support the idmConfigTool. If you have not completed that, revisit the steps to set them before continuing. Run the idmConfigTool using the -prepareIDStore, setting the mode equal to OIM as in the next example.

Run this in the OAM home location:

```
/home/oracle/IAMMiddleware/Oracle_IAM1/idmtools/bin
./idmConfigTools.sh -prepareIDStore mode=OIM input_file=preconfigOIMProperties
```

You will be prompted to enter the orcladmin password and set the password for the OIMLDAP user and XELSYSADM users. If everything completes as expected, you should be prompted for the OIM ldap user passwords and see the following output:

```
Enter ID Store Bind DN Password :
*** Creation of oimLDAP ***
Jan 5, 2016 1:20:01 PM oracle.ldap.util.LDIFLoader loadOneldifFile
INFO: -> LOADING:  /home/oracle/IAMMiddleware/Oracle_IAM1/idmtools/templates/oid/oim_user_
template.ldif
Enter User Password for oimLDAP:
Confirm User Password for oimLDAP:

Jan 5, 2016 1:20:06 PM oracle.ldap.util.LDIFLoader loadOneLdifFile
INFO: -> LOADING:  /home/oracle/IAMMiddleware/Oracle_IAM1/idmtools/templates/oid/oim_group_
template.ldif
Jan 5, 2016 1:20:06 PM oracle.ldap.util.LDIFLoader loadOneLdifFile
INFO: -> LOADING:  /home/oracle/IAMMiddleware/Oracle_IAM1/idmtools/templates/common/oim_
group_member_template.ldif
```

```
Jan 5, 2016 1:20:06 PM oracle.ldap.util.LDIFLoader loadOneLdifFile
INFO: -> LOADING:  /home/oracle/IAMMiddleware/Oracle_IAM1/idmtools/templates/oid/oim_groups_
acl_template.ldif
Jan 5, 2016 1:20:06 PM oracle.ldap.util.LDIFLoader loadOneLdifFile
INFO: -> LOADING:  /home/oracle/IAMMiddleware/Oracle_IAM1/idmtools/templates/oid/oim_
reserve_template.ldif
*** Creation of Xel Sys Admin User ***
Jan 5, 2016 1:20:06 PM oracle.ldap.util.LDIFLoader loadOneLdifFile
INFO: -> LOADING:  /home/oracle/IAMMiddleware/Oracle_IAM1/idmtools/templates/oid/idm_
xelsysadmin_user.ldif
Enter User Password for xelsysadm:
Confirm User Password for xelsysadm:
Jan 5, 2016 1:20:14 PM oracle.ldap.util.LDIFLoader loadOneLdifFile
INFO: -> LOADING:  /home/oracle/IAMMiddleware/Oracle_IAM1/idmtools/templates/oid/oim_group_
template.ldif
Jan 5, 2016 1:20:14 PM oracle.ldap.util.LDIFLoader loadOneLdifFile
INFO: -> LOADING:  /home/oracle/IAMMiddleware/Oracle_IAM1/idmtools/templates/common/group_
member_template.ldif
The tool has completed its operation. Details have been logged to automation.log
```

Integrate OIM and OAM

Much like you did to configure OAM for integration, you will be using the idmConfigTool.sh command to perform the integration of OIM and OAM. This involves creating a property file and using it to run idmConfigTool.sh –configOIM.

Prior to running the idmConfigTool.sh command, you must ensure that the environment variables are set properly. Failure to do so will result in a variety of errors, not all of which will point to the cause. Set the environment variables as follows:

```
MW_HOME=/home/oracle/OIMMiddlewareHome
JAVA_HOME=<JDK Installation Directory>
IDM_HOME=/home/oracle/OIDMiddlewareHome
ORACLE_HOME=/home/oracle/OIMMiddlewareHome/Oracle_OIM1
IAM_ORACLE_HOME=/home/oracle/OIMMiddlewareHome/Oracle_OIM1
```

Create a property file called OIMConfigPropertyFile with these contents:

```
LOGINURI: /${app.context}/adfAuthentication
LOGOUTURI: /oamsso/logout.html
AUTOLOGINURI: None
ACCESS_SERVER_HOST: 10.0.70.229
ACCESS_SERVER_PORT: 5575
ACCESS_GATE_ID: Webgate_IDM
COOKIE_DOMAIN: .centroid.com
COOKIE_EXPIRY_INTERVAL: 120
OAM_TRANSFER_MODE: SIMPLE
WEBGATE_TYPE: ohsWebgate11g
OAM_SERVER_VERSION: 11g
OAM11G_WLS_ADMIN_HOST: 10.0.70.229
OAM11G_WLS_ADMIN_PORT: 17001
OAM11G_WLS_ADMIN_USER: weblogic
```

```
SSO_ENABLED_FLAG: true
IDSTORE_PORT: 3060
IDSTORE_HOST: 10.0.70.229
IDSTORE_DIRECTORYTYPE: OID
IDSTORE_ADMIN_USER: cn=oamLDAP,cn=systemids,dc=mycompany,dc=com
IDSTORE_LOGINATTRIBUTE: uid
IDSTORE_USERSEARCHBASE: cn=Users,dc=mycompany,dc=com
IDSTORE_GROUPSEARCHBASE: cn=Groups,dc=mycompany,dc=com
IDSTORE_WLSADMINUSER: weblogic_idm
MDS_DB_URL: jdbc:oracle:thin:@10.0.70.229:1521:IDM1
MDS_DB_SCHEMA_USERNAME: dev_mds
WLSHOST: 10.0.70.229
WLSPORT: 27001
WLSADMIN: weblogic
DOMAIN_NAME: idm_domain
OIM_MANAGED_SERVER_NAME: oim_server1
DOMAIN_LOCATION: /home/oracle/IDMMiddleware/user_projects/idm_domain
```

The values of each of the parameters in this file should be populated with information specific to your environment. Refer to Table 11-4 for a description of the values.

Table 11-4. OIMConfigPropertyFile Parameter Values

LOGINURI	This value is taken from the original file; do not modify
LOGOUTURI	You can leave this as the default; however, if you have a custom logout page that conforms to the requirements, enter the URL here
AUTOLOGINURI	Set this to none
ACCESS_SERVER_HOST	Enter the name of the host where OAM is installed
ACCESS_SERVER_PORT	Enter the Oracle Access Management Port 5575.
ACCESS_GATE_ID	Enter the name of the Oracle Access Gate created in the previous step
COOKIE_DOMAIN	Enter the name of the domain in which the cookie is valid
COOKIE_EXPIRY_INTERVAL	Enter the number of minutes the cookie is good for
OAM_TRANSFER_MODE	Enter the same value for communication mode as the previous step; for example, open or simple
WEBGATE_TYPE	Indicate the WebGate version being used; valid values are ohsWebGate11g and ohsWebGate10g
OAM_SERVER_VERSION	Enter 11g as the version of the Access Server
OAM11G_WLS_ADMIN_HOST	Enter the hostname where OAM's WebLogic Server Administration Server is installed
OAM11G_WLS_ADMIN_PORT	Enter the port the Administration Server listens on
OAM11G_WLS_ADMIN_USER	Enter WebLogic
SSO_ENABLED_FLAG	Enter whether SSO is to be enabled; for example, true
IDSTORE_PORT	Enter the port where OID or other LDAP server is listening; this should match the location of the Identity Store
IDSTORE_HOST	Enter the hostname of where OID or other LDAP server is installed

(continued)

Table 11-4. (*continued*)

IDSTORE_DIRECTORYTYPE	Enter the type of LDAP server being used; for example, OID
IDSTORE_ADMIN_USER	Enter the username OIM should use to connect to the Identity Store; for example, cn=oimldap,cn=systemids,dc=mycompany,dc=com
IDSTORE_LOGINATTRIBUTE	Specify the Identity Store attribute that is used for login names
IDSTORE_USERSEARCHBASE	Specify the top level of the Identity Store where OIM should search for users
IDSTORE_GROUPSEARCHBASE	Specify the location where OIM should look for groups
IDSTORE_WLSADMINUSER	Enter weblogic
MDS_DB_URL	Enter the Metadata database connect information; it should be in the format jdbc:oracle:thin:@hostname:port:servicename
MDS_DB_SCHEMA_USERNAME	Enter the username to be used to connect to the metadata repository database schema
WLSHOST	Enter the hostname where OIM is installed
WLSPORT	Enter the administration port of the OIM WebLogic environment
WLSADMIN	Enter the username for WebLogic administration
DOMAIN_NAME	Enter the name of the WebLogic domain where the OIM managed server is installed
OIM_MANAGED_SERVER_NAME	Enter the name of the managed server used by OIM
DOMAIN_LOCATION	Enter the complete filesystem path to the domain files

With the file created, you can now run the idmConfigTool with the -configOIM option to set OAM up for integration. When run, this step will configure the OIM Identity Store and set the necessary system MBeans. You will be prompted to enter passwords for the SSO Access Gate, Identity Manager MDS database schema, ID Store password, and Admin Server password. You will also need to supply passwords for the ssoKeyStore.jks and SSO Global passphrase. If no errors are reported, restart the OIM environment, including the OIM managed server, SOA managed server and Administration Server. You should check the Automation.log file for any errors.

Configure Oracle HTTP Server WebGate

At this point, you have configured OAM and OIM in an integrated environment. OAM provides an SSO environment for your applications and protected resources. In Chapter 8, you installed and configured OHS and Oracle WebGate 11g. OAM and WebGate work in sync to protect resources and perform authentication and authorization services. With the addition of the OIM components, you must configure the OHS, WebGate, and OAM with the resource policies necessary to enable SSO and the automatic process flows.

Within the OAM home directory, there is a file located in IAM_HOME/server/setup/templates, called oim.conf. Copy this file to your OHS configuration directory and modify it with the OIM information that pertains to your installation. This will configure the various locations that the HTTP server hosts to be protected by the WebGate. At a minimum, this file should contain the following entries.

```
#Callback webservice for SOD
<Location /sodcheckservice>
    SetHandler weblogic-handler
    WebLogicHost 10.0.70.229
```

```
    WeblogicPort 14000
    WLLogFile "${ORACLE_INSTANCE}/diagnostics/logs/mod_wl/oim_component.log"
</Location>

#oim self and advanced admin webapp consoles(canonic webapp)
<Location /oim>
    SetHandler weblogic-handler
    WLCookieName    oimjsessionid
        WebLogicHost 10.0.70.229
    WeblogicPort 14000
    WLLogFile "${ORACLE_INSTANCE}/diagnostics/logs/mod_wl/oim_component.log"
</Location>

#xlWebApp - Legacy 9.x webapp (struts based)
<Location /xlWebApp>
    SetHandler weblogic-handler
    WLCookieName    oimjsessionid
        WebLogicHost 10.0.70.229
    WeblogicPort 14000
    WLLogFile "${ORACLE_INSTANCE}/diagnostics/logs/mod_wl/oim_component.log"
</Location>

#Nexaweb WebApp - used for workflow designer and DM
<Location /Nexaweb>
    SetHandler weblogic-handler
    WLCookieName    oimjsessionid
        WebLogicHost 10.0.70.229
    WeblogicPort 14000
    WLLogFile "${ORACLE_INSTANCE}/diagnostics/logs/mod_wl/oim_component.log"
</Location>

#used for identity.
<Location /identity>
    SetHandler weblogic-handler
        WebLogicHost 10.0.70.229
    WeblogicPort 14000
    WLLogFile "${ORACLE_INSTANCE}/diagnostics/logs/mod_wl/oim_component.log"
</Location>

#used for sysadmin.
<Location /sysadmin>
    SetHandler weblogic-handler
        WebLogicHost 10.0.70.229
    WeblogicPort 14000
    WLLogFile "${ORACLE_INSTANCE}/diagnostics/logs/mod_wl/oim_component.log"
</Location>

#used for provisioning-callback.
<Location /provisioning-callback>
    SetHandler weblogic-handler
        WebLogicHost 10.0.70.229
```

```
    WeblogicPort 14000
    WLLogFile "${ORACLE_INSTANCE}/diagnostics/logs/mod_wl/oim_component.log"
</Location>

#used for FA Callback service.
<Location /callbackResponseService>
    SetHandler weblogic-handler
        WebLogicHost 10.0.70.229
    WeblogicPort 14000
    WLLogFile "${ORACLE_INSTANCE}/diagnostics/logs/mod_wl/oim_component.log"
</Location>

# OIM Callback webservice for SOA. SOA calls end up at this OIM webservice
<Location /workflowservice>
    SetHandler weblogic-handler
        WebLogicHost 10.0.70.229
    WeblogicPort 14000
    WLLogFile "${ORACLE_INSTANCE}/diagnostics/logs/mod_wl/oim_component.log"
</Location>

#spml dsml profile
<Location /spmlws>
    SetHandler weblogic-handler
        WebLogicHost 10.0.70.229
    WeblogicPort 14000
    WLLogFile "${ORACLE_INSTANCE}/diagnostics/logs/mod_wl/oim_component.log"
</Location>

#spml xsd profile
<Location /spml-xsd>
    SetHandler weblogic-handler
        WebLogicHost 10.0.70.229
    WeblogicPort 14000
    WLLogFile "${ORACLE_INSTANCE}/diagnostics/logs/mod_wl/oim_component.log"
</Location>

# Fusion role-sod
<Location /role-sod>
    SetHandler weblogic-handler
        WebLogicHost 10.0.70.229
    WeblogicPort 14000
    WLLogFile "${ORACLE_INSTANCE}/diagnostics/logs/mod_wl/oim_component.log"
</Location>

<Location /reqsvc>
  SetHandler weblogic-handler
  WLCookieName oimjsessionid
  WeblogicHost 10.0.70.229
  WeblogicPort 14000
  WLLogFile "${ORACLE_INSTANCE}/diagnostics/logs/mod_wl/oim_component.log"
</Location>
```

```
<Location /oam>
  SetHandler weblogic-handler
  WeblogicHost 10.0.70.229
  WeblogicPort 14100
</Location>

<Location /oamfed>
  SetHandler weblogic-handler
  WeblogicHost 10.0.70.229
  WeblogicPort 14100
</Location>
```

After updating this file, stop and restart the OHS to pick up the changes. The next step will be to add OIM-specific resources to the OAM authentication policies.

You will use the OAM Adminstration Console to add OIM-specific authentication policies.

Log in to the OAM Administration Console by navigating a browser to http://<oam-hostname>:<OAMWLSAdminPort>/oamconsole. Use the OAMAdmin username and the password you set earlier. The Access Management landing page is shown in Figure 11-1.

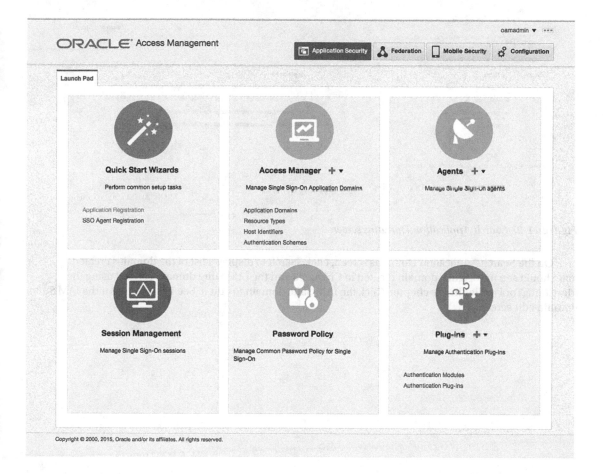

Figure 11-1. *Oracle Access Manager Administration Console*

> ■ **Note**   <OAMWLSAdminPort> should be set to the WebLogic Administration Server port number. You can
> access the OAM Administration Console even when the OAM managed server is not running.

On this screen, under Access Manager, click the Application Domains link. The OAM Application
Domain tab shown in Figure 11-2 shows the existing domains that are created out of the box. Notice that
IAM Suite and Webgate were created for you.

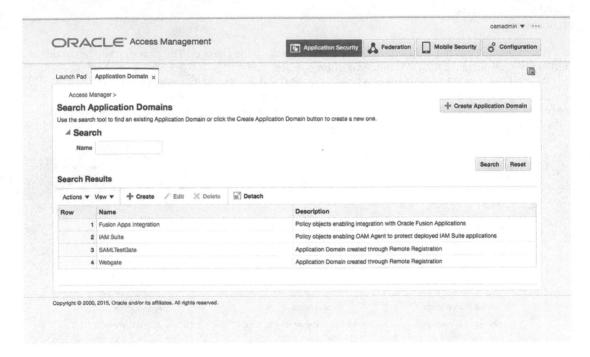

Figure 11-2. *Search Application Domains screen*

On the Search Application Domains screen, click Search to display a list of the domains created.
You should see the original domain created in Chapter 8 and the IAM Suite domain created using the
idmConfigTool earlier in this chapter. Click the IAM Suite domain to edit it. See Figure 11-3 for the IAM Suite
domain edit screen.

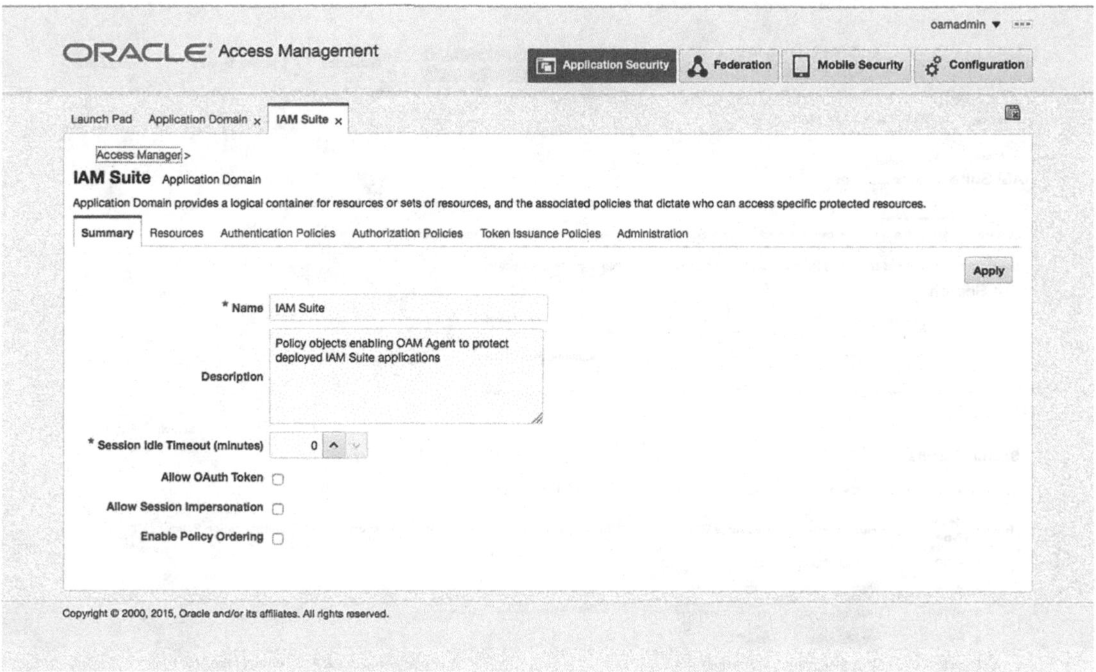

Figure 11-3. *IAM Suite domain summary*

On the first page you are shown the Summary details regarding the IAM Suite domain, as depicted in Figure 11-4. Click the Resources tab to display all of the protected resources in this domain.

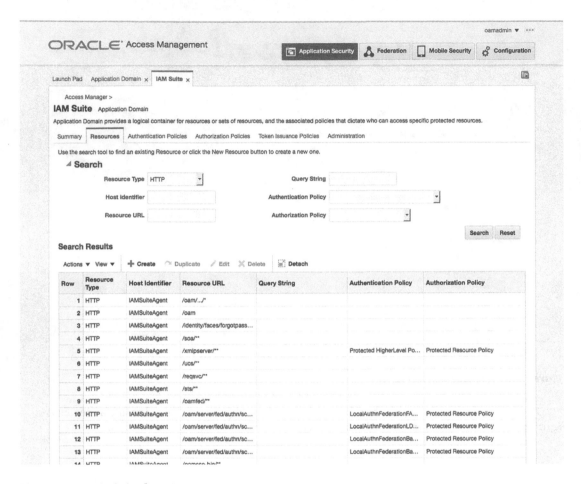

Figure 11-4. *IAM Suite domain resources*

Once on the Resources tab, click Search to display all of the resource URLs and configurations. Scroll until you find the /identity/** resource. Click it to edit the resource. This opens the edit resource screen shown in Figure 11-5.

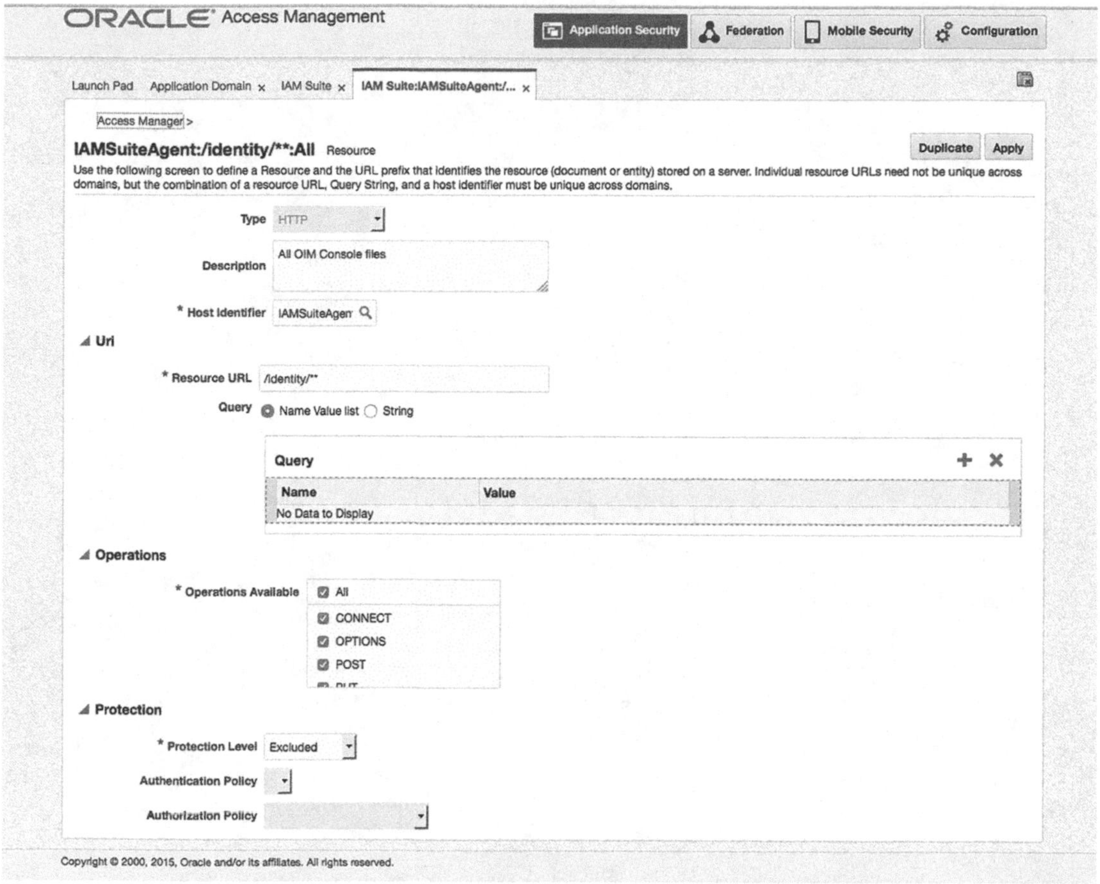

Figure 11-5. Edit resource screen

On the edit resource screen, set Protection Level to Excluded. Ensure that the Authentication Policy and the Authorization Policy fields are empty. Click Apply

While on this page, click Duplicate to create a new resource. Set the Resource URL to /provisioning-callback/**. Click Apply to save the changes.

You have now set up the OIM URLs as resources within the OAM environment.

Summary

After the installation of the software components of OIM and OAM, it was necessary to configure each tier for the integration. At this point in the process, you should have an environment that allows you to create users using the OIM utility. With the newly created user, you can log in and are prompted immediately to change the password and set up challenge questions. After setting up this basic profile, the user should be taken directly to the originally requested resource. In the next chapter, the process flow is demonstrated, along with a process for testing the integration.

■ ■ ■

## CHAPTER 12

Oracle Identity Management and Identity Stores

Many organizations have multiple identity stores to support various business units and processes. These identity stores might be in the form of Lightweight Directory Access Protocol (LDAP)-compatible directories, database tables, or other formats. In many cases, Oracle Identity Manager (OIM) can be used to manage these various directory formats using Oracle Virtual Directory (OVD). Although this book concentrates on using Oracle Internet Directory (OID) as the primary identity store using LDAP synchronization, it is important to consider this configuration as a possible solution when your environment necessitates it. You might also find it useful to configure the LDAP synchronization to use OVD to start with and prepare the environment for multiple data stores.

Most large companies have investments in a variety of user identity stores. They might use Microsoft Active Directory for their network LDAP user accounts and they might use other user directories for various applications. OID or Oracle Unified Directory (OUD) could be in place, providing support for applications such as Oracle E-Business Suite or OBIEE. Other business units might employ a file-based or OpenLDAP-based identity store to support other applications such as homegrown custom utilities. The result of this tends to include a single user possessing many accounts and passwords. Not only is this a problem for the user, but from a security standpoint, this could result in orphaned accounts and even malicious accounts that no one is aware of.

Use Cases

OIM provides solutions to help prevent these occurrences. It is possible for any LDAP-compatible application to use IOD using standard LDAP authentication calls and many third-party applications are able to leverage the Security Assertion Markup Language (SAML) assertion protocols used by Oracle Access Manager (OAM). This only covers the authentication and authorization aspects of the enterprise tools. Managing these multiple identity stores can be challenging, as most stores have proprietary management tools and are unable to manage other brands or types of directories.

In the past, OID provided the ability to synchronize with other LDAP directories, such as Active Directory, ODSEE, OpenLDAP, and others. Although this is a useful tool for providing application access to users from multiple stores, it does not address the management of the user accounts.

OVD increases the level of consolidation of identity store management by presenting multiple disparate directories as a single source. This can be useful not only for providing a single LDAP interface for all of the existing applications, but also by acting as a single source for OIM to handle account governance.

As discussed previously, OIM is an identity governance tool. As such, it provides the ability to manage user life cycle support from on-boarding to new permissions to off-boarding. One of the most common uses of the OVD and OIM combination might be the instance of combining OID users and Microsoft Active

© Kenneth Ramey 2016

K. Ramey, *Pro Oracle Identity and Access Management Suite*, DOI 10.1007/978-1-4842-1521-0_12

Directory users in a single source for management. When presented properly to OIM, both of these sources can be managed, ensuring a consistent handling of user accounts no matter how they were created.

Topologies

Split profile and distinct user populations are two main types of deployments when using OVD to present identity stores to the OIM environment. A split profile might be useful when user account information is stored in one location and the corresponding application user information is stored in other locations. In this case, the network identity directory might be Active Directory, whereas application-specific account information might exist in OID or OUD, or even another LDAP directory. The other deployment topology involves having multiple distinct user and group populations. This might be common in environments where external users are stored in an application identity store and internal employee users are managed in Active Directory. In this common configuration, the two sets of users must be managed through a single interface.

Split Profiles

Companies might choose to implement a split profile configuration if they have a single user population but the identity data is split between multiple identity stores. This could occur if the employee user accounts are stored in a network LDAP directory and one or more applications employ their own stores for account access. For example, Active Directory is used for network resource access and OID is used for access to Oracle E-Business Suite (EBS). Although it might be possible to extend the Active Directory schema to include the EBS data, it is not always the best method for all organizations. OID is treated as a secondary or shadow identity store containing the necessary attributes. OVD merely serves to consolidate the user attributes for OIM to handle. However, the user population from Active Directory and OID in this case are the same.

In a split profile environment each user repository serves a distinct role. Active Directory, or another enterprise directory, is responsible for storing the enterprise user accounts and groups, whereas OID manages the application user accounts and groups. In this case, OID is considered a "shadow" repository. Application roles and membership are handled by OID and managed by OIM. Active Directory handles enterprise or network users. It should be noted that in this configuration, OIM can be used to manage application-level security, however it will not be able to manage the enterprise-level accounts.

When considering the implementation of split profiles for your environment, the following prerequisites should be met.

- OID should be configured as the identity store for Oracle Fusion Middleware products and applications. In other words, the users, groups, and permissions required for access to the applications must be stored within the OID store. This will become the shadow directory.

- The OID should have "referential integrity" turned off. This will ensure that groups created in OID can contain members that are not located within the same directory. The users contained within the groups might be part of the enterprise identity store.

- Login names and accounts must be unique across all identity stores, regardless of the number of stores.

- Active Directory or the enterprise identity store should contain user information but not the application attributes.

Figure 12-1 shows how the enterprise repository and the application identity store are combined to provide the Identity Management suite a single view of the user and group permissions. This combination provides the authentication credentials from the enterprise directory and the authorization context from the application directory.

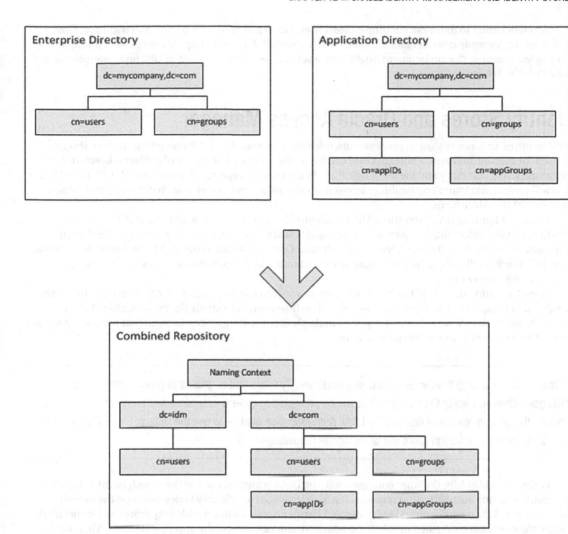

Figure 12-1. *Split domain directory structure*

Distinct User and Group Populations

A growing number of organizations have resources available to the public as well as private content available only to employees. In this situation, it is not always possible to include all users, external and internal, in the company network LDAP directory. Most enterprise deployments dictate that these two sets of users are stored separately and not in a system that provides network access. Although other LDAP directories could be involved, one example has OID containing all external users, and internal users are created and maintained in Active Directory. This is a very common architecture, but the application security might still require that all users are stored together in a general-use directory that allows for storage of application-level attributes.

OIM provides a couple different solutions for this architecture. The use of OVD allows multiple user identity stores to appear and be managed as a single store for applications and services and the Directory Integration Platform (DIP) allows the synchronization of multiple LDAP repositories into a single OID instance.

When deciding to implement multiple directories within a distinct user population within an OIM environment, a couple considerations should be kept in mind. First, user populations exist in multiple directories, meaning the environment might have a set of external users stored in OID and enterprise users stored within Active Directory.

Identity Stores and Oracle Access Manager

OAM requires an identity store to process authentication requests. An LDAP-compliant ID store should be used for this requirement. Although OAM can be configured to use a variety of different directories, including Active Directory and the WebLogic built-in LDAP, it is suggested that you use OID, OVD, or OUD. This will ensure maximum compatibility across the applications most often used within an Oracle single sign-on (SSO) environment.

When configuring OAM, you should first configure the security realm within the WebLogic Admin Console. Performing this step will ensure that you are able to use any user login specified as an administrator to log in to the WebLogic Administration Console as well as the OAM Administration Console later. This is especially helpful in preventing shared administrative accounts as well as lost or forgotten WebLogic user passwords.

Steps for setting up the OID as an identity provider within the WebLogic security realm for OAM were presented in Chapter 9. There, you were instructed on how to create a single data store within OAM. It should be noted that Access Manager supports multiple identity stores. Keep in mind that only one store can be used as the default store or the system store.

■ **Note**   When setting the System Store, you must specify users and or groups to grant administration privileges. When you apply the changes, you will be prompted to enter a username and password of a user that is within the groups. You must also set the LDAP Authentication Module to use the Default Store. Failure to do so could lock the administration users out of the Admin Console.

Within the OAM Identity Store configuration, the Default Store is used as the search location for user information during authentication requests. It is also leveraged for Identity Federation and the Security Token Service. When configuring OAM Federated Partner Applications, the Identity Store can be specified. If multiple stores are configured in OAM, the administrator can choose the appropriate store. This could be useful if a partner application is in use by only a small group within the enterprise and it uses its own LDAP repository. If no Identity Store is specified during this configuration, OAM will use Default Store for authentication.

The System Store is leveraged when a user attempts to log in to the administration tools. This store must contain all users that are designated as administrators. When setting this up, you should specify the same LDAP store that was used as the identity provider within the OAM WebLogic Security Realm. Doing this will ensure that the administration users are able to log in with their proper permissions and that administration groups and roles are properly leveraged. Figure 12-2 shows the ability to set both System and Default identity stores.

User Identity Stores

◢ Default and System Store   Apply

        * Default Store   OID   ▾

        * System Store   OID   ▾

Figure 12-2. Default and System identity stores

■ **Note** If you mistakenly set the System Store or Default Store and lock the administration users out of the Administration Console, you can undo the change using wlst:

Run $ORACLE_HOME/common/bin/wlst.sh

```
wls:/offline> connect("t3://<hostname>:<port>", "weblogic", "<password>")
wls:/base_domain/serverConfig> displayUserIdentityStore('UserIdentityStore1')
wls:/base_domain/serverConfig> editUserIdentityStore(name="UserIdentityStore1",isPrimary="tr
ue",isSystem="true")
```

When OAM is integrated with OIM, it should be noted that a shared identity store will be created within OAM. This will coincide with the LDAP repository that was configured to synchronize with OIM. In many cases, this will be the proper identity store to be used for an Access Manager environment. However, in some environments, it might be desirable to use different stores for different federation applications or authentication modules. Figure 12-3 displays an example of an OAM environment in which there are multiple available identity stores. You will note that there is the Embedded_LDAP, which is configured as the same store information used in the WebLogic security realm. The OID Identity Store shown is an overall OID configuration. In this example, the Base DN is configured as the top-level container of the OID directory. As mentioned previously, the OIMIDStore was created during the integration of OIM and OAM. In many cases, this might be the entire LDAP store or a subset of users.

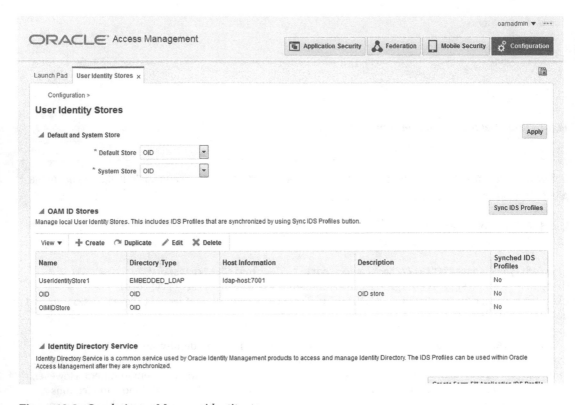

Figure 12-3. *Oracle Access Manager identity stores*

Summary

The OIM and OAM suite of applications can be configured to use various combinations of identity stores. Although the environment could be configured using OVD to present a single interface for managing multiple disparate stores, using directory synchronization profiles can leverage simpler configurations. Furthermore, the existence of multiple stores can be used to provide authentication services depending on the applications integrated into the SSO environment. This chapter served as a description of some of the possibilities.

■ ■ ■

## CHAPTER 13

Identity Manager Policy Administration

Oracle Identity Manager (OIM) serves a large number of functions for managing an organization's identity data. By providing a wide variety of tools to assist administrators, managers, help desk staff, and end users in maintaining a consistent and auditable identity, OIM has become a key tool within the enterprise. OIM policies such as password policies, access policies, and approval policies can assist organizations as they push toward increasing efficiency while maintaining tight security. Using the OIM policies, the system can be configured to allow many combinations of user privileges, including the ability to self-register, request new permissions, manage other users, and grant new privileges.

Access Policies

Most organizations have differing user populations. For instance, managers might have the ability to grant permissions to their employees, help desk employees might be able to unlock or reset user passwords, and user administrators can create, modify, and decommission user accounts. Although OIM allows significant flexibility to various user types, this functionality must be carefully allocated to the proper users to ensure proper security in the overall system. Access policies provide this security by allowing roles to be assigned to individual users, groups of users, or users who match a certain criteria. These options are invaluable in making a manageable setup.

Access policies define what permissions a user has within the system. External customer users may be able to register their account and manage attributes such as passwords and personal information. However, the enterprise might decide not to allow external users to unlock their account without calling the help desk. Help desk users, on the other hand, are usually granted many more permissions. Their access could include the ability to create and decommission accounts. The organization may set up access policies that allow employees to request new permissions, and managers can use the workflow to approve or grant those permissions. OIM provides the framework for the enterprise to set up simple and complex rules governing identity data management.

Sample Access Policy Configuration

If a management tool is difficult to configure or use, the end product could suffer. With identity information, this can result in poor security. OIM ensures configuration of access policies is performed in a standard, easy-to-use manner. Figure 13-1 displays the Identity Manager management screen. On this screen you can manage users, roles, password policies, administration roles, and so on. In the case of access policies, you will be navigating to the Administration Roles. These roles are used to control which users in the LDAP store can perform certain operations.

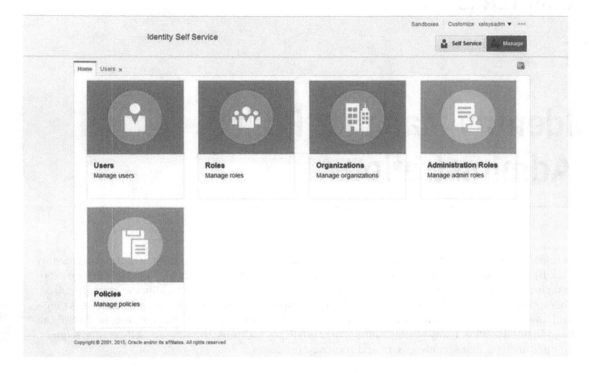

Figure 13-1. Oracle Identity Manager management screen

Figure 13-2 displays the default list of Oracle Identity Manager administration roles provided out of the box. These can be added to and disabled as needed in your environment. At creation none of these roles has members. It is left up to the administrator to determine what groups of users should receive the ability to manage accounts. It should be noted that these are, in effect, templates that can be used to grant permissions to various users and control what data users can see and modify.

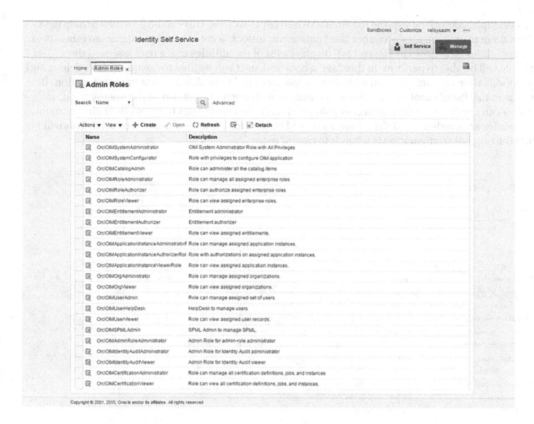

Figure 13-2. *Administration roles*

Editing a role is fairly simple. You are provided with a series of tabs that allow you to edit the basic information, capabilities, membership rules, and the organizations for which it applies. Figure 13-3 displays the tabs available for a given role.

Figure 13-3. *Role management*

In this example, you will be viewing the OrclOIMUserHelpDesk role. This can be provided to help desk staff to allow them to manage user accounts, reset passwords, unlock accounts, and grant roles to other users.

The Capabilities tab, shown in Figure 13-4, displays a list of the abilities that a user assigned the HelpDesk role will be able to perform. In this case, a help desk user will be able to create, update, delete, and otherwise modify user accounts that fall within the scope of control to be discussed later in this section. If for some reason this list of capabilities is not in accordance with the requirements of the organization, an administrator can create a new custom access policy with only the capabilities to match their environment. If custom policies are needed, the default policies should be left alone and new policies created. This will ensure that the original configuration is left as is in case of issues.

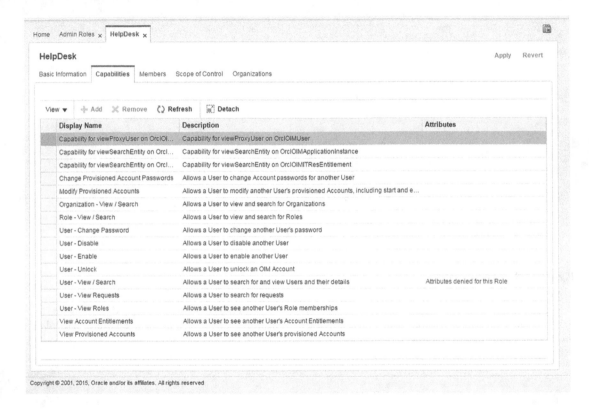

Figure 13-4. *Role capabilities*

Once the access policy is defined and the capabilities configured, the administrator must determine who in the system will be granted the new access. Standard access, such as searching and viewing user information, might be granted to all users. However, the ability to edit accounts might only be granted to a select few. Determining user membership is simple enough: You have options to add users directly to the role or create rules governing membership.

In the example shown in Figure 13-5, the administrator has created a rule that only users that begin with the text HPDSK will be granted the HelpDesk role. In this case, it could be that the help desk employees work for a contractor or are created with the prefix indicating the department for which they work. This rule could easily be modified to be based on other LDAP attributes such as department or employee type. An example of configuring a rule-based membership query is shown in Figure 13-6.

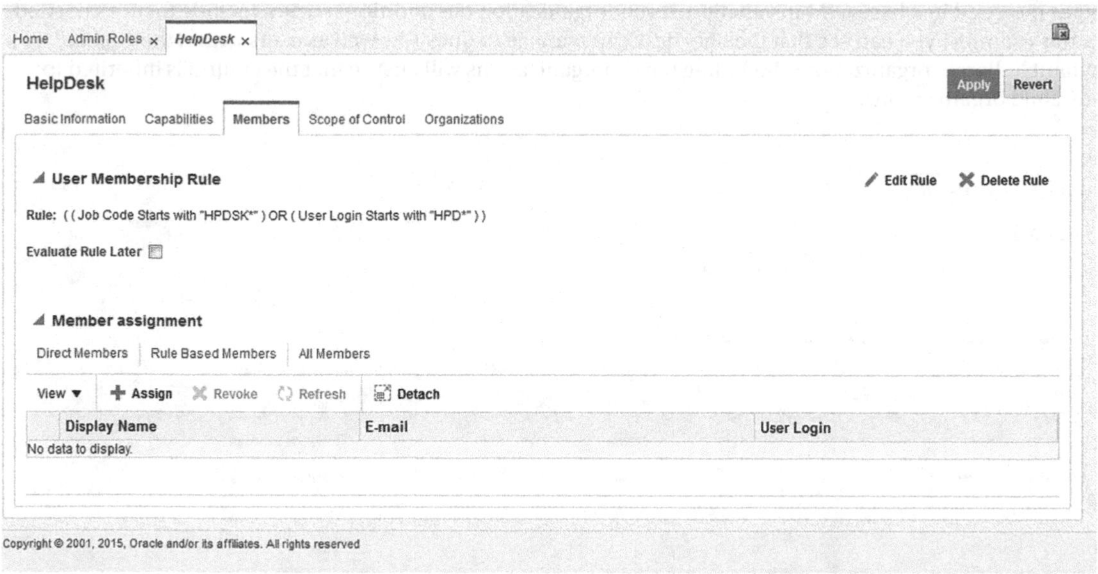

Figure 13-5. *Role membership*

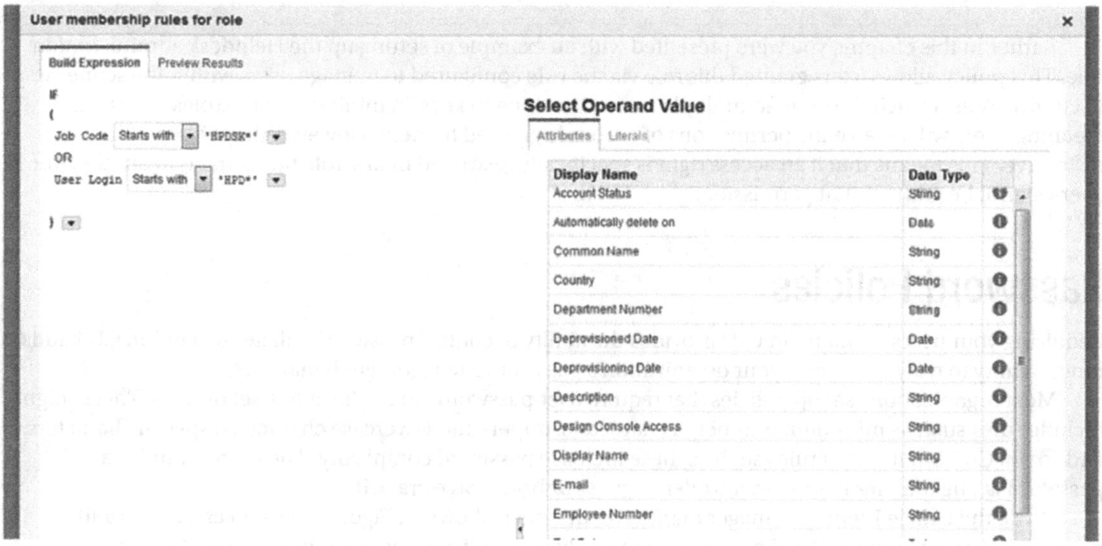

Figure 13-6. *Rule-based role membership query*

Access policies are often granted a scope of control. This is used to define user populations that the role can be used to control. For instance, a requirement might be that the customer support group can only manage external customer accounts, whereas the help desk can only handle internal employee accounts. The Scope of Control tab can be used to specify these rules. It should be noted that if the organization has requirements such as these, additional roles might need to be created for each of the subgroups. In Figure 13-7, you can see that the scope of control for the help desk has been set to include the default user types included in a base OIM installation. If your organization has additional types, include them as needed. In this example, you can see that the help desk can manage Requests as well as users within the Top and default Xellerate organizations. Including the suborganizations will ensure that the control is inherited to any child organizations.

Figure 13-7. *Scope of control*

Earlier in this chapter, you were presented with an example of setting up the Helpdesk administration role. This policy allows users granted this role via the rule configured to manage users within the scope of control. A user might be granted multiple roles. One thing to keep in mind is that the roles will stack, meaning users will receive the permissions of each role granted to them. However, they will remain restrictive. This means that if an access right is specifically restricted in one role but granted in another, the user will not be granted that permission.

Password Policies

Requiring your users to maintain OID provides the ability to control password policies to a point. OIM adds functionality to truly customize your organization's password management behavior.

Most organizations set up policies that require user passwords to conform to a set of rules. These might include rules such as minimum number of characters, upper- and lowercase characters, special characters, and so on. Combinations of rules such as these increase password complexity. The more complex a password is, the tougher it is for an intruder to guess or brute force crack it.

Using the Oracle Identity Manager management screen shown in Figure 13-8, you can create and maintain password policies for the organization by clicking Policies and selecting Password Policies.

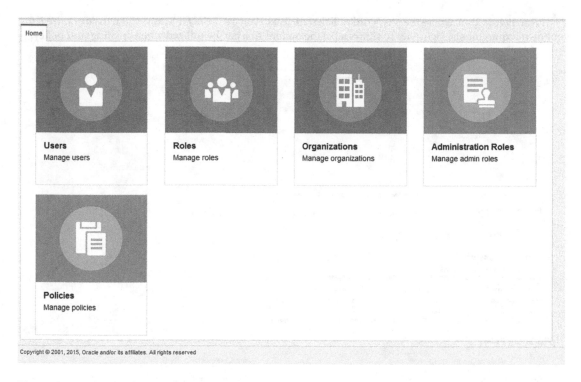

Figure 13-8. Identity Managermanagement screen

After clicking Manage Password Policies, you are presented with a list of the available password policies. You can create new policies or use the default. After creating the password policies, you must assign the policy to the proper user populations. OIM provides the ability to assign different password rules to different user groups based on requirements. For instance, human resources employees might be required to maintain a higher level of password complexity due to the sensitive personal data to which they have access. The list shown in Figure 13-9 displays the default password policy created for OIM users and an example password policy. Although you can modify this password policy, it is recommended that you create your own.

Policy Name	Description	Minimum Length	Minimum Password Age (Days)	Warn After (Days)	Disallow Past Passwords	Expires After (Days)
Default Policy	This is the Default OIM Password Policy	6		113		120
MyOrg_PW_Policy		10	1	75	10	90

Figure 13-9. Password Policies list

From Figure 13-9, where the password policies are listed, you can select one and edit it to customize it for your own requirements. Figure 13-10 shows all of the options that can be utilized when creating your policy.

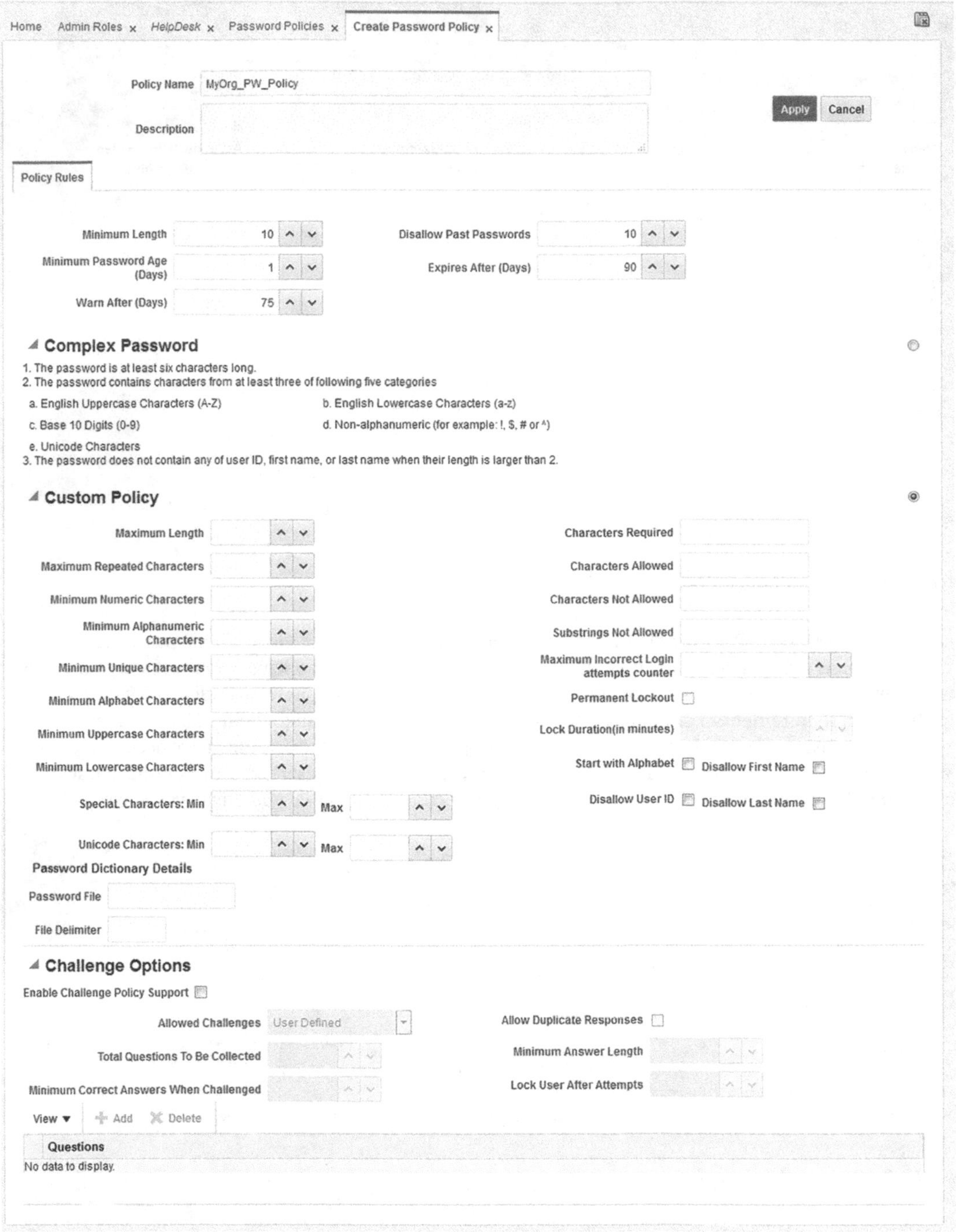

Figure 13-10. *Password policy configuration screen*

When creating the password policy, it is important to note the sections of the screen.

- The first section defines the basic rules of a password.

  - *Minimum Length*: This specifies the number of characters a password must be to pass the complexity rules.

  - *Minimum Password Age (Days)*: This number defines the number of days a user must have the password before changing it again. Use the number 0 to allow password changes on the same day.

  - *Warn After (Days)*: This is the number of days before the system will send out a reminder notification to the user that his or her password will expire. This is usually sent three to five days prior to the expiration.

  - *Disallow Past Passwords*: Enter a number to exclude the user from reusing previous passwords. This is often set to disallow the previous five passwords.

  - *Expires After (Days)*: This number determines the maximum age of a password before the user is forced to change it.

- The second section, Complex Password, can be used to use a preconfigured password complexity rule. It includes the following rules:

  - The password must be at least six characters long.

  - The password must meet three of these five rules:

  - Must contain uppercase characters.

  - Must contain numeric characters.

  - Must contain lowercase characters.

  - Must contain special characters (!@#$%^&*).

  - Must contain Unicode characters.

  - Must not contain the user's login name, first name, or last name.

■ **Note**   It should be noted that the minimum number of characters listed in the default Complex Password selection is actually based on the number of characters defined in the first section of the screen. If you entered 10 characters in that section, the Complex Password rule selection will actually require 10 characters, not six as indicated.

The third section of this configuration page, Custom Policy, allows a full customization of the preceding Complex Rules. It should be noted that you can only use Custom Policy or Complex Password for a single password policy. Here you are able to precisely define the rules you wish to enforce. You could require five uppercase characters and three special characters or more numeric characters. This section provides you with full control of the complexity rules. However, keep in mind that if the password policy is too restrictive, it could result in users writing down passwords.

The final section of the page is Challenge Options. This section is used to configure OIM to allow users to answer one or more challenge questions in case they forget their password or lock their account. This option could help reduce help desk calls dramatically by allowing users to manage their own locked and forgotten passwords.

Click the Enable Challenge Policy Support check box and the configuration options will appear. Here you can configure the system with custom questions that suit your organization's requirements. You could also the users to type in their own questions and answers. After defining the questions, you will also have the options to require users to input unique answers, define the number of characters an answer might be, or both. To further customize this system, you can enter as many questions as you wish, but allow the user to choose and answer a minimum number defined in the total questions to be answered.

Summary

The use of policies within OIM can encompass user permissions and passwords. This allows administrators to configure a secure identity management system while also minimizing the amount of day-to-day management that must be performed. Access policies can be used to control what functions users are permitted to use based on job title, role grants, group membership, and so on. Furthermore these can be used to provide granular access to groups of users. Password policies can help maintain a secure system by ensuring that the user population is leveraging secure complex passwords.

CHAPTER 14

■ ■ ■

Oracle Identity Manager Forms and Customization

In the previous chapters, you have seen that Oracle Identity Manager (OIM) provides a wide variety of tools that the organization can provide to its users, allowing them to be more or less self-sufficient. The use of these tools can eliminate help desk calls and allow faster, more efficient processing of permission requests and on- and off-boarding tasks. These also provide a higher level of security by removing the number of people that must process a request and removing steps in the processes managing accounts. These benefits can be a boon to many organizations, as they can see money saved and increased security. However, out of the box, the many forms available might not meet the look and feel or functionality needs of every organization.

Oracle has provided multiple methods of tailoring OIM to the individual organization. OIM allows a significant amount of customization. These customizations can range from simple logo and color changes, to localization of prompts, to full custom forms and reports. Depending on the individual requirements of an organization, the level of customization will change. In many cases, color changes, logo changes, and page layouts will suffice. Occasionally, the creation of custom forms might be required and can be created using the forms creation utility. There are some cases where an entire custom application or full customization is required and can leverage the OIM application programming interface (API) to create. Using the API to create a custom application is outside the scope of this book. However, this chapter covers customization and using the forms creation utility.

Basic Customization

Customization of OIM falls under a few different levels of complexity. At the most basic, OIM allows administrators to change things like the background colors, logos, and visual components of the various pages. Most of these changes will affect all pages due to how they are performed. The most basic modifications involve changing files such as Cascading Style Sheets (CSS) or replacing image files.

CSS have been used in web development for a long time. These files allow the designer to define items such as fonts, colors, backgrounds, and so on, one time for the project instead of trying to keep track of them on each page in a deployment.

Figure 14-1 displays the OIM Identity Self Service home page. Using a browser tool such as HTTPFox or Google Chrome that enables you to view the elements of a web page will allow you to determine the CSS files, elements, and properties used throughout the page. This information will be key to making changes to the OIM application pages.

© Kenneth Ramey 2016

K. Ramey, *Pro Oracle Identity and Access Management Suite*, DOI 10.1007/978-1-4842-1521-0_14

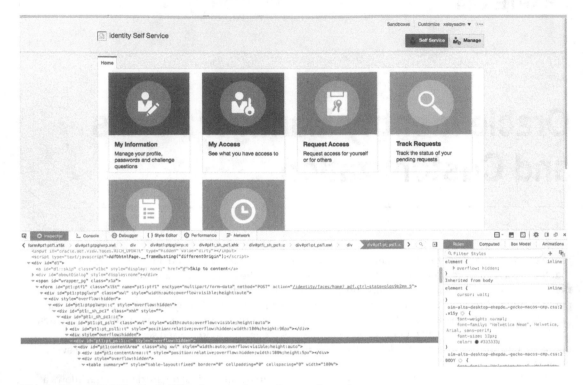

Figure 14-1. *OIM Identity Self Service page inspecting an element*

User Interface Customizations

In its simplest form, customizing the out-of-the-box user interface (UI) can be performed using the online form editing tools and OIM's concept of sandboxes. A sandbox allows editors to make changes to the forms in the current instance without affecting other editors or current users. The changes made in an individual sandbox are limited to that sandbox instance. The changes will be written in line with the live system on publishing the sandbox. Figure 14-2 displays the Oracle Identity Manager home page with the Sandboxes link at the top. Note that you must be logged into the system as a user with edit or administrative permissions to see this link. You can also access this link via the sysadmin console pages.

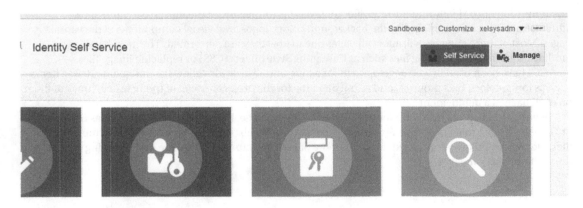

Figure 14-2. *Creating a sandbox*

Clicking the Sandboxes link available to administrators will bring up a screen that displays the currently available sandboxes and their status, as shown in Figure 14-3. On this screen, you can activate a current sandbox, publish an individual one, create a new sandbox, or delete an existing one. Click the Manage Sandboxes tab to view the existing sandboxes. This screen will show the status along with who last modified it. If the sandbox is active, a green light will appear in the Active column.

Figure 14-3. Current sandboxes

To create a new sandbox, click the Create Sandbox link. You will be presented with the Create Sandbox dialog box shown in Figure 14-4. Provide the new sandbox a name and description. If you would like to immediately start to work on customizations, select the Activate Sandbox check box. This will create the new environment and activate it.

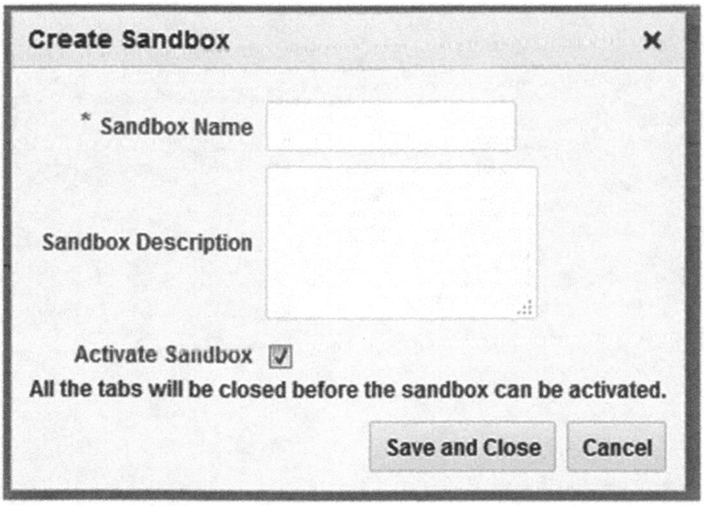

Figure 14-4. Create Sandbox dialog box

291

After creating a new sandbox, you will see it has been activated at the top of the screen. Next to the Sandboxes link, the name of the currently selected sandbox will appear, as shown in Figure 14-5. To customize the page or other pages, click the Customize link.

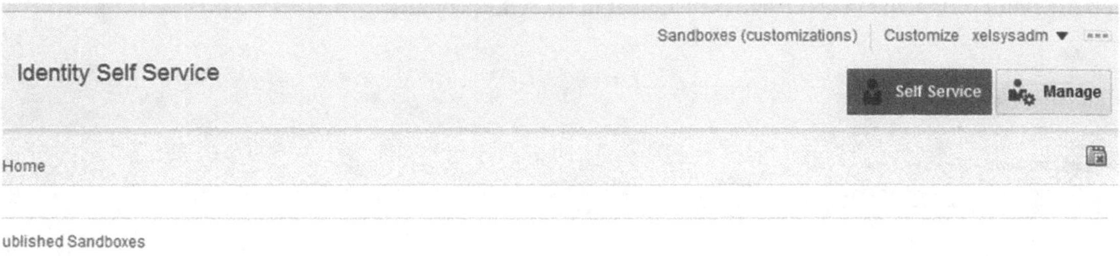

Figure 14-5. *Active sandbox*

Once in a sandbox, you will be able to make a number of changes. It is important to be familiar with the various views. By default you will be presented with Add Content view, depicted in Figure 14-6. This view of the editor will allow you to enter data into the form. This functionality is useful when dealing with multistep forms. In OIM, there are a number of forms that require multiple UI steps, such as the Forgot Password page. You can use the Add Content view to enter data and move to the next page in the process.

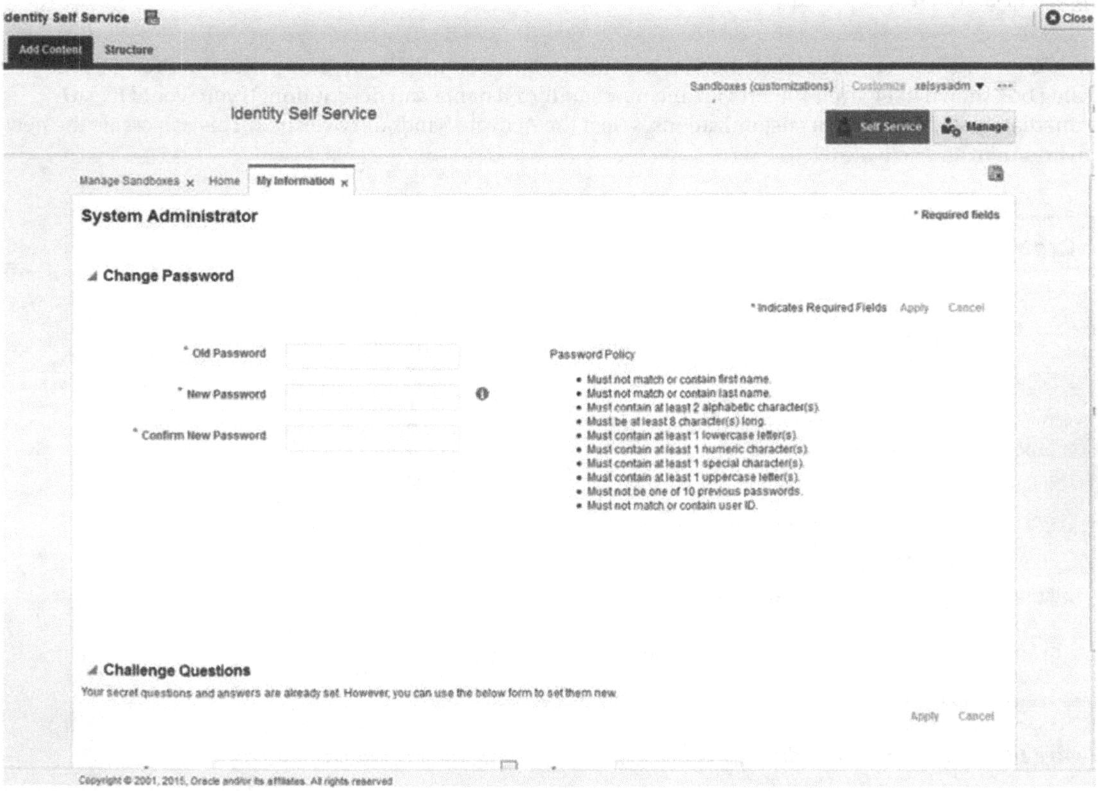

Figure 14-6. *Sandbox customization Add Content view*

After entering required data or data you wish to process using the Add Content screen, you can switch to the Structure view as shown in Figure 14-7. This screen displays both the overall page as well as a tree structure view of the page components. Each of the listed components on the right side of the screen represents an item or an area on the page displayed on the left. Clicking on a page item within the left side of the screen selects the corresponding element in the structure on the right. Using this interface can greatly assist finding the area or element you wish to edit or add to. You can use the structure list on the right to select the element directly.

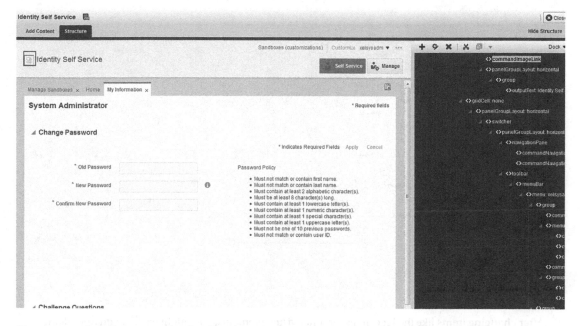

Figure 14-7. Sandbox customization Structure view

Once you have selected an item or area, you can right-click and select Edit. This opens the screen seen in Figure 14-8. In this example, the branding logo was selected. Here you can make a change to the logo to include your company or brand logo file. In Figure 14-8, the properties of the CommandImageLink item that represents the logo are shown. On this screen, you can enter a new value for the file or change other properties. It should be noted that when changing the logo using this method, relative URLs will not work. The value used in the field will default to the /identity/ context root if you do not use a direct URL value. If you do not wish to host a logo elsewhere in your environment such as within the web server, you can put your logo within the self-service application jar file and redeploy the file. However, many organizations decide to host images for their web sites on a content server or other image hosting service.

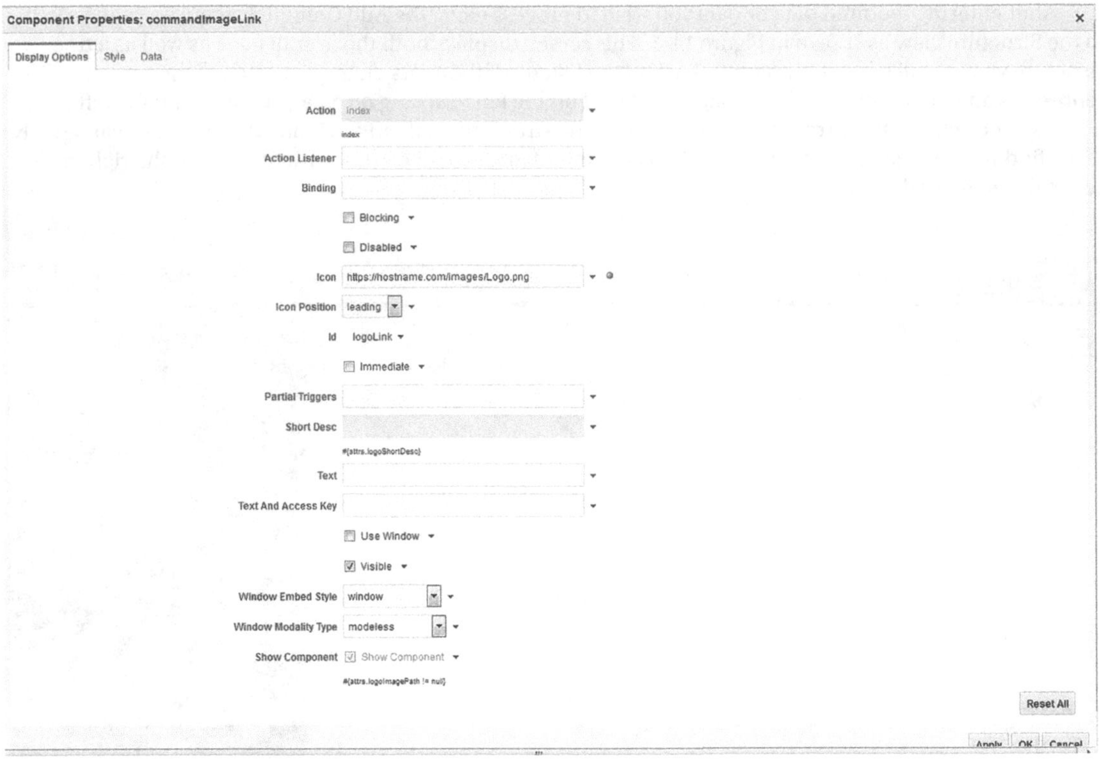

Figure 14-8. *Edit logo image*

After changing items like the logo, lines, or other visual elements, you might wish to add new elements such as hint text or new fields. Much like changing visual elements, you must first locate the region or area you wish to modify. This can be done using the structural pane on the right side or the content area on the left. Note that as you select areas or items on the page, the corresponding structural element will be selected on the right. Depending on where you wish to add the element, you should find the parent container and add it there. You can use the container editor to reorder the items. Figure 14-9 displays the structural pane with a panel selected. In this example, the new element to be added is some help text displayed to guide the user through changing their password. This will be added to the panel form layout that contains the password fields.

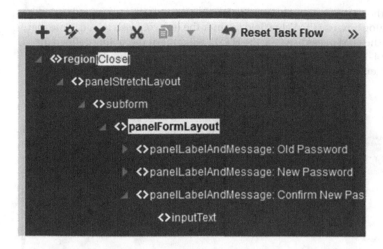

Figure 14-9. *Adding a new element*

After selecting the container in which to add the new element, use the plus on the main menu to bring up the Add Content dialog. Within this dialog box, you can choose from various page components. If you are planning to create data elements, you can use the Data Components. Clicking the Open link on any available component will display the individual components that can be added. In this case, you are adding a text box that can contain HTML markup to display some information for the user. In Figure 14-10, the Add Content dialog box shows a list of the various components that can be added. Expand Web Components and select Text Box.

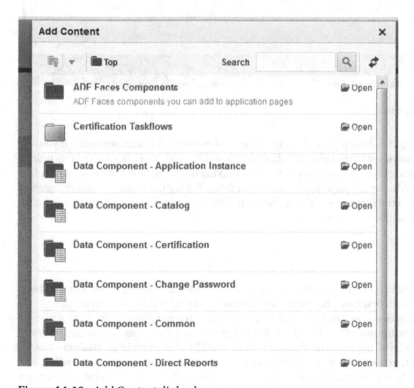

Figure 14-10. *Add Content dialog box*

After selecting the location and the type of content to be added to the page, you are presented with the properties of the new item. In this dialog box, use the Value field to enter the text you wish to add. Note that this field will accept HTML. Because the OIM pages use CSS, the HTML will inherit the styling defined for the rest of the application. In Figure 14-11, the new HTML field has been populated. It should be noted that if you wish to override the standard Identity Manager CSS, you can use the Style tab to enter customized style information.

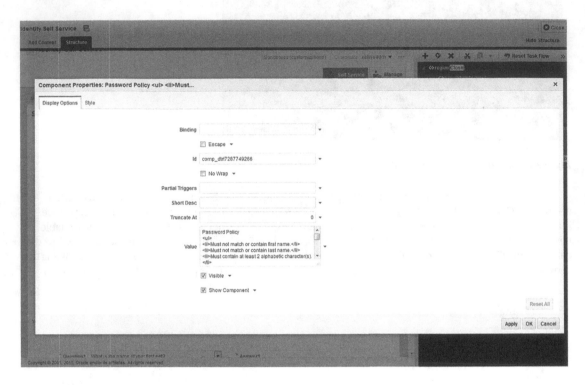

Figure 14-11. *New content properties*

At this point you have changed out the logo and added a text field to the My Information page. If you recall, customizations are all completed within an individual sandbox. The changes created up to this point are only visible when your sandbox is active, and only to the user making the edits. Users of the system still see the standard pages without edits or the previously published edits. Clicking the Publish Sandbox option will merge the changes made into the main line of the application. This functionality is useful for testing and making changes to the UI without affecting current users.

Summary

OIM provides a significant number of forms that can help streamline environments with high turnover, or where organizations wish to put power into their users' hands to handle requests and reset their passwords. This automation and plethora of self-service application forms can greatly reduce the number of help desk calls and administrator assistance. However, the out-of-the-box UI might not meet the requirements of all organizations. As such, Oracle has provided an easy to use sandbox type form editor that allows changes to be made to a live instance without the fear of affecting users with an untested change. The system allows developers to make changes in the sandbox and test those changes. Only when the sandbox is actually published will the changes go into the live system. This chapter demonstrated two types of commonly made changes to the UI.

■ ■ ■

## CHAPTER 15

Integrating Access Manager with E-Business Suite

A large number of organizations have an investment in Oracle E-Business Suite (EBS) along with auxiliary applications and products such as Oracle WebCenter Content and Imaging, Oracle Business Intelligence, and Service-Oriented Architecture (SOA) Suite. In an effort to increase user productivity while maintaining a high level of security, Oracle Access Manager (OAM) enables single sign-on (SSO) capabilities, tying these products together so that users are not prompted to log in throughout the day as they move from one application to another.

Architecture

Oracle EBS has been designed to integrate with Oracle Internet Directory (OID) serving as its identity store. This configuration allows the use of OAM to provide SSO capabilities. EBS administrators will be aware that the suite houses its own user store in the form of the FND_USER table. In an SSO environment, the EBS users are synchronized with OID by events raised by the workflow-based Business Event System.

OAM uses agents called AccessGates to integrate with EBS. These, along with Access Manager WebGates, discussed earlier, are used to provide a seamless transition from log in to application.

There is a flow of operations that occurs within an OAM integrated EBS environment. As the HTTP server receives an EBS request, the OAM WebGate intercepts the request and routes it to OAM. On receipt of the request, OAM determines if the resource is protected and the level of authentication and authorization required. Although OAM provides the credential collection, it hands off the credentials to OID for authentication. The overall process is detailed as follows:

1. A user attempts to access one of the Oracle EBS resources using a browser and is redirected to the EBS AccessGate.

2. The AccessGate is protected by Oracle HTTP Server (OHS) with WebGate.

3. The HTTP server and WebGate check for an existing authenticated session. If a session exists, the user is allowed to access EBS. If no session exists, the request is routed to OAM.

4. OAM performs credential collection.

5. OAM validates the submitted user credentials against the identity store.

6. OAM provides the user information to the Oracle EBS AccessGate.

© Kenneth Ramey 2016

K. Ramey, *Pro Oracle Identity and Access Management Suite*, DOI 10.1007/978-1-4842-1521-0_15

7. The EBS AccessGate submits the user information and request to the EBS database.

8. The Oracle EBS database checks for a user in EBS that is linked to the identity store user.

9. If no linked OID user is found, the user is redirected to the EBS linking page to associate his or her Oracle EBS username.

10. The originally requested resource is returned with a valid authenticated Oracle EBS user session.

Prepare EBS AccessGate Files

After downloading the Oracle EBS AccessGate files, available in Patch 13704814, unzip them to $MW_HOME/appsutil/accessgate/{instance}. For example:

```
mkdir -p $MW_HOME/appsutil/accessgate/ebsAG
cd $MW_HOME/appsutil/accessgate/ebsAG
unzip [location to patch 13704814]/p13704814_R12_GENERIC.zip
```

The AccessGate zip file contains the required files for configuring the AccessGate for EBS. These files will be referenced later in the configuration steps.

- *fndauth.war*: This is the Oracle EBS AccessGate application that will be deployed within the managed server created in the next steps.

- *fndext.jar*: This file contains Java libraries required to enable communication between application servers and the EBS database.

- *txkEBSAuth.xml*: This is an ANT script that is used to help automate the deployment of Oracle AccessGate.

- *fndauth_deployment_plan.tmp*: This is a template file used in the deployment automation tool.

- *LogConfig.properties*: This file can be used as an example for setting up logging.

- *samplecleanup.html*: This is an example HTML file used to clean up session information after an EBS logout.

Create EBS AccessGate Installation Directory

The Oracle EBS AccesGate must be installed within the Middleware Home directory. From the command line, create a directory for AccessGate at $MW_HOME/appsutil/accessgate/ebsAG. If you used a different instance name for your AccessGate, replace ebsAG with that name. Next, copy AccessGate files to new instance directory. The MW_HOME directory, in this case, is the Middleware installation where OAM is installed.

Prepare EBS and OID

Prior to beginning the integration process, you should ensure that the necessary patches and updates are applied on both the EBS and Oracle Identity and Access Management environments. Check with Oracle support to plan and implement the required compatible updates.

Register EBS Home with OAM

The first step of integrating EBS with OAM is to register the EBS home with OAM. This must occur prior to attempting to integrate OID. Registering the instance is only required to occur once per EBS deployment. This is true even within multiple-node instances of EBS.

■ **Note**   You must register the EBS Home with OAM before attempting to integrate with OID.

To begin, run the txkrun.pl script located within the EBS FND_HOME directory.

```
$FND_TOP/bin/txkrun.pl -script=SetSSOReg -registerinstance=yes -infradbhost=10.0.70.221
-ldapport=3060 -ldapportssl=3131 -ldaphost=10.0.70.229 -oidadminuserpass=*****
-appspass=*****
```

In this command, set the parameters as described in Table 15-1.

Table 15-1. SSO Registration Parameters

Parameter	Description
-script	SetSSOReg sets up the txkrun.pl script to run the register process for EBS instance with OID.
-registerinstance	Set this to yes to ensure the EBS instance is registered.
-infradbhost	This parameter should be set to the OID database host name. Note that this is not the same as the EBS database.
-ldapport	Set this to the non-Secure Sockets Layer (SSL) Lightweight Directory Access Protocol (LDAP) port.
-ldapportssl	Set this to the SSL LDAP port of OID.
-ldaphost	Set this to the hostname of the server on which OID is running.
-oidadminuserpass	Enter the orcladmin password here.
-appspass	Enter the EBS apps database administrator (DBA) password.

Register EBS with OID

After successful completion of registering the EBS instance with OAM, you can continue with registering EBS and OAM. To do this, you will run the same txkrun.pl as in the previous step.

```
$FND_TOP/bin/txkrun.pl -script=SetSSOReg -registeroid=yes -ldaphost=10.0.70.229
-ldapport=3060 -oidadminuserpass=***** -appspass=***** -instpass=***** -provisiontype=4
```

Table 15-2 shows the parameters set by this script.

Table 15-2. *OAM Registration Parameters*

Parameter	Description
-script	SetSSOReg sets up the `txkrun.pl` script to run the register process for EBS instance with OID.
-registeroid	Set this flag to yes to register EBS with OID.
-ldaphost	Set this to the OID hostname. This should be set to the actual hostname, not a VIP if you are using a load balancer
-ldapport	Set this to the LDAP port used by the OID instance.
-oidadminuserpass	This should be set to the orcladmin password or other administrative password.
-appspass	Set this to the Apps DBA password.
-instpass	This should be set to the same as the OID Adminstrator password.
-provisiontype	This value can be set to values 1, 2, 3, or 4. In this case set the value to 4 for Bi-Directional – No Creation Provisioning. Other values are: 1. Bi-Directional Provisioning: This is the default value. 2. In-Bound Provisioning: EBS to OID. 3. Out-Bound Provisioning: OID to EBS. 4. Bi-Directional, No Provisioning

After completing this step, the EBS middle tier services must be restarted.

Create EBS Connection User

After registering the EBS home with OAM and registering EBS with OID, it is time to create the required local EBS users for connection to OID. The new EBS user should be created with the UMS/Apps schema permissions. Once you have created this user, use the EBS Local Login to log in and reset the new user's password. Validate that the user can connect to EBS and has the proper role: UMX|Apps Schema Connect.

Configure EBS AccessGate

Because Oracle EBS uses a number of cookies and session information, configuration of the EBS AccessGate requires that it be installed within the same domain as the middle-tier servers used by EBS itself. In the example, the .example.com cookie domain was created. Ensure that the AccessGate is installed using the same information necessary for your environment.

Create Managed Servers for AccessGate

During the configuration of OAM, the WebLogic Server (WLS) domain was created for OAM. As such, you can use the same WLS and domain for the new AccessGate. After logging into the OAM WLS Administration Console, navigate to Environment ➤ Clusters, and create a new cluster. Assign the cluster a name appropriate to your environment. In this case, the name ebsAG_cluster is used. Use the following values to configure the cluster parameters.

- *Messaging mode*: Unicast.

- *Unicast broadcast channel*: Leave blank.

- *Multicast Address*: Use the default value.

- *Multicast Port*: Use the default value.

Once the new cluster has been created, it is time to configure the managed servers. Navigate to Environment ➤ Servers. On the list of existing managed servers, click New. Populate the fields with the following values:

- *Server Name*: ebsAG_server1

- *Server Listen Host*: <OAM host name>

- *Server Listen Port*: 17043 or other open post

- *Cluster*: Choose the cluster name created in the previous step.

After creating the managed server, edit the new server and assign it to an existing machine.

■ **Note** When creating this in a clustered environment, make sure you create two managed servers and assign each to the appropriate machine within the cluster.

Copy Artifact Files

Earlier in this chapter, you downloaded the AccessGate files and created the installation directory. You were presented with the files that are included in the downloaded zip file. Here, you will copy the files into the proper locations within the installation directory created.

First, copy samplecleanup.html from the $MW_HOME/appsutil/accessgate/ebsAG/sample directory to the /public directory created within the htdocs location within the OHS installation. Rename the file oacleanup.html as follows:

```
cp $MW_HOME/appsutil/accessgate/ebsAG/sample/samplecleanup.html
<OHS_HOME>/instances/instance1/config/OHS/ohs1/htdocs/public/oacleanup.html
```

After the file has been copied to the proper directory, access it using a web browser. Navigate to http://10.0.70.229:7777/public/oacleanup.html.

Because this page is not an OAM protected resource, you should be able to access it without being prompted for login information. However, this page will appear empty. This URL is used in the upcoming steps where you will deploy the actual WebGate and configure a centralized logout page.

Next you will copy the fndext.jar file to the OAM lib directory. Perform the following commands to complete this.

```
cp $MW_HOME/appsutil/accessgate/ebsAG/fndext.jar $MW_HOME/user_projects/domains/
OAMDomain/lib
```

Restart the OAM managed servers and Administration Server to pick up the new fndext.jar file you copied to the lib directory.

Generate DBC File in EBS

EBS uses a Database Connection (DBC) file to create a connection pool for the AccessGate to use for connecting to EBS. In this section, you use the EBS AdminDesktop utility to generate the required DBC file.

Set up the environment variables and ensure that JAVA_HOME is set to the OAM instance JAVA directory. Use the following command to generate the DBC file for your instance.

```
java oracle.apps.fnd.security.AdminDesktop apps/<apps password> CREATE NODE_NAME=10.0.70.229
DBC=$FND_SECURE/ebsAG.dbc
```

In the preceding command, the NODE_NAME is the host of the OAM instance. For easier reference in environments with multiple EBS AccessGates, name the DBC file something related to the AccessGate and EBS instance. Copy the generated file to the OAM server under the directory where EBS AccessGate was installed, in this case <MW_HOME>/appsutil/accessgate/ebsAG.

Add EBS AccessGate Host to List of External Tables

During the deployment of the EBS AccessGate, a Java database connectivity (JDBC) connection was defined. By default, the EBS database does not allow communication from an external machine. To allow this, the WLS hosting the OAM AccessGate must be registered within the EBS database as a trusted machine. To do this, you will use the EBS Java Development Kit (JDK).

For security purposes, Oracle recommends Internet Protocol (IP) address restriction to prevent unauthorized access. By adding the EBS AccessGate hostname to the EBS profile, you can set up the proper restrictions. Set the FND_SERVER_DESKTOP_USER profile at the User level to the list of hostnames that contain the AccessGate. It should be noted that this value can accept a comma-separated list of external machines. Failure to perform this step could lead to invalid username/password errors when users attempt to authenticate.

Use txkEBSAuth.xml to Deploy AccessGate

You have configured the necessary components to set up the AccessGate. As part of those steps, you staged the software, registered the AccessGate host, configured an AccessGate cluster and managed servers, and set up the Middleware Home directory structure. It is now time to deploy the AccessGate application using the WLST utility.

Before starting, it is important to ensure the environment variables are set correctly. Failure to do this can cause configuration issues. You can run setDomainEnv.sh located in the $DOMAIN_HOME/bin directory to perform this step:

```
. ./setDomainEnv.sh
```

You can also set the environment variables manually:

```
export MW_HOME=/home/oracle/OAMMiddleware
export DOMAIN_HOME=$MW_HOME/user_projects/domains/oam_domain
```

Next set up the WLST environment using setWLSEnv.sh located in the WLS home directory.

```
$MW_HOME/wlserver_10.3/server/bin/setWLSEnv.sh
```

Change to the directory where you installed Oracle EBS AccessGate in the previous step; for example:

```
cd $MW_HOME/appsutil/accessgate/ebsAG
```

Deploying the EBS AccessGate requires that you create a data source for the managed server to use. Performing this step utilizes ANT and the txkEBSAuth.xml template discussed earlier. This file is located in the AccessGate installation directory. When running the following command, it should be noted that it could take a significant amount of time to complete. Let the process run without interruption. At the end, you will see a completion message.

```
ant -f txkEBSAuth.xml createDataSource \
  -Dwlshosturl=10.0.70.229:17001 \
  -DdataSourceName=EBS_DS \
  -DdataSourceJNDIName=jndi/EBS_DS \
  -DasadminUser=OAM_EBS_USER \
  -DdbcFile=$MW_HOME/appsutil/accessgate/ebsAG/ebsAG.dbc \
  -DserverName=ebsAG_server1 \
  -DdeploymentName=ebsauth_dev \
  -DfndauthWarFile=$MW_HOME/appsutil/accessgate/ebsAG/fndauth.war \
  -DplanPath=$MW_HOME/appsutil/accessgate/ebsAG/plan/Plan.xml \
  -DSSOServerRelease=11 \
  -DSSOServerURL=http://10.0.70.229:14100 \
  -DWebgateLogoutURL=http://10.0.70.229:7777/public/oacleanup.html
```

Build Successful: 38 minutes, 29 seconds

The command will be saved within the instance home. The full path and filename are:

```
$MW_HOME/appsutil/accessgate/EBS_DB/createDS.sh.
```

Once the data source has been created, you will use the WLS Administration Console to target the data source to the proper managed servers within the environment. Use a browser to navigate to the OAM WebLogic Admin Console. Go to http://10.0.70.229:17001/console, and log in using the weblogic user.

Once in the WebLogic Admin Console, navigate to Services ➤ Data Sources. Select the new data source called EBS_DS. Click the Targets tab and select the new ebsAG managed server created previously. Once done, click Save to finalize the configuration. No restarts should be necessary at this step.

After ensuring the data source has been configured and targeted to the proper managed server, you can deploy the AccessGate application on WLS. Again, you will use ANT to perform this step; for example:

```
ant -f txkEBSAuth.xml deployApplication \
  -Dwlshosturl=10.0.70.229:17001 \
  -DdataSourceName=EBS_DS \
  -DdataSourceJNDIName=jndi/EBS_DS \
  -DasadminUser=OAM_EBS_USER \
  -DdbcFile=$MW_HOME/appsutil/accessgate/ebsAG/ebsAG.dbc \
  -DserverName=ebsag_server1 \
  -DdeploymentName=ebsauth_dev \
  -DfndauthWarFile=$MW_HOME/appsutil/accessgate/ebsAG/fndauth.war \
  -DplanPath=$MW_HOME/appsutil/accessgate/ebsAG/plan/Plan.xml \
  -DSSOServerRelease=11 \
  -DSSOServerURL=http://10.0.70.229:14100 \
  -DWebgateLogoutURL=http://10.0.70.229:7777/public/oacleanup.html
```

This command is interactive. Although you can provide the values inside the command, it is recommended that you run it interactively and enter the values as prompted to prevent entering the password in clear text and prevent typographical errors that could cause implementation issues. Use Table 15-3 as a reference to enter the script variables as prompted.

Table 15-3. *AccessGate Deployment Parameters*

Script Variable	Description
-dDeploymentName	Enter a value that can be used to identify the application deployment. In this case, the value is prepended with ebsauth_ then has the EBS instance being used, dev. This value will also be used as the context root to be protected by the WebGate.
-DasadminUser	Enter the EBS user created previously with the UMX/APPS schema connect permission. You should ensure that you can log in locally with this user in EBS.
-DasadminPassword	This is an optional parameter when running the script. For security reasons, you might decide not to include it. If you do not include it in the command, you will be prompted for it when the command is run.
-DWebGateLogoutURL	This value should be set to the complete URL to the oacleanup.html file created earlier. For example, this should be entered as http://10.0.70.229:7777/public/oacleanup.html. Do not use a relative URL.
-DOAMLogoutURL	Enter the complete URL for the OAM global logout; for example, http://10.0.70.229:7777/oam/server/logout.
-DserverName	Set this value to the deployment server you are using within the WebLogic environment. In the previous step, you created a managed server. As a best practice, do not deploy anything to the Admin Server. It is best to use a dedicated managed server. In this case use ebsag_server1.
-Dwlspwd	Enter the weblogic user password when prompted. Although you can include this in the command, it is best to not include the clear text password in the command.

The Oracle EBS AccessGate application has now been deployed within the OAM WLS environment. You have also created the necessary data sources to support the application. The application has been configured to know how to connect to EBS using the admin user.

Validate the AccessGate Application Deployment

After configuring the Oracle EBS AccessGate application resources and deploying the application to the managed server, it is recommended that you validate the operation and check for any misconfigurations before continuing. If you see any problems, this is the time to correct them. To verify the application settings, you can use the OAM WLS Administration Console located at http://<hostname>:<adminserver_port>/console; for example, http://10.0.70.229:17001/console.

Once logged into the WLS Administration Console, navigate to Environment ➤ Servers, and ensure the newly created EBS AccessGate managed server ebsag_server1 is running on the specified port.

Next, check the data source created for the EBS AccessGate managed server. Using the left side menu, go to Services ➤ DataSources, and check that the DataSource that you created during deployment (e.g., ebsAG_ds) exists, and is targeted to the correct managed server (e.g., ebsag_server1). Click the data source link to review the settings. Within the Settings view, use the Connection Pool tab to ensure the values for

Properties user and dbcFile are correct according to those specified in the deployment parameters. You should also ensure that the data source is enabled and running using the Monitoring tab. If desired, on the Monitoring tab, you can also use the Testing utility to test the connection.

After validating the managed server and data source, navigate to Deployments, and look for the Oracle EBS AccessGate application named ebsauth_dev. It should be deployed, in Active state, and OK health. If this is not the case, try to stop and start the deployment. Check the WLS logs for any errors that might indicate a configuration issue.

If all of the components are up and running, you should be able to access the AccessGate URL using a browser. Navigate to http://<hostname>:<EBSAccessGatePort>/<accessgatename>/ssologout_callback; for example, http://10.0.70.229:17043/ebsauth_dev/ssologout_callback. If successful, you will see an empty page. Check the server for issues if you receive any error pages.

Configure Resources in Oracle Access Manager

After configuring the AccessGate application, it is time to configure OAM and the appropriate WebGates to protect the EBS application URLs. For this you will use the OAM oamadmin screens shown in Figure 15-1. After using a browser to log in to the OAMConsole, navigate to the Application Security Launch Pad and click Application Domains to retrieve the list of domains currently configured. You will use the WebGate domain created earlier in this book. Within this domain, you will create new resources to be protected by OAM.

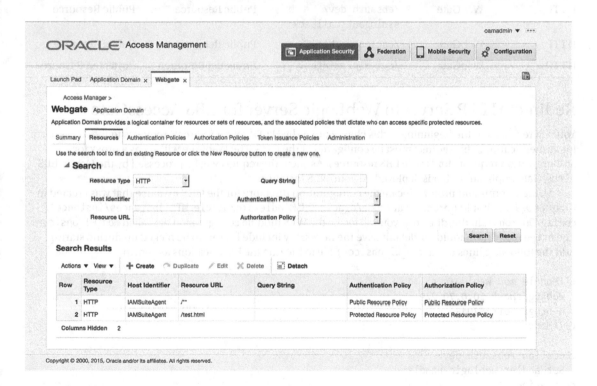

Figure 15-1. *Oracle Access Manager WebGate configuration*

The new resources should be configured as shown in Table 15-4.

Table 15-4. *Protected and Public Resources for EBS Integration*

Resource Type	Host Identifier	Resource URL	Authentication Policy	Authorization Policy
HTTP	WebGate	/**	Public Resource	Public Resource
HTTP	WebGate	/public/index.html	Public Resource	Public Resource
HTTP	WebGate	/excluded/index/html	Excluded	Excluded
HTTP	WebGate	/ebsauth_dev/	Protected Resource	Protected Resource
HTTP	WebGate	/ebsauth_dev/…/*	Protected Resource	Protected Resource
HTTP	WebGate	/ebsauth_dev/ OAMLogin.jsp	Public Resource	Public Resource
HTTP	WebGate	/ebsauth_dev/style/	Public Resource	Public Resource
HTTP	WebGate	/ebsauth_dev/style/…/*	Public Resource	Public Resource
HTTP	WebGate	/ebsauth_dev/ ssologout.do	Public Resource	Public Resource
HTTP	WebGate	/ebsauth_dev/ ssologout_callback	Public Resource	Public Resource
HTTP	WebGate	/oacleanup.html	Public Resource	Public Resource
HTTP	WebGate	/cgi-bin/printenv	Protected Resource	Protected Resource

Redirect HTTP Server to WebLogic Server for EBS AccessGate

You will recall, from the beginning of this chapter, that the HTTP server redirects requests to the AccessGate for authentication. This redirect must be configured at the OHS. The WebGate will act as a proxy for authentication requests for Oracle EBS resources. As such, the request will be processed by the Oracle EBS AccessGate application that is deployed on your WLS instance.

Using a command prompt, locate the configuration directory for the OHS instance that was created in Chapter 9. This should be located at /home/oracle/OHSMiddleware/Oracle_WT1/instances/instance1/config/OHS/ohs1. In this directory, you will locate the WLS module configuration file called mod_wl_ohs.conf. The httpd.conf file should, by default have the necessary include for this to be picked up during startup. Add the following lines to the mod_wl_ohs.conf file to include the EBS locations as shown.

```
<IfModule mod_weblogic.c>
  WebLogicHost 10.0.70.229
  WebLogicPort 17043
</IfModule>

<Location /ebsauth_dev>
  SetHandler weblogic-handler
</Location>
```

This entry configures the OHS to redirect requests for EBS authentication to the managed server with the AccessGate deployment. Ensure the WebLogicHost and WebLogicPort point to the correct location for the installation. Restart OHS.

You should now be able to access the Oracle ECBS AccessGate resource via your HTTP server and WebGate from your browser; for example, `http://10.0.70.229:7777/ebsauth_dev/ssologout_callback`.

This URL was configured within the OAM Application Domain Resources under the Public Resource Policies. As such, you should not be prompted for authentication at this point. OHS is now configured to proxy the EBS AccessGate application deployment as the authentication service provider.

Configure Centralized Logout

You might recall that OAM acts as a credential collection agent and authenticates the user against the configured identity store, in this case OID. When a user logs in to a protected resource, OAM creates the required sessions and cookies necessary to ensure a seamless transition to other protected resources and provides the SSO environment. During the logout process, OAM cleans up its own session information. However, it does not clean up partner application sessions. Thus, a user might be logged out of OAM, but the Oracle EBS session cookies might remain until the browser is completely closed. The AccessGate software installation provides the files necessary to ensure the EBS session information is cleaned up during a logout operation for increased security. Configuring a centralized logout will ensure the cleanup is performed and EBS sessions are eliminated when a user logs out of the SSO application.

Configure the Cleanup File for Logout

When you extracted the EBS AccessGate zip file, you were provided a file called `oacleanup.html`. During the deployment, you copied this file to the `/public` subdirectory within the OHS `htdocs` directory. Locate the file and use a text editor to update the context root as needed to ensure the script is called properly.

Find the following line within `oacleanup.html`:

```
<script type="text/javascript" src='/CONTEXT_ROOT/ssologout_callback?mode=cleanup'></script>
```

Update the entry by replacing `<CONTEXT_ROOT>` with the name of the resource configured in OAM. This should match the name of the managed server; for example,

```
<script type="text/javascript" src='/ebsauth_dev/ssologout_callback?mode=cleanup'></script>
```

Configure Additional Logout Callbacks

Some environments might have multiple EBS AccessGate instances or additional applications for which you might wish to perform a session cleanup after logout. If this is the case, you can add a callback for each additional AccessGate or custom application as follows. Search the `oacleanup.html` file for the following line:

```
function doLoad()
```

Add the callback for additional applications.

```
logoutHandler.addCallback('/<AccessGateInstance>/ssologout_callback');
logoutHandler.addCallback('http://webgatehost2.example.com:7777/<AccessGateInstance>
/ssologout_callback');
```

During the logout process, this ensures that the AccessGate calls the cleanup process to destroy Oracle EBS sessions. The OAM centralized logout should also include the cleanup for other partner applications protected by the OAM configuration.

In this example, the Oracle 11g WebGate has been used. As such, the 11g WebGate Logout Callback URL can be leveraged for a centralized logout process. Use the OAM Console Administration screens to set the URL for Logout Callback.

In the OAM Administration Console, click the System Configuration tab. In the Access Manager section, click the SSO Agents node and then select OAM Agents. Click Search and select the SSO agent created previously. Figure 15-2 shows the configuration parameters that are used when setting up the SSO Agent Webgate.

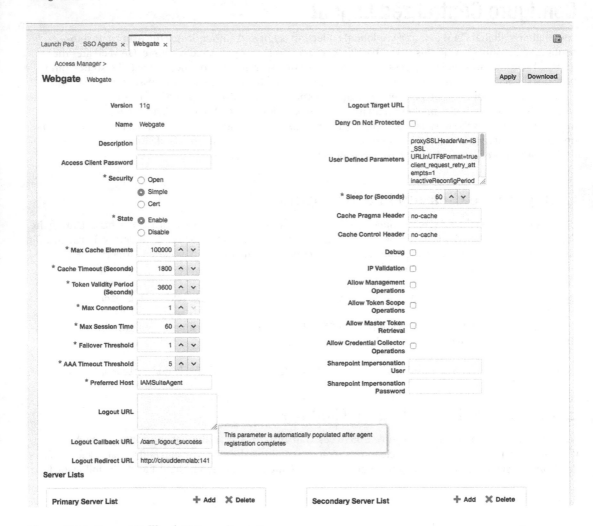

Figure 15-2. *Logout Callback URL configuration*

Set the value of the Logout Callback URL to http://<ebshost>.<domain>:<port>/OA_HTML/ AppsLogout.

This concludes the configuration of the OAM and AccessGate centralized logout process.

EBS Profile Configuration

After configuring the Oracle EBS AccessGate application and OAM resources, it is necessary to set up the login profiles within the actual EBS environment. Set the Oracle EBS profile options in Table 15-5, or have the EBS administrator set them.

Table 15-5. *EBS Profile Configuration Parameters*

Profile	Level	Value
Application Authenticate Agent (APPS_AUTH_AGENT)	Site	`http://<webgatehost>:<port>/ebsauth_dev/`
Applications SSO Type (APPS_SSO)	Site	`SSWA w/SSO`
Applications Single Sign On Hint Cookie (APPS_SSO_HINT_COOKIE_NAME)	Site	`<blank> (null)` This should be null; if there is a value such as `ORASSO_AUTH_HINT`, remove it.

Restart the applications services on your Oracle EBS middle tier, and then restart Oracle EBS AccessGate deployment WLS and managed servers.

Test E-Business Suite Single Sign-On

Now that all of the necessary components have been deployed and configured, and you have set up the Oracle EBS profiles for SSO, you can test the overall environment. Previously, you have set up a test URL for ensuring that the proper authentication mechanisms were in place. For this step, you will attempt to log in to the Oracle EBS system and subsequently log in to another protected resource. If everything is working, you should only be prompted one time for authentication within the browser session. Additional requests to protected resources should use the existing session information and cookies. On logout, all session information should be cleaned up and subsequent requests will be prompted for authentication. Use a browser to navigate to the EBS login.

```
http://<ebshost>.<domain>:<port>/OA_HTML/AppsLogin
```

According to the steps described at the beginning of this chapter, you should be redirected to the OAM authentication page. Using a set of valid credentials that exist in the identity store, log in. After successful authentication, you should be redirected to your Oracle EBS home page.

It should be noted that only users who have the Local Login Allowed profile within EBS will be able to log in using the EBS Local Login. This is helpful for administrative users and troubleshooting.

Summary

In this chapter, you were presented with the order of operations and data flow that exists when you integrate Oracle EBS and OAM. It should be noted that to integrate OID and EBS, OAM is required, as this integration utilizes the EBS AccessGate deployment. This chapter provided the steps required to instantiate a single AccessGate on a single node supporting a single EBS instance. These steps can be modified to support a clustered environment, providing higher availability and fault tolerance if one of your AccessGate managed servers happen to go down. Multiple AccessGate deployments can also be used to support multiple EBS instances.

■ ■ ■

## CHAPTER 16

Troubleshooting and Common Issues

You have followed Oracle's documentation to ensure that your environment meets a certified environment. Your operating system (OS) is up to date and the system requirements have been met. You run the installation software and things are looking good. All of a sudden the installer seems to hang. In the words of Douglas Adams, "Don't panic."

Considering the number of components that must be installed, patched, configured, and then integrated to make a successful implementation of the Oracle Identity and Access Management Suite, there is a chance that you will run into issues. These issues might crop up during installation and initial configuration; they could also come to the surface while you are attempting to integrate the components with each other or with other applications. No matter when you run into issues, they can be frustrating and sometimes no solution will be apparent. Many times there is a patch that was missed or a simple typographical error in a configuration file. Some issues are an easy fix, whereas others could require significant research. The aim of this chapter is to provide a list of some common issues and resolutions as well as a few uncommon problems that an implementer might need to resolve. These come from a compilation of many installations and notes from colleagues.

Installation Problems

The beginning of this book introduced you to the various components that make up Oracle's Identity and Access Management Suite. Following that, you were presented with the installation procedure for each of the main components to make the environment work. Although installation might seem fairly straightforward, it is not uncommon to run into a few issues. If you are not too far into the process, it can be easy enough to restart the installation software. However, at this stage, you are likely to run into the problem again unless you have taken steps to resolve the underlying issue.

During the installation stage, you are laying down the application binaries. The Oracle Universal Installer will check your OS to ensure that it meets the minimum specifications. The most commonly encountered issues are found during this precheck. Ideally you have already checked to make sure you have the proper OS packages installed. However, there is a large list and if any are missing, the Oracle Universal Installer will point them out for you to resolve. If you have root or sudo access, these issues can be easy to resolve. Dependent on your chosen OS, you can just install them and continue.

Using UNIX-based systems, you can either use yum to install a missing package or download the missing package rpm files and install. Note that this will require either sudo or root access. Installing missing packages from rpm files can be a lengthy process, as you will need to find the package and all required packages to install them properly. Most times a package installation tool such as yum will perform the download and installation of all required packages. Missing OS packages are some of the easiest problems

© Kenneth Ramey 2016

K. Ramey, *Pro Oracle Identity and Access Management Suite*, DOI 10.1007/978-1-4842-1521-0_16

to diagnose and resolve. See Table 16-1 for a list of the required packages for each of the main components covered in this book. Depending on your environment, these packages might need to be installed on all of your servers, or only select servers, depending on the components installed on each.

Table 16-1. *Oracle Identity Management Operating System Package Requirements*

Identity Management Component	Required Components
Oracle Internet Directory 11.1.1.9	binutils-2.20.51.0.2-5.28.el6 compat-libcap1-1.10-1 compat-libstdc++-33-3.2.3-69.el6 for x86_64 compat-libstdc++-33-3.2.3-69.el6 for i686 gcc-4.4.4-13.el6 gcc-c++-4.4.4-13.el6 glibc-2.12-1.7.el6 for x86_64 glibc-2.12-1.7.el6 for i686 glibc-devel-2.12-1.7.el6 for i686 libaio-0.3.107-10.el6 libaio-devel-0.3.107-10.el6 libgcc-4.4.4-13.el6 libstdc++-4.4.4-13.el6 for x86_64 libstdc++-4.4.4-13.el6 for i686 libstdc++-devel-4.4.4-13.el6 libXext for i686 libXtst for i686 libXext for x86_64 libXtst for x86_64 openmotif-2.2.3 for x86_64 openmotif22-2.2.3 for x86_64 redhat-lsb-core-4.0-7.el6 for x86_64 sysstat-9.0.4-11.el6 xorg-x11-utils* xorg-x11-apps* xorg-x11-xinit* xorg-x11-server-Xorg* xterm

(*continued*)

Table 16-1. *(continued)*

Identity Management Component	Required Components
Oracle Access Manager 11.1.2.3	binutils-2.20.51.0.2-5.28.el6
	compat-libcap1-1.10-1
	compat-libstdc++-33-3.2.3-69.el6 for x86_64
	compat-libstdc++-33-3.2.3-69.el6 for i686
	gcc-4.4.4-13.el6 gcc-c++-4.4.4-13.el6
	glibc-2.12-1.7.el6 for x86_64
	glibc-2.12-1.7.el6 for i686
	glibc-devel-2.12-1.7.el6 for i686
	libaio-0.3.107-10.el6
	libaio-devel-0.3.107-10.el6
	libgcc-4.4.4-13.el6
	libstdc++-4.4.4-13.el6 for x86_64
	libstdc++-4.4.4-13.el6 for i686
	libstdc++-devel-4.4.4-13.el6
	libXext for i686
	libXtst for i686
	libXext for x86_64
	libXtst for x86_64
	openmotif-2.2.3 for x86_64
	openmotif22-2.2.3 for x86_64
	redhat-lsb-core-4.0-7.el6 for x86_64
	sysstat-9.0.4-11.el6
	xorg-x11-utils*
	xorg-x11-apps*
	xorg-x11-xinit*
	xorg-x11-server-Xorg*
	xterm
	pdksh-5.2.14

(continued)

Table 16-1. (*continued*)

Identity Management Component	Required Components
Oracle Identity Manager 11.1.2.3	binutils-2.20.51.0.2-5.28.el6 compat-libcap1-1.10-1 compat-libstdc++-33-3.2.3-69.el6 for x86_64 compat-libstdc++-33-3.2.3-69.el6 for i686 gcc-4.4.4-13.el6 gcc-c++-4.4.4-13.el6 glibc-2.12-1.7.el6 for x86_64 glibc-2.12-1.7.el6 for i686 glibc-devel-2.12-1.7.el6 for i686 libaio-0.3.107-10.el6 libaio-devel-0.3.107-10.el6 libgcc-4.4.4-13.el6 libstdc++-4.4.4-13.el6 for x86_64 libstdc++-4.4.4-13.el6 for i686 libstdc++-devel-4.4.4-13.el6 libXext for i686 libXtst for i686 libXext for x86_64 libXtst for x86_64 openmotif-2.2.3 for x86_64 openmotif22-2.2.3 for x86_64 redhat-lsb-core-4.0-7.el6 for x86_64 sysstat-9.0.4-11.el6 xorg-x11-utils* xorg-x11-apps* xorg-x11-xinit* xorg-x11-server-Xorg* xterm pdksh-5.2.14

(continued)

Table 16-1. (*continued*)

Identity Management Component	Required Components
Oracle HTTP Server/WebGate 11g	binutils-2.20.51.0.2-5.28.el6
	compat-libcap1-1.10-1
	compat-libstdc++-33-3.2.3-69.el6 for x86_64
	compat-libstdc++-33-3.2.3-69.el6 for i686
	gcc-4.4.4-13.el6 gcc-c++-4.4.4-13.el6
	glibc-2.12-1.7.el6 for x86_64
	glibc-2.12-1.7.el6 for i686
	glibc-devel-2.12-1.7.el6 for i686
	libaio-0.3.107-10.el6
	libaio-devel-0.3.107-10.el6
	libgcc-4.4.4-13.el6
	libstdc++-4.4.4-13.el6 for x86_64
	libstdc++-4.4.4-13.el6 for i686
	libstdc++-devel-4.4.4-13.el6
	libXext for i686
	libXtst for i686
	libXext for x86_64
	libXtst for x86_64
	openmotif-2.2.3 for x86_64
	openmotif22-2.2.3 for x86_64
	redhat-lsb-core-4.0-7.el6 for x86_64
	sysstat-9.0.4-11.el6
	xorg-x11-utils*
	xorg-x11-apps*
	xorg-x11-xinit*
	xorg-x11-server-Xorg*
	xterm
	pdksh-5.2.14

Other issues that might be encountered during installation or even later in the process during configuration or runtime are related to the OS environment and configuration. The following information will provide an overview of setting up the environment for success.

The following kernel parameters need to be set:

```
kernel.sem  256  32000  100  143
kernel.shmmax 10737418240
```

To set these parameters, edit the sysctl.conf file located in the /etc directory.

```
[root@clouddemolab home]# vi /etc/sysctl.conf
```

Add or edit the following lines in this section of the file:

```
# Controls the maximum number of shared memory segments, in pages
kernel.shmall - 4294967296
kernel.sem = 256 32000 100 142
kernel.shmmax = 10737418240
```

After setting these values in the sysctl.conf file, you must activate and verify the new values are shown using this command:

```
 [root@clouddemolab home]# /sbin/sysctl -p
net.ipv4.ip_forward = 0
net.ipv4.conf.default.rp_filter = 1
net.ipv4.conf.default.accept_source_route = 0
kernel.sysrq = 0
kernel.core_uses_pid = 1
net.ipv4.tcp_syncookies = 1
net.bridge.bridge-nf-call-ip6tables = 0
net.bridge.bridge-nf-call-iptables = 0
net.bridge.bridge-nf-call-arptables = 0
kernel.msgmnb = 65536
kernel.msgmax = 65536
kernel.shmmax = 68719476736
kernel.shmall = 4294967296
kernel.sem = 256 32000 100 142
kernel.shmmax = 10737418240
```

The open file limits must be set to 4096 to support the instance. To do so, edit the limits.conf file.

```
[root@clouddemolab home]# vi /etc/security/limits.conf
```

If the environment is to be installed on Oracle Linux or RedHat Linux, you must perform the edit in /etc/security/limits.d/90-nproc.conf as well. If this is missed, the values in this file might override the values in the limits.conf file.

In both of these files, ensure the following lines are added or edited:

```
* soft nofile 4096
* hard nofile 65536
* soft nproc 2047
* hard nproc 16384
```

After editing this file, the server must be rebooted to ensure all the changes take effect.

Most installation issues can be resolved or prevented by ensuring the aforementioned prerequisites are met prior to starting the installer.

Common Configuration Issues

Because there are three main components of the Oracle Identity and Access Management Suite—Oracle Internet Directory (OID), Oracle Access Manager (OAM), and Oracle Identity Manager (OIM)—this section covers related issues separately.

Oracle Internet Directory

As the back-end directory for OIM and OAM, if the OID environment is not configured properly, the rest of the stack is guaranteed to have problems. Although the configuration wizard performs most of the work during this stage, there can still be issues. The OS packages listed in Table 16-1 will suffice for an OID installation, as will the previously mentioned kernel parameters. Just as OAM and OIM have Java version ranges, OID versions are quite sensitive to Java Development Kit (JDK) versions and updates. For OID 11.1.1.9, ensure that you are using JDK 1.7 update 80. OID can be installed in an environment higher than update 80, but careful verification of the compatibility will be required. Most commonly, the installation will appear to run correctly. However, during the configuration stage, you might run into issues while the deployment of the domain is running.

Many organizations use an Active Directory environment as their network Lightweight Directory Access Protocol (LDAP). It is common practice to set up a Directory Integration Platform (DIP) to keep the OID environment in sync with Active Directory. Sometimes this synchronization will require users that meet certain criteria to be added to one OID subtree, whereas others will be put into another tree. Other environments might only want to synchronize a subset of Active Directory users that meet a complex set of rules. The OID 11.1.1.9 Directory supports multiple sets of synchronization profiles and each can have its own set of filtering rules. However, you could run into issues with complex rules. Many times this will only be apparent because users are not synchronizing, and when trying to load the DIP profile in the EM console, the console will hang. You will notice a spike in memory on the server at this time as well. In a case where a rule such as `searchfilter=(&(objectclass=user)(|(company= BB*))(!(objectclass=computer))` is needed, add double quotes around the search filter so it will be in the following format: `searchfilter="(&(objectclass=user)(|(company= BB*))(!(objectclass=computer)"`.

Oracle Access Manager

OAM handles the single sign-on (SSO) functionality for the Identity and Access Management environment. During configuration, a few issues can arise. This section covers a few common issues and resolutions.

■ **Note**   Prior to making any changes to the OAM configuration, you might find it useful to make a backup copy of the `DOMAIN_HOME/config/fmwconfig/oam_config.xml` file.

Changing identity stores can be a little tricky within the Access Manager console. However, you might be changing out your identity store, or migrating it to a new environment. In these cases, if you follow a couple guidelines, this activity can be carried out with little hassle. First ensure that you create a user or users within the new LDAP store that you plan to manage with the Access Manager administration. Ideally you will keep a user called oamadmin and a group of users in the Administrators group. In Figure 16-1, the OAM Administration Console is shown with multiple identity stores. Each of these contains at least one user configured as an administrator. Creating a new identity store and setting it up as the System Store will spawn a new section to this page where you will be able to select the users and groups to administer the instance, as shown in Figure 16-2.

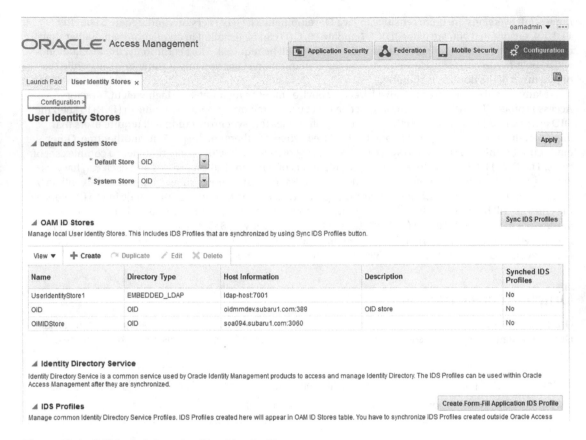

Figure 16-1. *OAM administration User Identity Stores screen*

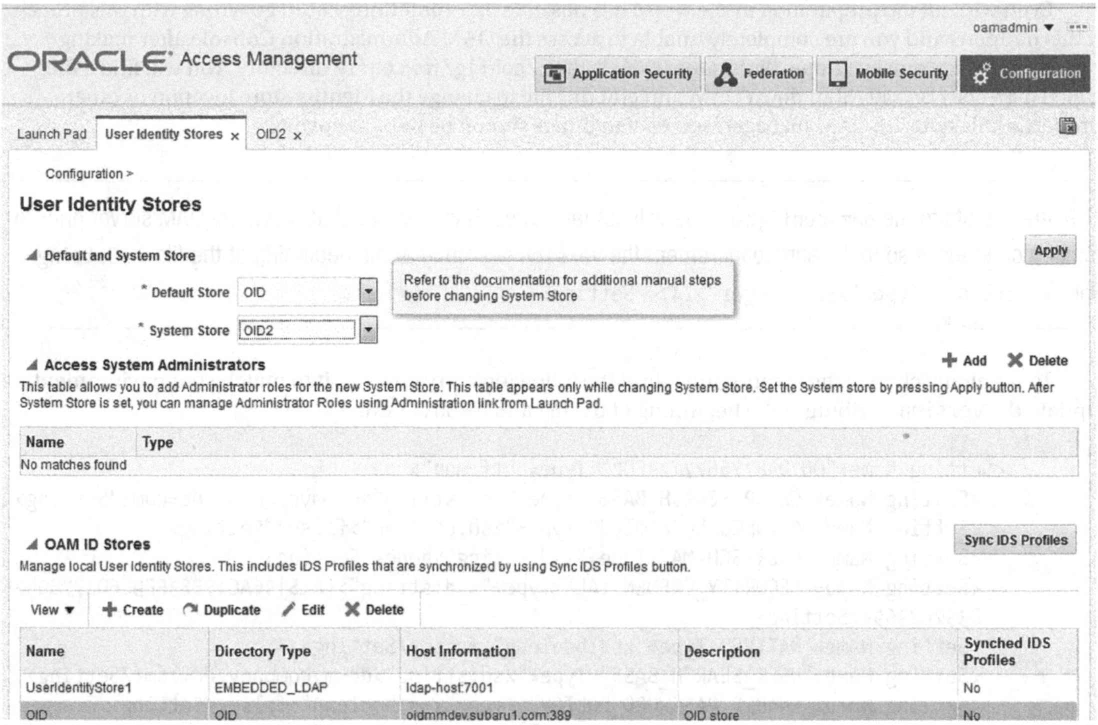

Figure 16-2. *OAM identity store selection*

After performing these tasks, it is important to ensure that the LDAP Authentication module or other Authentication module in use is configured to use the new identity store. Failure to perform this step could prevent you from accessing the OAM Console in the future. Check Figure 16-3 for this screen example.

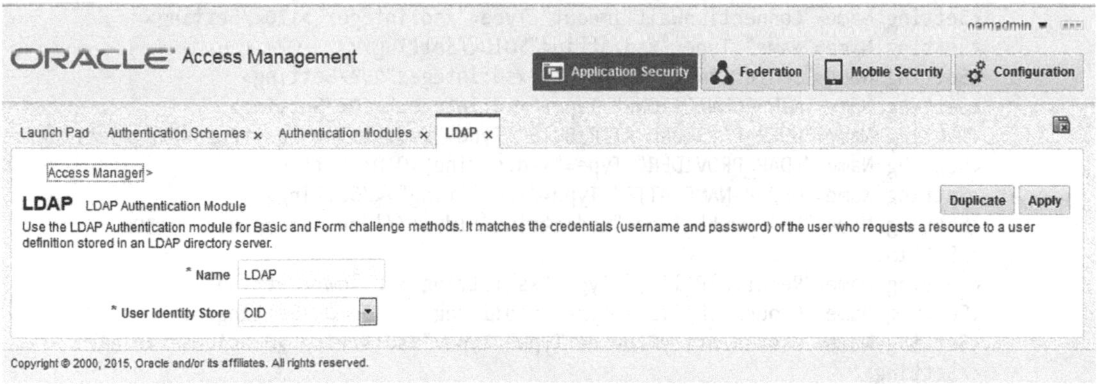

Figure 16-3. *OAM Authentication module configuration*

Even with all the preparation in the world it is possible that something could go wrong with this process. If this happens and you are completely unable to access the OAM Administration Console after making changes, there is one last hope. Within the DOMAIN_HOME/config/fmwconfig directory, you will find a file called oam-config.xml. Shut down OAM and edit this file to change the identity store location or other properties. Restart the OAM managed server, and things should be back to normal.

■ **Note** Edits to the oam-config.xml file will not take effect if you do not shut down the OAM server prior to making changes. Also make sure to increment the Version tag found at the beginning of the file: `<Setting Name="Version" Type="xsd:integer">247</Setting>`

To manually change the identity store, find the following entry and edit it to match your environment. Update the version attribute at the beginning of the file and restart OAM.

```
<Setting Name="DD7DA8776677123FD2" Type="htf:map">
  <Setting Name="GROUP_SEARCH_BASE" Type="xsd:string">dc=mycompany,dc=com</Setting>
  <Setting Name="GroupCacheEnabled" Type="xsd:boolean">false</Setting>
  <Setting Name="USER_SCHEMA" Type="xsd:string">none</Setting>
  <Setting Name="SECURITY_CREDENTIAL" Type="xsd:string">{AES}36AC17B83FF9C6D177B092F
  D352CB369</Setting>
  <Setting Name="NATIVE" Type="xsd:boolean">false</Setting>
  <Setting Name="USER_SEARCH_BASE" Type="xsd:string">dc=mycompany,dc=com</Setting>
  <Setting Name="ENABLE_PASSWORD_POLICY" Type="xsd:boolean">false</Setting>
  <Setting Name="MAX_CONNECTIONS" Type="xsd:integer">50</Setting>
  <Setting Name="GroupCacheTTL" Type="xsd:integer">0</Setting>
  <Setting Name="SECURITY_PRINCIPAL" Type="xsd:string">cn=orcladmin</Setting>
  <Setting Name="Description" Type="xsd:string">OID Store</Setting>
  <Setting Name="ConnectionRetryCount" Type="xsd:integer">3</Setting>
  <Setting Name="USER_NAME_ATTRIBUTE" Type="xsd:string">uid</Setting>
  <Setting Name="IsSystem" Type="xsd:boolean">true</Setting>
  <Setting Name="IsPrimary" Type="xsd:boolean">true</Setting>
  <Setting Name="ConnectionWaitTimeout" Type="xsd:integer">120</Setting>
  <Setting Name="Name" Type="xsd:string">OID</Setting>
  <Setting Name="SearchTimeLimit" Type="xsd:integer">0</Setting>
  <Setting Name="MIN_CONNECTIONS" Type="xsd:integer">10</Setting>
  <Setting Name="USER_PASSWORD_ATTRIBUTE" Type="xsd:string">userPassword</Setting>
  <Setting Name="LDAP_PROVIDER" Type="xsd:string">OID</Setting>
  <Setting Name="GROUP_NAME_ATTR" Type="xsd:string"></Setting>
  <Setting Name="LDAP_URL" Type="xsd:string">ldap://ldap.mycompany.com:3060
  </Setting>
  <Setting Name="ReferralPolicy" Type="xsd:string">follow</Setting>
  <Setting Name="GroupCacheSize" Type="xsd:integer">10000</Setting>
  <Setting Name="UserIdentityProviderType" Type="xsd:string">OracleUserRoleAPI
  </Setting>
</Setting>
```

Oracle Identity Manager

By itself, OIM is not a difficult product to install and configure. When using it with OID or another identity store, the configuration is very straightforward. Some confusion can be encountered when integrating OIM with an SSO product such as OAM. There are several steps involved with this integration, and issues can be encountered at various stages. Take your time and follow the steps carefully, and you should be successful. This section covers some of the commonly faced issues.

Installation of the Oracle Identity Management binaries is usually a smooth operation. Very few things go wrong. If they do, they are usually due to the previously mentioned items like missing OS packages or incorrect JDK versions. That said, the actual configuration of OIM can be a little confusing. Many times, a screen full of messages can scroll by and a step might seem to complete properly. Unresolved or missed problems at one stage can manifest in later steps, however.

As mentioned previously, unlike OID and OAM, where there is a single config.sh or config.bat file, there are actually two required for OIM. For OIM, you must run the config.sh file located in the <ORACLE_HOME>/common/bin directory to create the domain. Later, you will run <ORACLE_HOME>/bin/config.sh to actually configure OIM. This could be confusing to someone familiar with OID or OAM environments installing OIM for the first time. Running the incorrect file at the wrong time will result in errors that do not indicate the actual problem.

On the subject of the configuration tool, installing the incorrect version of Service-Oriented Architecture (SOA) required for OIM can cause many issues. This is further compounded by the fact that the Repository Configuration Utility (RCU) version required for OIM does not match the actual OIM version. OIM 11.1.2.3x requires SOA 11.1.1.9. The SOA 11.1.1.9 software is available as a separate download from OIM. There is no OIM 11.1.2.3 RCU available. Instead, you will use the Fusion Middleware 11.1.1.9 version.

When configuring the identity store using idmConfigTool.sh with the -configOIM tag, it is possible to encounter an error regarding the JMXCLIENTLIB variable. In the Oracle documentation, it is a little unclear that you must create the wlfullclient.jar file even if you are not installing the OIM Developer Console. This file must be present if you are configuring an OAM and OIM integration. In the documentation, instructions for generating the wlfullclient.jar file are presented within a separate section regarding the Developer Console. Although you do not need to copy the file anywhere, missing this step will lead to an error when running the idmConfigTool.sh file. To resolve this issue, generate the wlfullclient.jar file. If you are installing OIM and OAM on the same server, but in different WebLogic Server (WLS) instances, make sure you run idmConfigTool.sh from the OIM Home, not the OAM Home. This is known as a split domain configuration. Second, you might need to modify your CLASSPATH to point to the location of the wlfullclient.jar instead of the JMXCLIENTLIB directory.

It occasionally becomes necessary to change or update the connection to the identity store. This could be due to a change in architecture or a loss of OID that necessitates a host change. If your environment is configured similarly to the one in this book, it is using the libOVD connector. This connector can be updated to reflect the new OID or LDAP directory host and connection information. There is a file called adapters.os_xml located in <DOMAIN_HOME>/config/fmwconfig/ovd/oim. Prior to modifying this file, ensure the Administration Server and OIM managed server are shut down. Look for the following sections and update as necessary to reflect the new LDAP host. Note that this should only be done using this method if the new identity store is of the same type and version and the connector user and password are the same; for example, OID 11.1.1.9. If this is not the case, you can rerun the LDAP synchronization tools presented in Chapter 10.

Summary

There are a number of points during the installation and configuration of the Oracle Identity and Access Management Suite where problems can crop up. After the installation, you can run into issues with synchronization, authentication, and authorization. This chapter served as an introduction to some of the steps for troubleshooting and resolving some commonly encountered problems, from installation issues to runtime and modification issues.

Index

Get the eBook for only $4.99!

Why limit yourself?

Now you can take the weightless companion with you wherever you go and access your content on your PC, phone, tablet, or reader.

Since you've purchased this print book, we are happy to offer you the eBook for just $4.99.

Convenient and fully searchable, the PDF version enables you to easily find and copy code—or perform examples by quickly toggling between instructions and applications.

To learn more, go to http://www.apress.com/us/shop/companion or contact support@apress.com.

Printed in the United States
By Bookmasters